Drag and Drop Code

with Thunkable

An App Camp in a Book

David Wolber and Rafiki Cai

draganddropcode.com

1st Edition, Version 1.0.
July 2022

ISBN 979-8-6888881-1-9

Thunkable

This book teaches you app building with Thunkable. Thunkable is a free-to-use website for building apps at thunkable.com. There are two option to begin your app camp journey:

1. Use Thunkable's Free Version: Building apps with Thunkable is free! Register for a free account at thunkable.com and work on up to 10 apps at a time.

2. GO PRO! Special "App Camp" License, exclusively for purchasers of *Drag and Drop Code with Thunkable*. You get "pro" features for a major discount! Unlimited apps, downloads, and publishing!

Scan this QR code to take advantage of this exciting offer.

For Tomás and Cai Andrai

Advanced Praise

Drag and Drop Code will grab students on the very first page and gently guide them through the fundamentals of building mobile apps. Thunkable, a derivative of MIT App Inventor, is an ideal way to learn coding. Suitable for classrooms at multiple levels, teachers will find the presentation accessible and the coverage of basic coding concepts thorough. Students of all ages can use this book not only to learn how to code, but also to implement their own app ideas in a matter of days and weeks. Like Dave's other contributions, this book is a welcome step toward making computer science accessible to all. If there's a better way than *Drag and Drop Code* to introduce beginners to programming, I haven't seen it. And there's no one better than Dave at presenting these exciting concepts.

--Ralph Morelli
   Co-Founder, MobileCSP.org,
   Professor Emeritus, Trinity College

Drag and Drop Code is a great resource for beginning programmers! With easy to understand instructions, you will be able to create interesting apps designed to appeal to many people. The book introduces many fundamental concepts of programming, but leverages the power of building real world apps to engage the reader from the first to last page. For teachers and students, the chapter activities and the end of chapter conceptualize, customize, and create activities provide support aligned with the I Do, You Do, We Do model of teaching.

--Jennifer Rosato
   Director, National Center for CS Education (St Scholastica College)
   Board Chair, Computer Science Teachers Association (CSTA)
   Co-Founder, MobileCSP.org

TABLE OF CONTENTS

FOREWORD

Dave is unlike any Computer Science professor I have met! He has dedicated his energies to democratizing the power of computer science, and has been very clear eyed about how traditional computer science teaching techniques are not working for learners new to the field.

I have been working with Dave for more than a decade now. I run a global technology education nonprofit, Technovation, empowering children and adults, especially those from under-resourced communities to develop technology solutions to address critical issues that they face. Since the start of the program, almost 10 years ago, Technovation girls and instructors have been using Dave's App Inventor book and tutorials at appinventor.org. With this book we are excited that the Technovation community has top-notch guidance on creating iPhone apps using Thunkable - another visual, block-based mobile app creating language.

Over the years, I have been blown away by Dave's enthusiasm, passion and patience for motivating novices to take their first tentative steps into building things with technology. But passion and enthusiasm are not enough. They need to be coupled with creativity, courage and persistence. Dave has been innovating in creating coding video tutorials, trying to move away from the mold of step by step instructions, by doing something really fresh and engaging - live teaching a novice learner and creating technology solutions for real-world problems - on the fly. This takes courage and a love for innovation! He has also been working with us to inspire a completely new set of learners—grandmothers! His patience and passion are clearly visible as he dedicates his weekends to inspiring this new set of learners. Together we launched the world's very first Grandmom's Coding Club, holding weekly sessions for learners ranging from age 8 - 75!

This book itself is a testament to what Dave believes in so strongly—democratizing technology, highlighting innovative apps that tackle a broad range of social issues and speak to different communities. And as Dave is a phenomenal teacher—with tremendous experience explaining complex and abstract concepts simply with real-world examples—the book makes for an engaging learning experience. You want to get started right away and build your own version of the app! Each chapter has some exciting real-world apps that will resonate with all of us. This is a big difference from many textbooks and tutorials that exist that tend to cover topics of commercial interest. Dave's empathy and passion for inspiring others to make change in the world, comes through clearly in the book and its content.

The book is the epitome of what technology enables—bringing high quality, world class information and experiences at low cost—to everyone.

Let's go out and build!

Tara Chklovski,
Founder and CEO, Technovation

PREFACE

Want to make apps, learn to code, and have fun? Thunkable is the answer. It is a visual "blocks" language, so coding is like plugging puzzle pieces together. Within fifteen minutes you can build your first app and test it on your phone or tablet!

This book is designed for absolute beginners and walks you step-by-step through the app creation process. You learn coding fundamentals while creating real-world apps for your friends, family, organization, or the app stores. Instead of laboring through boring coding exercises, you learn by creating—what a concept!

Thunkable was spawned from MIT App Inventor, which revolutionized drag and drop coding for Android app development. Thunkable is cross-platform, so you can install the apps you build on any iPhone, iPad, or Android device. You can even create web apps!

Thunkable may have the best user interface ever applied to coding. Imagine some really smart people from Google and MIT focusing their attention on building the ultimate coding environment for beginners. Imagine they made it easy and fun to build real apps for your mobile devices, and they made it so you could drag in code blocks and connect them together instead of trying to remember cryptic coding statements. This is Thunkable!

Now imagine an author who is a Computer Science (CS) professor dedicated to educating beginners, one who has been teaching non-CS students from the Humanities and Business School for years (as well as CS students). Then throw in a second author who is a code-whisperer, a technologist and "digital doctor" adept at translating tech talk to the layperson. You are in good hands and will have a blast learning to build apps with Thunkable and this book.

WHO SHOULD USE THUNKABLE?

Thunkable and this book are perfect for:

- Beginners who want a gentle and fun introduction to coding.
- Designers and artists who want to add to their creative arsenals.
- After-school groups and app clubs looking for creative fun.
- Teachers who want super-motivated students.
- Companies, schools, and organizations who want to automate processes and build software without involving IT or spending thousands of dollars.
- Anyone with a great app idea!

Beginning Coders

Thunkable is fun because, even as a beginner, you get to build apps with user interfaces, databases, sensors, animation, and all the features of a phone or tablet—you don't get to build such apps in the early stages when you learn with a language like Python or Java. It's easy because Thunkable was designed specifically for beginners. You don't have to remember and type code, but instead can choose from a set of pre-defined code blocks and plug them together like puzzle pieces. Figure P.1 shows some sample blocks from an "Asteroids" app that takes away a "life" when an asteroid collides with a sprite:

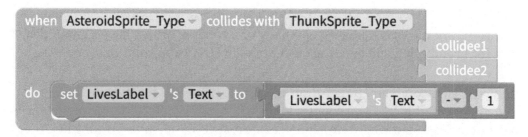

Figure P.1. Code blocks from an Asteroids game

Though visual in nature, Thunkable coding is "real" coding, and you'll learn universal coding fundamentals that apply to traditional text languages as well. Thunkable provides a user interface for coding so the introductory experience is gentler and more enjoyable. And because you can build full-fledged apps, you get a broader exposure to the entire software development process than with traditional languages. It is the best way to start and is a great launchpad to learning textual coding languages like Python and Java.

Designers

If you're a designer, Thunkable provides a perfect way to begin adding coding and the ability to specify interactive behaviors to your creative arsenal. Jump over the "coder divide" and learn to define interactive behavior and animation. Make your designs come alive!

Coding Clubs

Thunkable is perfect for outside-of-school learning, whether as part of formal groups like Technovation or Black Girls Code, or an informal family or multi-family coding club. Looking for a way to connect with your children, parents, or grandparents? Think of some app projects that the whole family can work on together! Imagine—doing something fun together and learning coding and technical skills along the way!

Teachers

With Thunkable, the dream of students learning by coding their own phone is here. I teach at the University of San Francisco. In my introductory coding course, in the first fifteen minutes of the first class, *before I even go over the syllabus*, I have my students build their first app. You should see their faces when they build an app that they can show their family and friends that night! If you want motivated students who drive the learning process, try Thunkable and this book!

Entrepreneurs and Organizations

Whether you work for an established company or a startup, or just have a great idea, Thunkable is terrific for prototyping and creating do-it-yourself (DIY) app solutions.

A prototype is an incomplete, rough-draft of an app. It is great for turning those great app ideas into something tangible that you can use to illustrate and promote your idea. PowerPoint slides are nice, but imagine showing your audience or prospective client a working app that they can install and play with on their phone.

There are many prototyping tools that let you design screens for an app, and many that provide a limited set of canned, interactive behaviors. Thunkable is different in that it is a general-purpose coding language and virtually any app behavior can be defined. You can build prototypes that not only look like the app you are dreaming of, but behave like it!

And you aren't restricted to building prototypes—you can build complete apps, either for in-house use or for publication on the App or Play Store. Does your company need a low-cost social app to help new employees learn everyone's name? Or an app that automates some laborious process now done manually? Thunkable is for you!

HOW THUNKABLE WORKS

Visual Blocks Language

Thunkable is a visual blocks language. Unlike traditional programming languages such as Java and Python, you don't have to remember and type code. Thunkable provides a set of pre-defined blocks, organized by topic, that you drag-and-drop into your app. You then plug those blocks together to specify the behavior of your app.

Get Started Quickly

With traditional coding tools, just getting setup is a challenge. Setting up Eclipse—one of the most popular tools for Android Java programming—can take hours for even a highly technical engineer.

Long setups and configuration issues can kill the beginner's spark right out of the gate. Such impediments are why many people give up on coding early on. Sites such as code.org and codeacademy.com are designed to immediately engage beginning programmers. They let you start coding and learning immediately upon reaching the site, then lead you through increasingly complex exercises.

Like these tools, Thunkable is a cloud tool that lets you get started quickly. But instead of working on coding exercises with no tangible result, you get to learn by creating an actual app for your phone or tablet. All you need is a computer, a phone or tablet, and a WiFi connection. You don't need to download any software to your computer. You just install a free app, Thunkable Live, on your phone or tablet, and you are ready to go.

Event-Response Programming

Computers were originally designed to compute—to take a large set of numbers and compute some formulaic result. The "computers" we now carry around and call "phones" still crank through formulas, of course, but their purpose has expanded far beyond that. We now socialize with our computers, take and share pictures, bank, learn, and communicate with satellites so that our location is known to the world. Our computers are more like augmentations of our minds than computing machines.

Though the purpose of our computing devices has changed, our coding languages have not. Popular languages like Python and Java are still based on a "recipe" model with a "main" program of sequential instructions. This recipe model makes sense for computing things, but is a poor fit for modern, highly interactive software. The languages don't make it easy for beginners to program the event-response behaviors of modern apps: reacting to the user touching a button, location information coming in from a GPS satellite, or a text arriving from a friend.

For experienced programmers, the dissonance between the language they use and the software they're trying to build isn't that big a deal. But for beginners, it makes learning to code really difficult. Think of a super simple app, say one in which clicking a button causes the button to turn red. Should be simple right? It's not. In Java, for instance, you first create an object called a Listener, then register that listener with the user interface object (the button), then program the handler to...well, you get the picture!

Creating an app that has a user interface or responds to a sensor is not a first hour or even first day exercise with traditional textual languages. The typical first engagement with coding is to write a program that displays "hello world" on a terminal screen or adds up a list of numbers. Beginners don't get to build anything fun and the computer barks error messages at them for typing things wrong—it is no wonder that many people don't stick with coding very long.

The key issue is that events, are not primitive objects in most programming languages. The events must be constructed by the programmer, and it is a complicated process.

Thunkable is different. "when event, do" is a first-class construct in the language, called an event handler. In Thunkable, you can code the simple "click to make a button turn red" app with just a few simple blocks, as shown in Figure P.2.

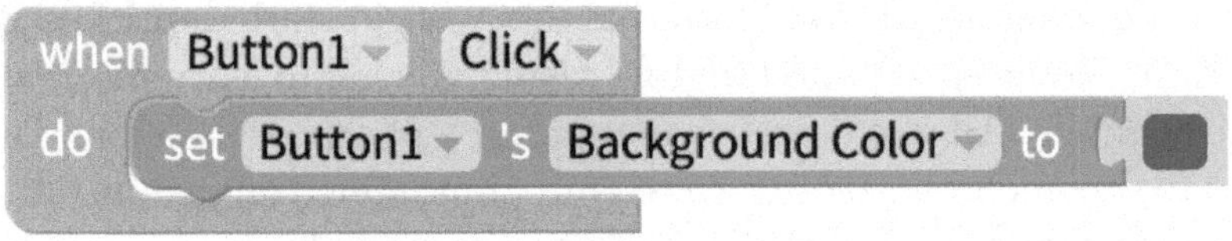

Figure P.2. Event handlers simplify coding

In Thunkable, the events you can respond to are pre-defined and organized into folders. You just click on a folder, find the event you're looking for, and drag it into your app. Then you drag blocks in to specify what should happen when the event occurs (e.g. change a button's background color to red). The fundamental software behavior– event-response– is the fundamental construct in the language.

Code Library Designed for Beginners

To program apps, you not only need to be proficient in a coding language, e.g., Swift for iOS, or Java for Android, you also need to learn a large code library. Traditional code libraries are designed for use by experienced coders, not beginners. They are designed with flexibility and code reuse in mind, so they are abstract in nature.

Thunkable was designed for beginners. The code blocks library provides you with a fixed set of concrete event and response blocks. Experienced programmers might balk at a lack of flexibility, but for beginners, the concrete nature allows you to learn faster and build far more complex software than you can build as a beginner with traditional, textual languages.

BROADENING AND DIVERSIFYING CODING

Software development has been restricted to the digital elite, the .1% of the world who know how to program; most people don't even dream of participating in the mysterious world of code.

Drag-and-drop tools like Thunkable help break down the "programmer divide" and radically broaden and diversifying the pool of software creators. Thunkable both heightens motivation—it's really fun—and lowers the barriers to learning. It provides a welcome introduction to designers, artists, women, people of color, scientists, health professionals, humanities majors, entrepreneurs, basically anyone who desires to add software to their creative problem-solving arsenal. The effect is two-fold: more people are empowered to thrive in today's increasingly digital society, and the software development field is infused with creative, big-picture thinkers.

HOW TO USE THE BOOK

The best way to use the book is to interleave reading with doing. As you read, code. Then, when you finish a chapter, reflect on what you've learned. Each chapter has conceptual questions at the end, with answers in the back to check your understanding.

The chapters also have "customize" and "create" sections. The customize sections present challenges involving modifications of the apps you built in the chapter. You aren't given step-by-step instructions, like you are in the chapter proper, so you'll have to explore the available blocks, try things out, read ahead, look things up—problem solve! If you want to become a coder, it is vital that you challenge yourself to complete these customizations.

The "create" sections suggest larger, creative ideas for you to think about, design, and build. The suggested ideas are not meant to be restrictive and you are encouraged to set a goal of building the app you've been thinking of, or brainstorming new ideas with your friends. You don't have to step through the chapters sequentially, but can jump around and learn the concepts you need in a just-in-time manner. Creative juices are the key to motivation for learning—let them lead instead of the table of contents!

When you complete the book, you'll be able to prototype and create apps, and you'll be able to talk the talk of coding fundamentals. You will have magical powers and an understanding of what goes on behind the coding curtain.

You may also be inspired to forge ahead, and use your new knowledge as a launchpad to learning more traditional and powerful languages like Python, Java and Swift. The coding concepts you learn will translate well.

Buckle-up—you are about to become a coder!

GREETINGS FROM THE AUTHORS

David Wolber

I'm interested in literature, basketball, history, psychology, and politics. I like to say I'm a writer trapped in the body of a computer science professor. I am passionate about demystifying the overly complex world of code for big picture thinkers, aiding designers and artists in crossing the "programmer divide", and helping to broaden and diversify the world of software.

At the University of San Francisco, I teach mostly beginners and never get tired of that challenge. I designed the app building course that many students from across the university take to fulfill their "math" requirement. Hundreds of students have sat in my office and told me, "I'm not good at Math". I force them to rephrase and say, "I haven't been successful at Math thus far in my life". Then I listen to their stories, often of grade school teachers who turned them off to Math or CS or told them they should try something else. Through building apps, these same students often end up at the top of the class and rediscover a love for logic and problem solving. You can do that, too, and build some great apps as you do it!

Rafiki Cai

Amongst my friends I'm called the "Digital Doctor" because I am committed to constantly finding ways that technology can make life better for marginalized individuals and for diverse communities. By the end of this learning journey, I'm hoping that you too will share this perspective and in your own personal way use app building as a tool for bringing good to the world around you.

Repetition can be the pathway to perfection, so in the 'Rafiki Breaks It Down' section at the end of each chapter, I'll help you review what's been covered. Not word-for-word, but through different lenses, so the material is reinforced and your grasp of it is strengthened. I look forward to offering you varying perspectives and to hearing your take on the content as well.

CHAPTER 1.EVENT-RESPONSE CODING

App: "SayIt"

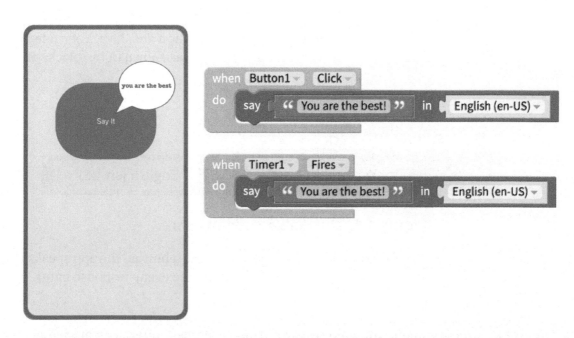

This chapter explains the basics of drag and drop coding and the fundamentals of app building. You'll build your first app: one that talks! And you'll learn that an app consists of a set of event handlers—blocks specifying how the app should respond to external events like the user clicking a button.

INTRODUCTION

Thunkable is a tool for making iPhone, Android, and web apps in a drag-and-drop manner. Even if you've never coded before, you can open a browser, navigate to thunkable.com, and immediately start building an app.

With Thunkable, you don't have to type cryptic code and suffer through hard-to-understand error messages as with more traditional coding languages like Python and Java. You code by dragging in blocks and plugging them together like puzzle pieces, as shown in the blocks of Figure 1.1:

Figure 1.1. Thunkable code blocks.

Can you tell what this app does? If you said, "when the user clicks a button, the app speaks the words, "You are the best!"" you are correct. The blocks illustrate the event-response nature of the Thunkable language.

With Thunkable, even beginners can build real-world apps with user interfaces, animation and databases—apps you can show off to your friends and family and even publish on an app store or the web. Figure 1.2 shows some of the apps you'll build with this book:

Figure 1.2 Some apps you'll build with this book

You'll build a soundboard app that plays speeches of civil rights leaders, a countdown app, a trivia app on inspirational women, a Meet My Classmates app for learning the names of the people in your organization, apps that listen and talk and describe images, an American Sign Language (ASL) app, an Asteroids game, a Math Blaster app for practicing arithmetic, and an Instagram-like posting app with user login. You'll also build a workout app, an app for supporting black-owned businesses, and a book search app using the Google Books API.

All of the apps in the book serve as templates that can be remixed to build your own custom apps. You can build soundboard apps for your history classes or of your friends saying silly things, countdown apps of varying types, study guides to help you and your friends practice for upcoming tests, language and translation apps to help you communicate in another language, games and animations bound only by your imagination, apps that bring in data from spreadsheets and other data sources, and social apps for posting different types of information and sharing it in the cloud.

Each chapter in the book provides "Customize" and "Create" sections for you to apply the knowledge you gain in the chapter. The "Customize" sections challenge you to modify the app in specific ways, with the goal of you gaining experience coding without explicit instructions and thereby refining your understanding of code. The "Create" sections encourage you to spread your wings and build apps that you can use in your everyday life, share with your friends, or even publish in the app stores.

HOW DOES APP BUILDING WORK?

Thunkable has two main screens, the Designer and the Blocks Editor. You first design the Screen and add the visual components you need in the Designer, then specify the app's interactive behavior in the Blocks Editor. In the Designer, you drag in all the images, text, buttons and other user interface components that will appear in the app, and lay them out on screens. In the Blocks editor you drag in blocks and plug them together to show how the app should respond to button clicks and other events. As you design and code the app on your computer, you test it with Thunkable's Live Testing app on your phone or tablet.

After you complete an app and test thoroughly, you can decide if you are ready to publish it to the Apple App Store or Android Play Store.

You toggle between the Designer and Blocks editor of Thunkable by selecting one of the tabs in the top-left corner, as shown in Figure 1.3:

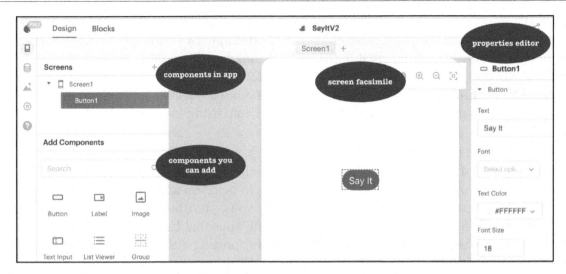

Figure 1.3. The Thunkable Designer.

DESIGNER: LAYOUT THE COMPONENTS

Thunkable's Designer is similar to those found in other app and screen design tools. If you have worked on such designs, this part of app building will be familiar.

Figure 1.3 shows the Designer in action. The top-left panel lists the components that have already been put in the app, in this case a single screen and button. The bottom-left panel lists the components in the Thunkable library which can be added to your app. The Thunkable component library is extensive and growing, so you can build virtually any type of app.

In Figure 1.3, one component, a button, has been added to the Screen that appears in the middle of the Designer. When you choose one of the components, its properties appear in the Properties panel on the right-side of the Designer. The Button1 component is selected, so its properties, such as Text and Font, are displayed. You can click on any of the components inside the screen to view and change its properties.

Try it

The best way to learn app building is to actually do it, and the best way to use this book is to follow along and build the apps being discussed. To get started, build a simple app in which clicking a button results in the app speaking some words.

- Start by opening a browser to Thunkable.com and registering for a free account (or signing in if you have one already).

- Create a new project and name it, "SayIt".

- When the Designer opens, drag a Button onto the screen. Set the Text property of the Button to "Say It".

Now you're ready to specify the behavior of the app.

BLOCKS EDITOR: SPECIFY THE BEHAVIOR

Specifying the interactive behavior of an app is the most challenging part because you aren't specifying something you can see, as with the Designer. Instead, you are specifying how the app should respond to events, like the user clicking a button. Figure 1.4 shows the Blocks Editor:

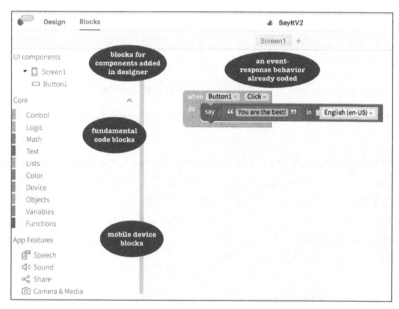

Figure 1.4. The Thunkable Blocks Editor.

The left-side panel organizes all of the blocks you can drag in for use in your app. The "UI components" area has blocks relating to the specific components you added in the Designer. The "Core" area with color tabs (Control, Logic, etc.) provides general coding blocks. The "App Features" area provides mobile device functionality like text-to-speech and playing a sound as well as blocks for accessing your data sources.

The main area of the Blocks Editor is where you drag in the blocks for the app you're building. In Figure 1.4, the coder has defined an app with a single event-response behavior-- an event of Button1 being clicked, and a response of words being spoken.

Try It

- In your "SayIt" project, select the Blocks tab. Unlike in Figure 1.4, your Blocks window will be blank because you haven't added any blocks yet. Click on Button1 in the top-left of the screen and drag in a when Button1.Click block.

- Click on "Speech" in the lower left of the screen and drag in a **say** block. Then click on the red "Text" folder in the middle-left and drag in a text ("") block, typing in whatever you want in the red box (e.g., "You are the best!").

You will notice that the blocks are gray when initially dragged in, as shown in Figure 1.5.

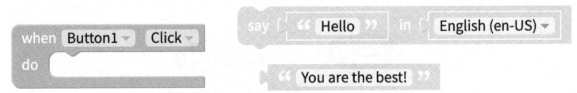

Figure 1.5. Blocks are gray until plugged into an event-response "when" block.

The blocks are gray to signify that they aren't valid until they are plugged into a "when event do" block. A function like **say** has no meaning until you specify *when* it should occur. In this case, you want to speak the words in response to the button being clicked.

- Drag the **say** block into the when Button1.Click block, then drag the red text block into the **say** block's text slot, replacing "Hello"

The blocks should appear as in Figure 1.6:

Figure 1.6. The Interactive Behavior for the "SayIt" app.

Test the App

You can test many apps directly in Thunkable. Just click the arrow in the top-right menu to test in preview mode.

It is also easy and fun to test the apps you build on your phone or tablet. Just open the App Store or Play Store on your device and install an app called, "Thunkable Live". Then launch the app and login with the same email account you use on the Thunkable website. Finally, back at Thunkable on your computer, click on the tiny device icon in the top-right to "Live test on a device". The app you are building should appear on the device.

Make sure the volume of your device is on and then touch the button. Does it speak the words, "You are the best!"? I hope so, because of course you are! But if you get tired of hearing it, you can modify the text in the red box to instruct the app to say something different.

Note: apps won't necessarily behave or look exactly the same in the Thunkable preview as they do on your device, and some app components only work when run from a device. So always, at some point, test your app on your phone or tablet, and not just in the previewer.

EVENT HANDLERS

Let's consider the "SayIt" app you just built and analyze the app's *grammar*, just as people analyze the subject-verb-object grammar of English (and other natural languages). Understanding the grammar and terminology of code is vital to becoming a software developer and being able to communicate within a software team.

The blocks in Figure 1.7 define an event-response behavior known as an event handler.

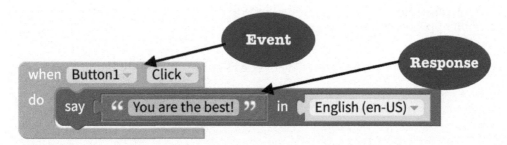

Figure 1.7. An event-handler consists of an event and a response.

An event handler is one of the most fundamental constructs in coding. It specifies that an app will perform a sequence of operations in response to an event. In the "SayIt" app, Button1 being clicked is the event. The response is a single operation of speaking the words, "You are the best!".

In general, the response to an event is a sequence of operations (rows of blocks), not just one operation as in Figure 1.7. Figure 1.8 shows a more complex event handler from the American Sign Language app you'll build in Chapter 7:

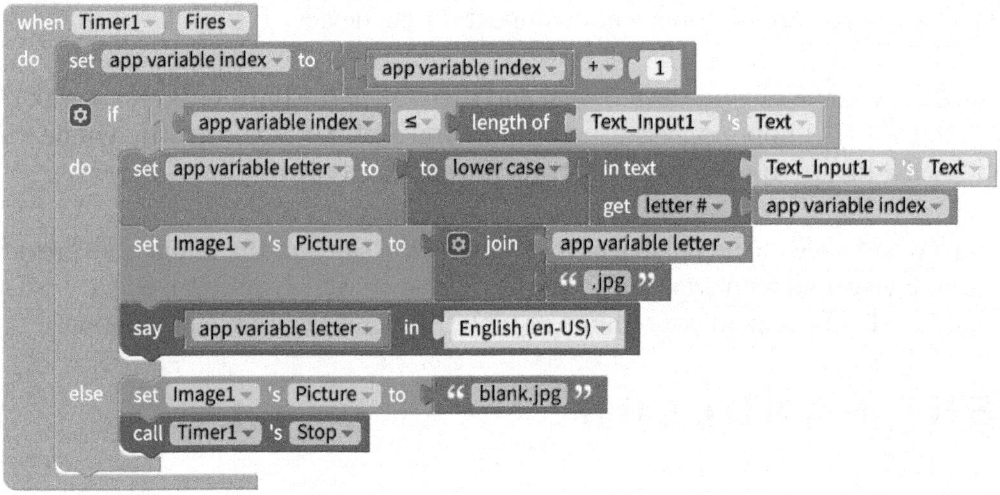

Figure 1.8. An event-handler with a response consisting of multiple operations.

Don't worry about the details of these blocks yet, and don't be scared! For now, just realize that an app responds to an event by performing a sequence of operations in order from top-to-bottom, and that a response can contain "if" blocks that specify operations that are only to be performed under certain conditions.

Now that you've seen the grammar of a single event-handler, you are ready for a more general definition of an app's behavior:

An app's interactive behavior consists of a set of event-handlers.

Figure 1.9 illustrates the fundamental architecture of an app's behavior. An app is an event-response machine, continuously reacting to external events by executing operations in response to those events.

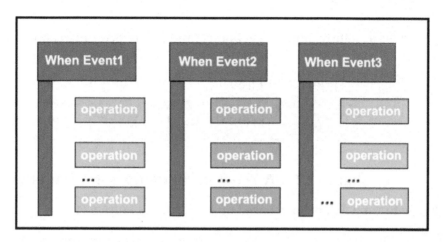

Figure 1.9. An app's interactive behavior consists of a set of event handlers.

EVENTS

An event is any external activity *that happens to* the device/app. Figure 1.10 illustrates the types of events that can occur.

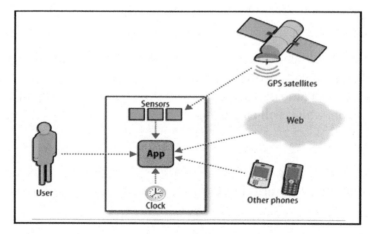

Figure 1.10. An event is something that happens to the app/device.

If you have a phone, you are probably familiar with such events. As a coder, you'll start thinking of these events in a new way: how you can code an app to respond to them.

The most common type of event is a user action, like the when Button1.Click event of the "SayIt" app. Sensor events detect something happening to the device, such as the device being shaken or its orientation changed, or location information coming in from GPS satellites. The passing of time is also considered an event, and is fundamental to coding animations and games.

Figure 1.11 provides a slightly modified version of the previous event-response behavior:

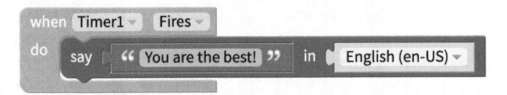

Figure 1.11. A Timer event triggers the response.

Can you tell how the app will behave based on the code in Figure 1.11?

If you answered that it is even more egotistical (and annoying) than the one triggered by the button click, you are correct. With this code, the app speaks "You are the best" over and over, forever!

Instead of a button click, the triggering event is when Timer1.Fires. The response of speaking the words is no longer triggered by the user clicking a button. Instead, it is triggered by the passing of time.

Try It

Open the Blocks Editor and click on the "+" near the "Timers" in the lower left panel of "App Features". The Timer's Interval property controls how often a when Timer1.Fires event will trigger, and has a default value of 5 seconds. Leave the default setting for it, but change Timer1's Loops property to true, which will cause the when Timer1.Fires to fire periodically, and set Enabled to true as well.

Next, in the Blocks Editor, drag in a when Timer1.Fires block and copy and paste the **say** blocks into it to get the configuration in Figure 1.11. Test your app--does the app say the words every five seconds?

RESPONSE OPERATIONS

An event's response is a sequence of operations performed by the app. An operation is a row of blocks and can be either a function call or a set operation.

Thunkable provides numerous functions that provide access to the "swiss-army-knife" capabilities of mobile phones. You've already seen the text-to-speech function **say.** There are also functions that let the user take pictures or select photos, functions for image and speech recognition, functions for playing and recording sounds, functions for working with a database, and many more. All of the functions you can call are found in the left side of the Blocks Editor.

It is important to understand the grammar of the function call. Function calls can have *parameters* denoted by slots to the right of the block, as shown in Figure 1.12.

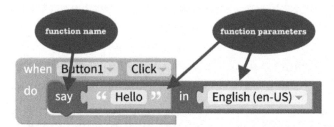

Figure 1.12. The say function requires two parameters

A parameter is information the function needs to do its job. The **say** call needs to know what text to speak, and what language to speak it in, so it has two parameters slots. Thunkable supplies a default parameter value, "Hello", for the text to be spoken, which you typically replace, and a default parameter value, "English" for the language to be spoken.

Function calls can also return a result. For instance, the **translation of** call returns text translated into another language. In Figure 1.13, the text the user enters in Text_Input1 is translated into Mandarin, returned from the function, and displayed in ResultLabel:

Figure 1.13. "translation of" returns the translation of the given parameter.

Figure 1.13 is also an example of the second type of operation that can appear in a response to an event: a set operation. set operations change component properties and store information in the app's memory (yes, an app has memory!).

SUMMARY

In this chapter, you learned some coding fundamentals: that an app's interactive behavior consists of a set of event handlers, that an event handler consists of an event and a response, and that the response consists of a sequence of operations, including function calls that provide access to the amazing capabilities of the tiny computers we carry around with us each day.

In the chapters that follow, you'll learn many more coding fundamentals, including:

- An app has a memory just like a person does, hidden from view, and coding is primarily about storing to and retrieving from that memory.

- An app can ask "if" questions, and "if-else" questions to provide the logic and artificial intelligence of the app.

- An app can repeat operations and process lists of data.

- An app can store data persistently in a database on the device or, for apps in which users share data, in the cloud.

You'll learn how to use these fundamentals to build more and more complex apps. In the process, you'll exercise your logic and problem-solving skills like never before.

With Thunkable and this book, you get to learn these coding and problem-solving skills in the context of building real apps with user interfaces, sensors, and database data. Such is not the common path to learning how to code: with traditional languages you usually learn through coding exercises and the creation of command-line programs. With Thunkable, you get early exposure to app development skills like user interface design, usability testing, data design, and system testing that are not typically part of beginning lessons. So, strap yourself in and get ready to build some cool apps and learn the fundamentals of code!

RAFIKI BREAKS IT DOWN

Congratulations, you've just navigated through your first experience with the fundamentals of app design. The principles you took in will give you the foundation you need to make things happen; creative things, productive things, engaging things.

Your app is a genie and an event is a wish—a command presented. Your job is to program the genie to fulfill the command. When a button is clicked, you are responsible for the genie fulfilling the wish.

That may sound trivial, because at this point you only have simple commands in your purview, but life as a genie-commander will get complex and demanding quickly. Don't despair though, there are ways that super-genies stay ahead of the wishes coming at them. They continuously think like a wisher and anticipate what might be desired next. By doing so, they can have wishes lined up for easy delivery before they're even asked for. Anticipation is a potent power in app development. Always be anticipating what a user might need or want, and how best to effectively deliver that, and you will succeed as a genie commander.

The Grammar of Genies

Remember your primary point of coding grammar, upon which you will build as we go along:

Natural Language: Sentence	Subject	Verb	Object
Coding: Event Handler	Event	Response (Sequence of Operations)	

VOCABULARY VIBE

EVENT and EVENT HANDLER

An event is something that your app can respond to, such as a user swiping a screen, clicking a button or the inflow of data from GPS satellites or sensors. The *agents* that facilitate such responses are event handlers and the process of them doing so is event-response.

OPERATION

An operation is an action that an app performs. *A genie's hands clappin' makes an operation happen.* The two operation types are **function call** and **set.** It often takes a collection of operations to execute a full cohesive action.

CONCEPTUALIZE

1. Match the terms with the definitions:

Term	Definition
Event	An event and the response it triggers.
Function call	The sequence of operations performed when an event occurs
Response	Something that happens to the app/device
Event Handler	When the app performs a task such as speaking words or playing a sound clip

2. Grammatically, what does an app's behavior consist of?

3. The red, purple, and green outline parts of the code. Name the part of code within each color.

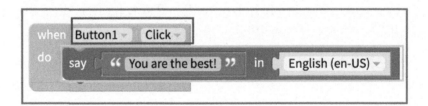

4. Which of the following are events?

a. Button1.Click

b. The passing of time

c. say

CUSTOMIZE

1. Modify the "SayIt" app so that it speaks one thing when the button is clicked, and another when it is long-clicked (held down longer). You'll need to drag in another event handler block from the Button1 folder.

2. Modify the "SayIt" app so that is speaks a language other than English.

CREATE

Create an app to help a traveler communicate in a foreign language. The app should have multiple buttons that each speak some important phrase, e.g., "Dónde está el baño?"

Share your creative apps with your authors and other *Drag and Drop* coders:

- Use #DragAndDropCode and #MadeWithThunkable on your social media platforms.

- @ us at @DragAndDropCode on Twitter and Instagram.

Chapter Resources: draganddropcode.com/bookCh1/

CHAPTER 2. I HAVE A DREAM

Apps: "I Have a Dream" and "I Have a Dream 2022

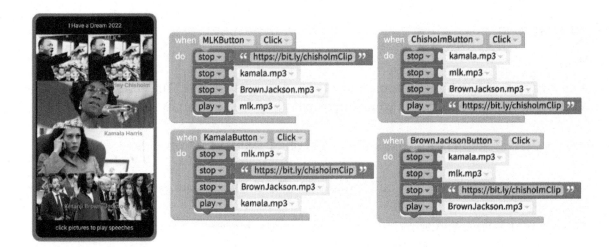

In this chapter, you'll start by building a soundboard app involving Martin Luther and his "I Have a Dream" speech, then expand it to include images and speech clips for Shirley Chisholm, Kamala Harris and Ketanji Brown Jackson. You'll learn how to layout components, work with media and play sound files, and you'll build an app with multiple event handlers.

INTRODUCTION

Most people have never even dreamed of building an app, primarily because software is this mysterious world of 0s, 1s, and computer nerds. The goal of this chapter is to show you that anyone can create in this medium.

In this chapter you will build two apps: "I Have a Dream", with a single picture of Martin Luther King that you click to play a clip from the famous 1963 speech he gave to 250,000 people on the steps of the Lincoln Memorial. You'll then expand the app to create "I Have a Dream 2022", a soundboard app that includes speeches by Shirley Chisholm, the first black woman to be voted to congress, Kamala Harris, the first woman to be the Vice President of the United States, and Ketanji Brown Jackson, the first black woman to sit on the Supreme Court.

This chapter instructs you on the detailed mechanics of app building and working with media. Later chapters will provide less step-by-step instruction, and more conceptual learning.

When you complete these apps, you'll be ready to build soundboard apps on any topic: You can build history lessons like this one, educational ones like a farm animal app for kids, or a personalized app with pictures and sound clips of your friends saying goofy things.

PART 1. I HAVE A DREAM

Perform the following steps to get started:

- In a browser, go to thunkable.com and sign in, or register for an account if you don't have one.

- Click on the Thunkable icon to open the Projects screen. If you've already created some apps, they will appear there.

- Click on "Create New App", name the app "IHaveADream", and choose to use the "drag and drop" interface.

Add Media

In this section, you'll add the media files needed for your app. You'll use the provided image of MLK and sound clip of his "I Have a Dream" speech.

- Open a browser page to https://draganddropcode.com/bookCh2/.

- Download the picture of MLK and his audio clip. If you are on an Apple computer, you can select control-click and choose "Save Image As" to download a picture, and control-click and "Save Audio As" to download an audio file. If you are on a Windows machine, use right-click instead. For now, just download the picture of MLK and the audio file that appears below it.

- Return to your app at Thunkable.com and upload the mlk.jpg and mlk.mp3 files you just downloaded into your app. You can upload files in the Designer, as shown in Figure 2.1.

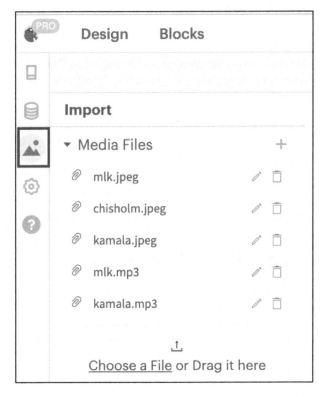

Figure 2.1. Drag image and sound files into Assets area

Click the assets icon and either drag files in or choose "Choose a File" and navigate to the folder to which you downloaded the image and sound files (by default, your "Downloads" folder). Do this twice to upload both the image and sound files for MLK

The files are now in your app, but the picture isn't on the Screen. In the next section, you'll add a Button component to the app's screen, and set a property so that the "MLK" image covers the button.

Add a Button Showing MLK

An app consists of visible components like Buttons, Labels, and Images, which appear on screen, and code blocks responsible for the event-response behavior of the app, in this case reacting to button clicks by playing sound clips.

In the "IHaveADream" app, the speech should play when the user clicks MLK's picture. You'll use a Button component and set its Button.BackgroundPicture property, instead of using an Image component, which is used to show images that don't respond to touch.

- Drag in a Button component from the left panel onto the Screen, as shown in Figure 2.2:

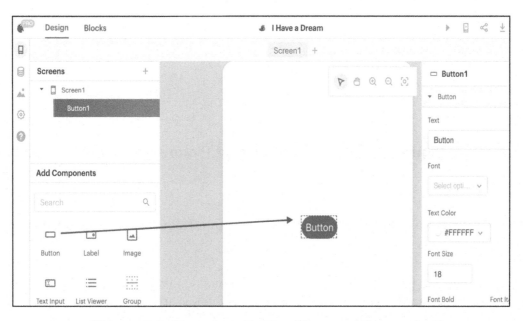

Figure 2.2. Drag in a Button then set its properties.

Components, like a Button, are defined by a set of properties which appear to the right of the screen when the component is selected. A component's appearance depends on how these properties are set. By default, the Text property of a Button is set to "Button" so that text appears on top of the button. The Background Picture property is not set by default, so no picture appears on the button.

- Click on the Background Picture property and you'll be prompted to either upload a file or choose a previously uploaded file. In this case, choose the file you uploaded earlier, "mlk.jpg". When you do, the image from the file will appear on the button. The image and button will appear very small, something you'll fix later. The text "Button" will also appear on it, so blank out the Text property, as shown in Figure 2.3:

Figure 2.3. Set the Background Picture and blank out the Text

Test the App

An important app building strategy is to test your apps frequently, after every couple of changes you make.

To test the app you just built, you'll need the "Thunkable Live" app on your phone or tablet. If you completed Chapter 1 you already installed it. If not, search for it in the App or Play Store.

Once it is installed, launch Thunkable Live and login with your Google account. Then back on your computer, at thunkable.com, click on the device icon in the top menu. In a few seconds, you should see your app appear with the single button in the middle of an otherwise blank screen.

Rename "Button1" to "MLKButton"

The Designer and Blocks Editor are in separate windows in Thunkable. When you switch to the Blocks Editor, you won't see the user interface and you can only refer to components by their name. For this reason, it is important to provide descriptive names to your components, especially the ones involved in interactive behavior.

Change the name of Button1 to MLKButton. A descriptive name isn't as important for this first
app which has just one button, but in the next app of this chapter you'll have multiple buttons
and the descriptive name will be helpful.

You can change the name of a component by clicking on its name near the top of the right
properties panel, as shown in Figure 2.4:

Figure 2.4 Change the name of the button to "MLKButton".

Resize the Button

The next step is to resize the button so that it fills more of the screen. With Thunkable's drag and
drop interface, you can click on a corner of a component and drag it to resize. Thunkable helps
you place things with red lines which denote that you have an item centered or aligned with
another item or with the screen. In this case, just enlarge the button and center it within the
screen.

When you change the button's properties, the changes appear both on your computer and your
phone or tablet. This live testing feature is helpful as you can immediately see how the app will
look on the device.

Set the Screen background and add labels

In this section, you'll set the screen background to black and you'll add two label components for
the title and instructions.

- Click the Screen1 component in the left-panel so that its properties appear in the right-
  panel. Then set its BackgroundColor property to black.

- Drag in two Labels and place one above the MLKButton and one below.

- Set the Text property of the top Label to "I Have a Dream!" and its Color property to white.

- Set the Text property of the bottom Label to "Click picture to play speech" and its Color property to white. When completed, your app should look like Figure 2.5:

Figure 2.5. Set the screen background to black and add labels.

Add the "Click to Play Speech" Behavior

You've completed the visual design of the app, but you haven't coded its interactive behavior. If you click on the MLKButton on your device at this point, the speech won't play.

The next step is to code the event-response behavior—specifying that clicking the button should play the sound. Choose the Blocks tab at the top, and you'll see a blank screen because you haven't coded any behaviors.

- Click on MLKButton in the left panel and drag the when MLKButton.Click block into the blocks area, as illustrated in Figure 2.6:

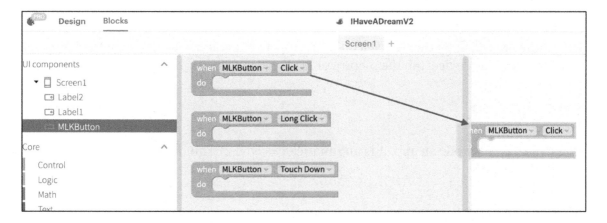

Figure 2.6. Click on MLKButton and drag in its "when MLKButton.Click" block.

The blocks you place within this "when" block will be executed when the button is clicked. In this case, you want the speech to play.

- Click on the "Sound" folder in the left panel and drag in the **play** block, placing it in the when MLKButton.Click block, as shown in Figure 2.7:

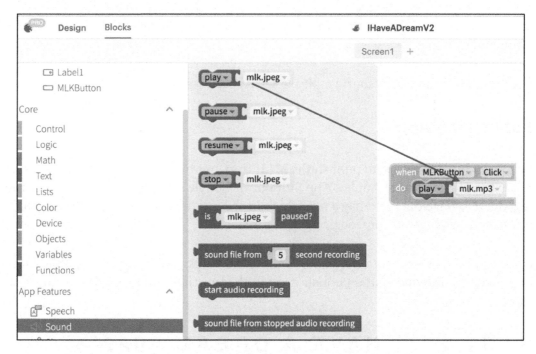

Figure 2.7. Drag a play operation into the "when" block.

When you drag in the **play** block, its parameter is set to one of your media files by default. Make sure to change it so that "mlk.mp3" is the chosen audio file.

Test the App

To test the app, click on the device icon in the top Thunkable menu. Then, in the "Thunkable Live" app on your device, tap the picture of MLK. The "I Have a Dream" speech should play.

Save the App

As you design and code an app, it is automatically saved in Thunkable's cloud. You do not need to save it explicitly.

Share the App

Thunkable is by nature open source. The apps you build, including the underlying source code blocks, are public by default and available in Thunkable's public gallery. To create private apps, you must register as a paid, "Pro" user.

You can share the apps you build explicitly by selecting the Share icon from the top right menu. Thunkable will generate a link that you can email your friends or colleagues. When that person clicks on the link, Thunkable will launch with a copy of the app open. The person doesn't have edit access to your original app, and there is currently no "Google Docs" like sharing in Thunkable.

For more information on sharing, please see Appendix C.

Publish the App

You probably don't want to publish the MLK App, but by the time you finish this book, you'll be ready to publish apps in Apple's App Store or in Google's Play Store. Both stores require you to register as a developer and pay a fee, which in the Summer of 2022 was $99 a year for the App Store, and $25 lifetime for Google's Play Store .

Once you've registered as a developer, Thunkable helps you through the publication process— just click the "Download and Publish" icon in the top-right menu and follow the steps from there.

PART 2: "I HAVE A DREAM 2022"

In Part 2, you'll transform "I Have a Dream" into a soundboard app with multiple images and sound clips. You'll learn how to layout multiple components on the screen and you'll add three more event handlers to the interactive behavior of your app.

The app you'll build is called, "IHaveADream2022". It has four sound clips: the "I Have a Dream" speech from MLK, a speech from Shirley Chisholm, who became the first African-American US congresswoman in 1969, a clip from Kamala Harris, the first African-American and Asian woman to serve as Vice President, and a clip from Ketanji Brown Jackson, the first black woman named to the US Supreme Court.

Start the app by copying the one you just created. In the Designer, choose the "more operations" icon (three vertical dots) from the top-right menu and choose "Duplicate Project". Then click on the Thunkable icon in the left-top corner to open your app list. You'll see "IHaveADream" as well as the copy, "IHaveADream copy" Click on the edit icon next to the second app and rename it to, "IHaveADream2022". Then click on it to re-open it for editing.

Add the Media

You need three more images and three more sound clips for this second app.

Open a browser page to https://draganddropcode.com/bookCh2/ and download the pictures of Shirley Chisholm, Kamala Harris, and Ketanji Brown Jackson. The files are named chisholm.jpg, kamala.jpg, and ketanjibrownjackson.jpg, respectively. Also, download the audio files for Kamala Harris and Ketanji Brown Jackson. You'll use a URL to refer to the clip of Chisholm's speech, so you won't download a file for it. Download the files, then upload them into your app in the Files area of the Designer.

Figure 2.8 shows how the app will look once you've added the components you need and set their properties.

Layout the Components

Figure 2.8 shows how the app should appear in the Designer, once you add the components.

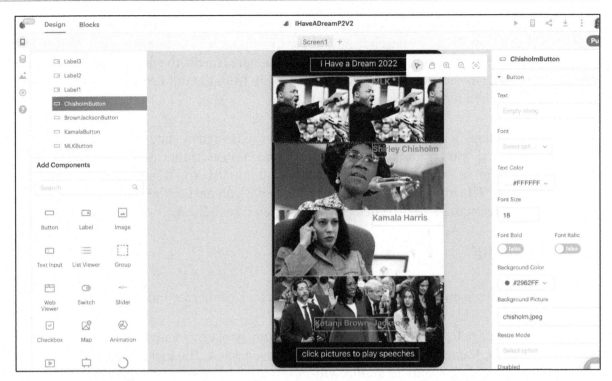

Figure 2.8. The "I Have a Dream 2022" app in the Designer

Design the app by using Figure 2.8 and these instructions:

- Set the top Label's Text property to "I Have a Dream 2022" and set its Font Size property to 24. Since this app will have a number of components, it is best to give the components descriptive names. Choose the pen icon next to the Label name in the right top panel and rename it to TopLabel.

- Click on one of the MLKButton's corners and resize it to fill the width of the screen. In its properties, change the Border Radius to 0 so that it is a rectangle and not rounded.

- You can duplicate a component by selecting it and choosing the "more operations" icon to the right of its name in the top-right properties panel. Duplicate the MLKButton three times. Name one of the duplicates ChisholmButton, one KamalaButton, and the other KetanjiButton, and place them in the configuration shown in Figure 2.8.

- Add four labels to the app and place one over each of the buttons. Set the text of each label to one of the names. Modify the Text Color to blue.

- Set MLKButton's Resize Mode to "repeat".

Test the App

The goal is for your screen to look like the one depicted in Figure 2.8. Be sure and test that the screen appears correctly on your phone or tablet.

Code the Interactive Behavior

Now you are ready to define the interactive behavior of the app. Open the Blocks editor and code it so that clicking on each button stops the other sound clips and plays the chosen one.

- Drag in three additional event handler blocks, when ChisholmButton.Click, when KamalaButton.Click, and when BrownJacksonButton.Click

- Drag in **play** and **stop** function call blocks from the "Sound" folder.

- Configure the blocks as shown in Figure 2.9:

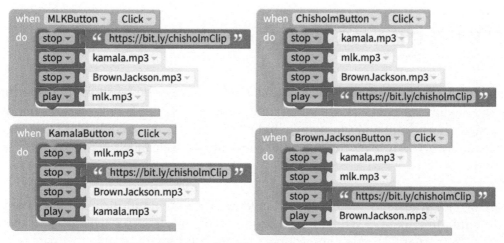

Figure 2.9. The Blocks for the "I Have a Dream 2022" app.

Note that for Chisholm's speech, red text blocks are used to refer to a URL, https://bit.ly/chisholmClip, instead of a file that has been loaded in. The advantage of using a URL instead of an uploaded file is you can only upload a limited number of bytes into your Thunkable media library. The disadvantage of referring to a URL is, if the website that the URL points to changes, or there is a problem connecting to the Internet, your app won't work correctly.

Test the App

Click on the device icon to test the app on your phone or tablet. When you click on each of the buttons, the currently playing speech (if any) should pause and the selected one should begin. The code doesn't provide a button for stopping all speeches—that behavior is left as an exercise in the "Customization" section at the end of this chapter.

SUMMARY

The apps you've built in this chapter introduce the mechanics of app building. You now know how to design and layout your components, include media in an app, and specify simple event-response behaviors. With this knowledge, you can build all kinds of soundboard apps, whether they be for educational purposes, promotion, or just for fun.

There is much more to app building than mechanics and simple event handlers, of course. In the following chapters you'll learn to build more complex apps that include conditional "if" logic, repeat blocks, database data, and more.

RAFIKI BREAKS IT DOWN

You've moved up in your app *grammar* from a single sentence being spoken, to sharing some meaningful media experience. With your genie-imagination, think about how a soundboard app might engage a user again and again and what media experiences people like most. My genie says, "music". Everybody loves music and once immersed we can listen to song after song on any given day.

Here's an idea for you: a music soundboard might make a great gift idea. It's like giving someone their own miniature Spotify. Who are your mom's and pop's favorite artists? How about your grandparents? Keep on Thunking and soon your genie power will be able to create a gift app that your friends and family would surely enjoy!

Flexing Thunk Muscles

The free Thunkable account allows you to export an app to "native" iOS or Android format. If you purchase a paid "Pro" account, you can also export to a web app format as well. A web app can be made immediately available, without going through an app store. Say you want to test how users will respond to an app idea you have. You can Thunk up a working prototype of your app, put it on the web, and share the URL. Your testers won't have to navigate to an app store, but can go straight to the URL you supply and immediately engage with your app.

1s and 0s

At the start of this chapter, there is a reference to a "mysterious world of 0s, 1s and computer nerds". I want to extrapolate on that description, just in case some of you may not be familiar with the story behind the 1s and 0s.

The impressive power of all our computing devices boils down to merely two numbers: 1 and 0, which represent an 'on' and 'off' state and whether electricity is flowing or not. This architecture is known as binary code and, at the end of the day, no matter our concepts and extravagant arrangements, everything ultimately gets built in patterns of the two bricks—1 and 0. That's all the computer understands! Fascinating isn't it? If you're interested in knowing more, check out this video created by the good people at Khan Academy and code.org.
https://youtu.be/ewokFOSxabs.

CONCEPTUALIZE

1. The green, blue, red, and yellow outline parts of the code. Coding has a grammar, just like natural language. Name the part of code within each color.

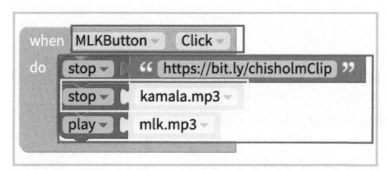

2. How many event handlers are defined in the "IHaveaADream2022" app?

CUSTOMIZE

1. Add a StopAllButton which stops all the sound clips.

2. Besides **play** and **stop**, there are also functions for **resume** and **pause,** and a block to check if a clip is paused. Add Buttons which allow the user to start from the beginning, pause, stop, and resume each clip. For some functionality, you'll need an if-block, which is in the Control folder (and which you'll learn about in Chapter 3).

CREATE

Create your own soundboard app with your own media. Here are some ideas:

- An app with four or five historical figures in which clicking each picture plays a speech or discussion of their accomplishments.

- An app that lets you click on pictures of your classmates or work colleagues to see their names and hear them say something goofy.

- A soundboard playing notes from your favorite musicians.

- Educational software for kids, e.g., a farm animal app

- A "Name that Tune" game that plays song notes and displays the song name (answer) after the user clicks a button.

- An app about your school/organization providing info about different places on campus.

Share your creative apps with your authors and other *Drag and Drop* coders:

- Use #DragAndDropCode and #MadeWithThunkable on your social media platforms.

- @ us at @DragAndDropCode on Twitter and Instagram.

Chapter Resources: draganddropcode.com/bookCh2/

CHAPTER 3. CONDITIONAL BLOCKS AND AN APP'S HIDDEN MEMORY

Apps: "CountDown"   and "Slideshow v.1"

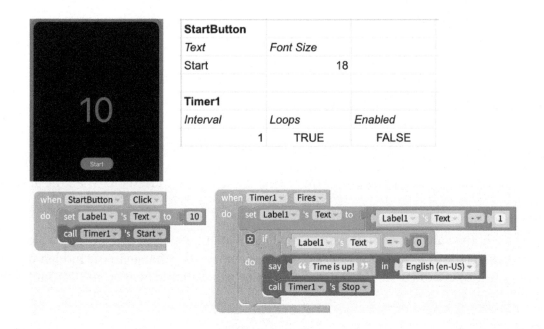

StartButton		
Text	Font Size	
Start	18	
Timer1		
Interval	Loops	Enabled
1	TRUE	FALSE

In this chapter, you'll learn that an app has hidden memory cells, just like a human does. You'll learn to store and retrieve from that memory, and have the app ask questions and make "if" decisions based on the data. With what you learn, you'll build a count-down app and a slideshow of inspirational women.

INTRODUCTION

An app has an internal memory, hidden from view, something like the spreadsheet shown in the introductory figure of this chapter. App users see only the user interface of an app, what appears on the screen. But a programmer knows that underlying that user interface is the app's hidden memory and that an app's code involves operations for storing values into that memory and recalling data from it.

An app also has logic, which just like your brain interacts with memory. In this chapter, you'll learn how to code an app to ask questions, often questions concerning the information in hidden memory.

Components and Initial Values

In previous chapters, you used the Designer's right-side Properties Panel to set the component properties, like a Label's Text, or an Image's Picture. What you set in the Designer was the *initial values* of component properties—the values the properties are set to when the app launches.

On app launch, the values specified in the Properties Panel are placed into the app's hidden memory cells. As the app runs, the values of those memory cells change in the hidden memory, but not in the Properties Panel. Really, the Properties panel should be labeled, "Initial Property Values".

To illustrate, consider a simple app named "ClickRed". The "ClickRed" app has a single button that starts out with a background color of blue. The app's behavior is simple: when the user clicks the button, its background color turns from blue to red.

Build "ClickRed"

- Go to Thunkable.com and create a new project named, "ClickRed".

- In the Designer, drag a Button into the screen. By default, the button's BackgroundColor is blue and its Text Color is white. Leave those settings as they are and set the Text property to "Click Me", as shown in Figure 3.1:

Figure 3.1. The ClickRed app in the Designer.

- In the Blocks editor, code the interactive behavior. From the Button1 folder, drag in a when Button1.Click block and a set Button1's BackgroundColor to block. From the Colors folder, drag in a red block. Plug them together so that they fit as shown in Figure 3.2:

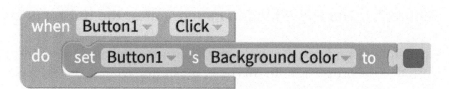

Figure 3.2. The Blocks for the ClickRed app.

Test the App

To test your app, launch the Thunkable Live app on your device, then back on your computer click the device icon in the top-right menu. When you click the button, does it turn red?

INITIAL PROPERTY VALUES

"ClickRed" is about as simple an app as you can build, but it helps illustrate how an app's memory works. When the app launches, the initial properties specified in the Designer are placed in the app's internal memory, which is totally hidden inside the device. Figure 3.3. shows the app screen on the left and a spreadsheet illustrating a portion of the app's hidden memory *if you could see it.*

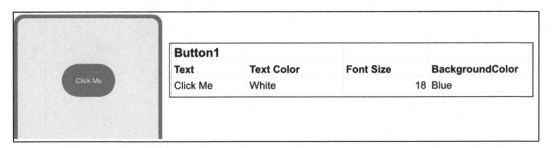

Figure 3.3. On launch, hidden memory is initialized to values from the Designer.

After the app launches, the hidden memory cells match the properties specified in the Designer. But once the user begins interacting with the app, the hidden memory changes. When Button1 is clicked, Button 1's BackgroundColor property is set to red. The hidden memory cell changes as shown in the right side of Figure 3.4.

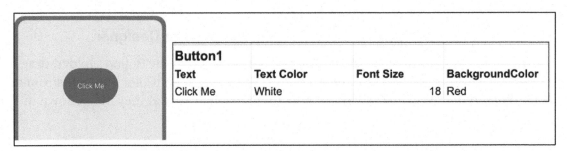

Figure 3.4. The app's hidden memory after the button is clicked.

After the event handler completes, the app's user interface is updated to manifest the changes that have occurred to the properties. In this case, the button changes color, as shown in the left side of Figure 3.4.

The button changes to red in the running app on your device, but in the Designer, you'll see that Button1's BackgroundColor property remains set to blue. Why do you think that is?

The reason is that the Designer displays the initial property values, how the app will look on launch. Only the app's hidden memory holds the current values as the app runs.

SCREEN.STARTS AND SCREEN.OPENS

When an app launches, the initial property values in the Designer are placed in the hidden memory and two events are triggered. when Screen.Starts is triggered when the app first launches. when Screen.Opens is triggered when the app launches, and also each time the user returns to a screen after opening another screen (you'll learn about adding screens later). You can add blocks in these event handlers to perform additional initialization for an app.

Code the when Screen.Starts event handler in your "ClickRed" app. Set the BackgroundColor to the blue block you find in the Color folder, as shown in Figure 3.5:

Figure 3.5. When the app launches, set the color with blocks

The app works the same, but now you know you can initialize properties with blocks as well as in the Designer.

ASKING "IF" QUESTIONS AND ACCESSING HIDDEN MEMORY CELLS

The previous example illustrates how to set a property to change the hidden memory and user interface when the app is running. "set" is synonymous with "change". It is the app equivalent of a person entering a value in a spreadsheet cell.

In addition to setting the values in memory cells, an app can also recall the data in memory cells, an operation called a "get". "get" is the equivalent of a person referring in a formula to a spreadsheet cell with something like "A3".

One purpose of a get operation is to ask a question as the app runs. For example, suppose you wanted to modify the "ClickRed" app so that each time the user clicks Button1, its background color toggles between red and blue. The algorithm is basically:

> When the user clicks, if the button is blue, change it to red, otherwise (if it is red) change it to blue.

Build "ClickRedBlue"

Copy your "Click Red" app. From your Projects page, choose the "..." by the "ClickRed" app and "Duplicate", and name the new app "ClickRedBlue". Then, in the Blocks Editor for the new app, change the blocks within when Button1.Click to implement the red-blue toggling behavior.

From the Button1 folder, you'll need a set Button1's BackgroundColor block, along with a "get" block, Button1 BackgroundColor, which is directly below the set in the folder.

You'll also need blue and red blocks from the Color folder, an = block from the Logic folder, and an if block. The if block can be found in the Control folder, as shown in Figure 3.6:

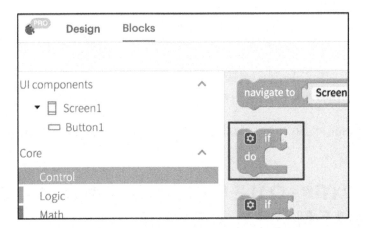

Figure 3.6. The "if" block is found in the Control folder of the Blocks Editor.

The if block in the Control folder doesn't have an "else" branch when you drag it in. By default, the block is set up to ask a single question and perform the blocks within it if the answer to the question is true. You can add additional branches and questions, however, by clicking on the blue icon in the top-left corner of the if block, which opens up a window like that in Figure 3.7:

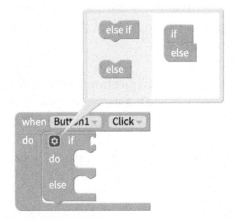

Figure 3.7. Adding branches to an "if"

For the "ClickRedBlue" app, you need to add an "else" branch. You add "else" (or "else if") branches by moving them into the top-right white area of the dialog, which results in the block being modified. The block is transformed into one with an "else" branch, as shown at the bottom of Figure 3.7. With an "if-else", if the question asked is true, the blocks in the "do" branch are performed. If the answer to the question is false, then the blocks in the "else" branch are performed.

Try it. Plug the blocks together so that they look like those in Figure 3.8:

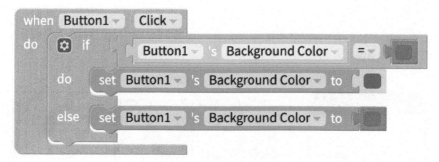

Figure 3.8. The blocks for "ClickRedBlue".

When Button1 is clicked, the app asks if the Button1.BackgroundColor property is blue. To ask the question, the app first "gets" the value in the memory cell using the Button1. BackgroundColor block. The app retrieves the value of the property from the hidden memory cell, which is initially blue. Because the BackgroundColor starts blue, the "if" question evaluates to true on the first click, so the "do" branch of the code is followed and the app sets Button1's Background Color property to red.

The second time Button1 is clicked, the value in Button1's Background Color property, in the hidden memory, is red, so the "if" question evaluates to false. If a question evaluates to false, the "else" (otherwise) branch is followed. In this case, the "else" branch changes Button1's Background Color back to blue.

If you follow this logic forward through more clicks, you'll see that the code blocks will indeed cause the button to change color back and forth with each click.

Test the App

Test the app. When you click the first time, does the button color change to red? When you click again, does it change back to blue?

If there is an issue, make sure that you have coded the when Screen.Starts to set the initial color of the button to blue, as shown in Figure 3.5, and make sure you use the same exact blue block there that you use in the "if" question. Otherwise, you may be checking for a slightly different shade of blue (the default blue set in the Designer is different than the blue block in the Blocks editor).

"ELSE IF" AND A SLIDESHOW APP

As a second "if" example, consider the "Inspirational Women in History" slideshow app, illustrated in Figure 3.9

Figure 3.9. A "Slideshow" app in which clicking "Next" switches the picture.

A picture appears when the app starts. Each time the user clicks the "Next" button, the app displays a different picture. When it gets to the fourth picture (Ruth Bader Ginsburg) and the button is clicked, the first picture reappears—the slideshow "wraps around".

There are a number of ways to code this app. In this chapter, you'll use an "if" block with "else if" branches. In chapter 4, you'll learn a better way that stores the pictures in a list variable and indexes through them.

Build the Slideshow App

Create a new app named "Slideshow". Then open a browser page to
https://draganddropcode.com/bookCh3/ and download the four pictures of inspirational leaders. The files "parks.jpg", "hopper.jpg", "vaughan.jpg", and "ginsburg.jpg" are pictures of:

- Rosa Parks, Civil Rights Activist
  https://www.womenshistory.org/education-resources/biographies/rosa-parks

- Grace Hopper, Computer Scientist
  https://www.womenshistory.org/education-resources/biographies/grace-hopper

- Dorothy Vaughan, NASA Mathematician
  https://www.nasa.gov/content/dorothy-vaughan-biography

- Ruth Bader Ginsburg, Supreme Court Justice
  https://www.womenshistory.org/education-resources/biographies/ruth-bader-ginsburg

Use the links to learn about these inspirational leaders, then upload the images into your "Slideshow" app. Recall that you upload media files by choosing the "Assets" icon in the left-menu of the Designer.

Once the pictures are uploaded, do the following:

- Drag in an Image component, set its Picture property to "parks.jpg", and resize it to your liking.

- Drag in a Button component and place it below the Image. Set the Button's Text property to "Next" and rename the button to NextButton. Recall that you can change the name of a component by clicking the name near the top of the right-side Property Panel. Your screen should appear like the one on the left-side of Figure 3.9

Next, open the Blocks Editor and code the blocks for having the picture change each time the button is clicked. Your goal is for the blocks to appear as shown in Figure 3.10:

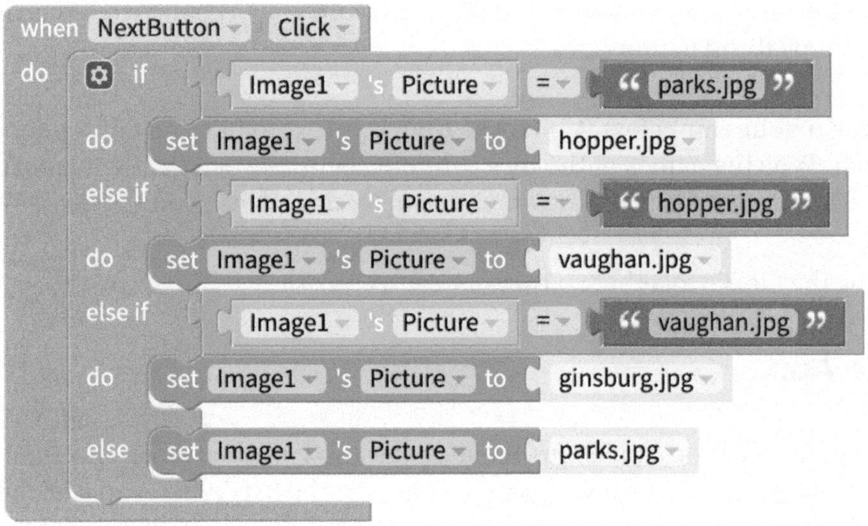

Figure 3.10. The blocks for navigating to the next picture

These are the steps required to build the blocks in Figure 3.10:

- Drag in the when NextButton1.Click block.

- Drag an if block from the Control folder. Click on the if block's blue transformer button and add the two else if branches and a final else branch, as shown in Figure 3.11:

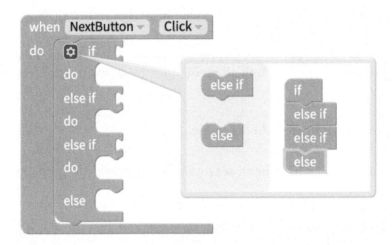

Figure 3.11. Click the blue icon to add branches to the "if" block

- There are three questions, each asking what the current picture is. There are four possible branches: the final "else" branch will be followed when none of the three questions are true. Drag in three = blocks from the Logic folder and plug them into the if slots.

- Drag in an Image1's Picture get block and copy it twice, and a set Image1.Picture block and copy it three times.

- Drag in four empty text ("") blocks from the Text folder and enter one of the file names in each. Type the names of the files carefully, being sure to get the name and extension exactly the same as the file names you uploaded. If you don't, the app won't work.

- Plug the blocks together so they appear as was shown in Figure 3.10.

Test the App

Test the app. Rosa Parks should appear when the app launches. Each time you click the NextButton, the app should show the next woman in the list. When you click on the last picture (Ruth Bader Ginsburg), the app should "wrap-around" and show Parks again.

How the Blocks Work

The picture of Rosa Parks initially appears because, in the Designer, Image1's Picture property is set to "parks.jpg". The first time the button is clicked, the first "if" question will evaluate to true and the first branch followed so that the picture changes to "hopper.jpg". Since the first question is true and that branch is taken, the following "else-if" and "else" branches are skipped and the event handler completes with the picture of Grace Hopper displayed

The second time the button is clicked, the value of Image1's Picture property is "hopper.jpg". The first "if" question evaluates to false (Image1's Picture is not parks.jpg), so the app asks the first "else if" question: is the picture "hopper.jpg". It is, so that branch is taken and Image1's Picture is changed to "vaughan.jpg".

On the third click, Image1.Picture is equal to "vaughan.jpg", so the third branch is taken and the picture is changed to "ginsburg.jpg".

On the fourth click, Image1.Picture is equal to "ginsburg.jpg". All of the "if" and "else if" questions evaluate to false. Thus, the final "else" branch is taken, and Image1's Picture is set back to "parks.jpg".

The "else" branch serves as a catch all—if all questions are false this final branch is taken. You could have added another "else if" asking if Images1's Picture is equal to "ginsburg.jpg". But the logic of the app is such that if Image1's Picture isn't any of the first three pictures, it must be "ginsburg.jpg". Thus, an additional "else-if" checking for "ginsburg.jpg" is unnecessary.

ANALYZING IF BRANCHES

Figure 3.12 illustrates the general way "if", "else if", and "else" branches are processed.

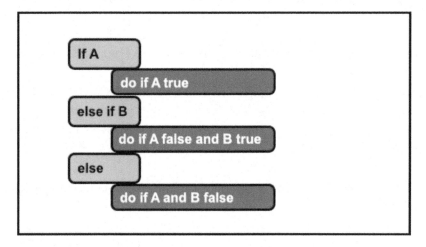

Figure 3.12. How "if", "else if" and "else" work

"A" and "B" represent *boolean* conditions, that is, some proposition that is true or false. The "if" branch is performed if the boolean condition A evaluates to true. The second branch, the "else if", is performed only if A is false *and* B is true—B is only asked if A is false. The third branch, the "else" clause, is only performed if both A and B evaluate to false.

It is easy to get the logic wrong in an app. Figure 3.13 provides some blocks that might appear to work as a slideshow, but don't. Can you tell how this app will behave?

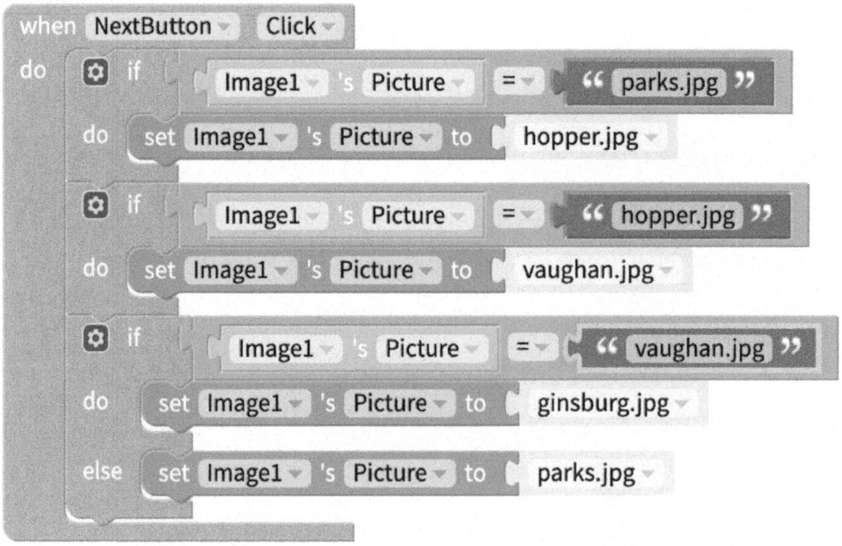

Figure 3.13. Three separate "if" questions.

These blocks are different from the previous ones in that there are three separate if blocks instead of a single if block with "else if" and "else" branches.

Assume that Image1's Picture starts out as "parks.jpg" and trace through the blocks with your finger. How will the app behave? Will it move to the next picture on each click, as with the previous version?

It won't. The blocks in Figure 3.13 will result in a slideshow of just two pictures, with the picture toggling between "parks.jpg" and "ginsburg.jpg". Because there are separate "if" blocks, they are all checked when the user clicks "Next".

On the first click, the first "if" question evaluates to true as Image1's Picture is indeed "parks.jpg". Image1's Picture thus gets set to "hopper.jpg". However, the event handler hasn't completed processing the initial click: the code immediately asks the next "if" question, asking if Image1's Picture is "hopper.jpg". It just got set to that, so Image1's Picture is set to "vaughan.jpg". Then the third question is asked. At that point, Image1's Picture is indeed "vaughan.jpg", so Image1's Picture is set to "ginsburg.jpg". Before the event handler for the first click has completed, Image1's Picture property has flipped through three of the pictures!

The image shown on the screen doesn't flip through the pictures, however. Typically, an app completes all of the blocks in an event handler before it updates the user interface. Even if a property in hidden memory changes a number of times within the event handler, the user doesn't see a change until the event handler completes. Despite all the internal property changes, the user only sees the picture of Parks change to a picture of Ginsburg on the first click.

Now consider the second time the button is clicked. Because Image1's Picture is set to "ginsburg.jpg", all of the "if" statements evaluate to false. Thus, the "else" branch of the final question is followed and Image1's Picture is set to "parks.jpg". The third click will go back to "ginsburg.jpg". The app just toggles between the pictures of Parks and Ginsburg with Hopper and Vaughan never shown.

INCREMENTING A PROPERTY VALUE

Now that you know how to ask questions, let's talk about numbers. To increment means to add to an existing value: 1 becomes 2, 3 becomes 4 or 8 becomes 9. Incrementing is a common operation in coding. When you score a point in a game app, the score in incremented. When an animated object moves across the screen, its x and y properties, which specify its horizontal and vertical location, are incremented.

As an example, consider the "ClickCount" app, shown in Figure 3.14. The app counts how many times a button is clicked, showing the count on the button:

Figure 3.14. The Button displays the number of times it has been clicked.

Build ClickCount

Create a new project named "ClickCount". In the Designer, drag in a Button and set its Text property to zero (0). Set the Text Color and Background Color as you see fit. Add a Label as well, with Text such as, "Number of times this button has been clicked".

In the Blocks Editor, drag in the when Button1 Click block along with set and get blocks for Button1's Text property. Then drag in a "+" block from the Math folder and configure the blocks as shown in Figure 3.15:

Figure 3.15. Increment Button1's Text on each click

Test the App

Test the app. Click the button a few times. Does the number on it increase by one each time?

How the Blocks Work

For most beginning coders, the blocks for incrementing shown in Figure 3.15 are a bit confusing. The blocks can be characterized as:

> when the button is clicked, set its Text property to *its current value plus one*.

If the value of Button1's Text is 0, set it to 1. If it is 1, set it to 2, and so on.

It helps to consider how a row of blocks is performed. Within each row, the blocks are performed in an inside-out manner. The set operation on the left isn't performed until the "+" operation is performed. The "+" operation isn't performed until the current value of Button1's Text is retrieved with the get block.

When Button1 is clicked the first time, the app first performs the get operation on Button1's Text to retrieve the current value (0 on first click). It then performs the "+" block, adding 0 to 1 for a result of 1. Finally, the left block of the row, the set operation, is performed and 1 is set into Button1's Text property.

Study this increment operation closely, as it is a fundamental operation used in almost every app.

INVISIBLE COMPONENTS AND TIMED BEHAVIORS

Visible components are those like Button and Label which appear in the app's screen. Invisible components are those that don't map to something the user sees. These invisible components are found in the Blocks editor in an ever-growing list that includes Timers, Alerts, Sensors and Ads.

The Timer component is used to control the timing of app behaviors—you can use it to build countdown apps, automated slideshows and animations. Think of the Timer component as an alarm clock inside the app.

The Timer component is found near the bottom of the left-panel of the Blocks Editor. When you click on the "+" near "Timer", a new Timer is created (e.g., Timer1) and a dialog appears prompting you to set some properties.

Before discussing the properties within Timer, it is important to note that a Timer has one associated event handler, the when Timer Fires block, shown in Figure 3.16:

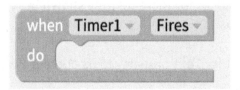

Figure 3.16. The event for the passing of time

No user event is needed to trigger this event handler: the blocks placed in it are performed in response to the passing of time.

Timer properties

Timer has three key properties, all of which modify how often the when Timer fires triggers. You can turn a timer on/off, specify that it should trigger periodically, and set how often it should trigger.

Figure 3.17 shows the properties of the Timer component.

Figure 3.17. Timer Component properties

Timer.**Interval**—specifies how often the when Timer Fires event will trigger, if it is enabled. You can set this in milliseconds (1/1000) of a second, or in seconds.

Timer.**Loops**—When true, the when Timer Fires will trigger periodically, instead of just once. If false, when Timer Fires will only trigger once. This property is set to false by default.

Timer.**Enabled**—When true, the when Timer Fires event handler will trigger. If false, when Timer Fires won't trigger at all.

Build a CountDown App

Consider the "CountDown" app shown in Figure 3.18:

Figure 3.18. A CountDown App.

When the "Start" button is clicked, the number on the screen starts getting smaller every second: 10-9-8, and so on, until it reaches 0. When the count reaches 0, the app speaks: "Time is Up" and the countdown stops.

This app increments a value like in the "ClickCount" app, except that one is subtracted instead of added each time (it "decrements"). The value change occurs in response to the passing of time as opposed to a button click.

The "CountDown" app follows a common pattern for animated behaviors: the user does something that enables the timer, the when Timer.Fires blocks begin repeating periodically, and then at some point the timer is disabled and the repeated activity ends.

Build the Countdown App

Create a new app named "CountDown". In the Designer:

- Drag in a Button, name it StartButton and change its Text to "Start".

- Drag in a Label, name it CountLabel, set its Text property to 10, and change its FontSize and Text Color as you see fit.

- Change the Screen's Background Color to any color you would like.

In the Blocks Editor,

- Click on the "+" near "Timer" to create a Timer component named Timer1. Set Timer1's Enabled property to false so the animation does not begin when the app launches—it should only start when the button is clicked. Set Timer1's Loops property to true so the when Timer.Fires event will trigger periodically, and set Timer's Interval to 1 second.

- Drag in a when StartButton Click event handler, and call **Timer1.Start**, which sets Timer1's Enabled property to true. Do not put the repeated activity—subtracting one from the Label—in this event handler.

- Drag in a when Timer.Fires event handler and place blocks in it for subtracting from the CountLabel's Text. Add an if block to check if the countdown should be ended. If it should be, call **say** to speak, "Time is Up", and call **Timer.Stop**, which sets Timer1's Enabled property to false. The blocks should look like those shown in Figure 3.19

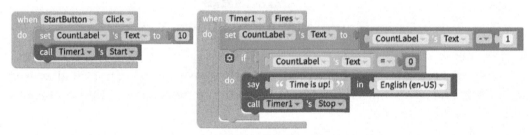

Figure 3.19. Blocks for the CountDown App.

Test the App

Open Thunkable Live on your phone or tablet, then back on your computer click the device icon in Thunkable's top-right menu. "10" should appear in the CountLabel. Click the StartButton. Does the number in the CountLabel decrease every second? Does the app speak when "0" is reached?

How the Blocks Work

When the user clicks the StartButton, the Timer is started--Timer's Enabled property is set to true. This "turns on" the second event handler, when Timer1.Fires, so that it begins triggering every second. Each time it triggers, it subtracts 1 from CountLabel.Text and checks to see if CountLabel.Text is equal to 0. If it is 0, the words, "Time is up!" are spoken and the Timer is stopped, effectively stopping activity until the button is clicked again.

SUMMARY

In Chapters 1 and 2, you learned that the fundamental construct of an app is the event handler and that your job as a coder is to specify how the app should respond to external events like the user clicking a button.

In this chapter, you learned more fundamentals:

- An app has a hidden memory, just like a human. The responses to events often involve setting values into memory cells, and retrieving values from those memory cells.

- An app can ask "if" questions with an arbitrary number of branches. Often those questions involve examining the values in the hidden memory.

- Incrementing a memory cell is a common operation which adds to or subtracts from the value in that memory cell.

- Some components are invisible. Changing the properties of an invisible component doesn't affect the way an app looks, but how it behaves. Timer is an invisible component that allows for animated behavior.

RAFIKI BREAKS IT DOWN

To code like a genie, you've got to think like a genie, which is to say you can't be intimidated by complexity. Not all incoming wishes will be snap-a-finger simple. Anticipating what your wish-makers may think to ask, before they themselves think of it, is genie-work and entails complexity.

Conditional blocks such as "if" and "if-else" are tools for managing complexity. In this chapter you saw them infuse a consistent rotation among images in an app. In other circumstances, they can facilitate your app with choice-power. Let's take the music soundboard app that we discussed last time, and consider ways that conditional blocks could help make it more interesting.

Thunkable has a Device folder in the Blocks Editor, inside of which is a block for identifying the day of the week, month or day of the month. Combined with a conditional "if", you can program an app to:

- Check the day of week. If it's Friday feature upbeat, spunky music. If it's Saturday, mix in a good amount of Jazz and Easy Listening. If it's Sunday, highlight inspirational artists.

- Check the month and the day. If it's granddad's birthday, play Stevie Wonder's "Happy Birthday".

Conditions are pivot points that give you creative power in app design. Like the multi-talented basketball players Lebron James and Nneka Ogwumike, you can be a wizard of surprise with a vast repertoire of moves.

VOCABULARY VIBE

BOOLEAN

The foundation of all computation is binary, a matter of 1s and 0s, on or off. The computing concept of boolean, true-false, mirrors this.

To the average ear, the word boolean rings kind of different. Actually, it's a nod to George Boole; a self-taught 19th century mathematician and logician who's work in algebraic theory laid the foundation for digital circuit design and all that followed from that—namely the Internet.

IF

The world is full of possibilities. Not everything aligns on a single track. To accommodate for this type of complexity in coding, there are conditional statements, all starting with if.

if is like a traffic light giving direction based on circumstances at hand. When conditions are a certain way, then proceed; if not. then move in a different direction. A simple concept, but imagine the knot that traffic would be tied into without this single factor: the traffic light. Consider this as well: by adeptly combining if-else conditions, you can engineer any artificial intelligence you want

CONCEPTUALIZE

1. How are an app's memory cells named differently than the memory cells in a spreadsheet?

2. Explain what a set operation and a get operation do.

3. Consider the following blocks:

a. Assume that CountLabel.Text has a 5 in it. What will the value of CountLabel.Text be after this row of blocks is performed?

b. In what order are the individual blocks in this row executed?

c. What is the term for the task completed by the row of blocks?

4. Consider an app with a Button that starts with the text "Go" on it. The following blocks are supposed to toggle the button's text between "Go" and "Stop" each time it is clicked.

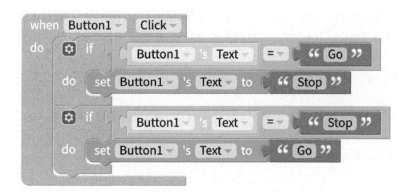

The code doesn't work. Explain, in detail, what actually happens when the button is clicked.

5. Consider the following diagram and suppose A, B, and C are boolean (true/false) conditions.

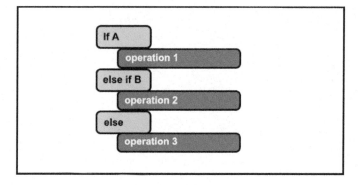

"operation 1" will be executed if A is true. Under what conditions will operation 2 and operation 3 be executed?

CUSTOMIZE

1. Write an app with a single button that starts with a zero on it. When clicked, the number on the button should increase by 1. When the number reaches 10, the app should speak, "Mission complete" and clicking the button again should no longer have an effect.

2. Write an app that has two buttons, both starting out with blue backgrounds. When the first button is clicked, it should toggle between blue and red. When the second button is clicked, it should become the current color of the first button.

CREATE

Create a simple arithmetic game for kids. Provide some simple math problems displayed in Labels, with adjacent input forms (TextInput and Button) for the user to enter answers. Check the user's answer and report if they are right or wrong using another Label or a **say** block.

Share your creative apps with your authors and other *Drag and Drop* coders:

- Use #DragAndDropCode and #MadeWithThunkable on your social media platforms.

- @ us at @DragAndDropCode on Twitter and Instagram.

Chapter Resources: draganddropcode.com/bookCh3/

CHAPTER 4. LISTS AND ITERATION

Apps: "Slideshow v.2"   and "TriviaApp"

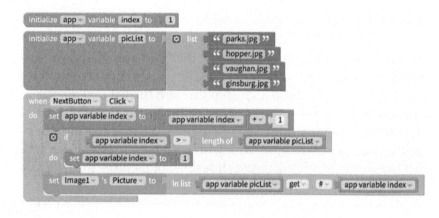

In this chapter, you'll learn how to define variables and lists of data, and you'll learn a fundamental coding task: how to iterate through a list of information using an index. With this knowledge, you'll transform the slideshow app from the previous chapter into a customizable multiple-choice trivia quiz app.

INTRODUCTION

One common software task is to process a list of data. Facebook processes your friend lists and your list of posts. Spotify processes your music lists. Your calculator app processes lists of numbers.

In this chapter, you'll learn how to define a list of data and how to walk through it to visit each item. You'll also learn how to add memory cells, called "variables", to your app.

You'll apply these techniques to recode the "Slideshow" app you created in Chapter 3. Instead of using "if", "else if", and "else" branches, as you did in that chapter, you'll place the picture files in a list, and you'll code blocks that step through the list and display a picture at a time. It is a better solution because it works generically, on any list of pictures, instead of particular ones. Such generality is important for code reuse—the new version can be used as a template for easily building your own slideshows with your own media. It also is a scheme that will work for apps in which the data is not fixed, e.g., a slideshow of pictures the user takes or uploads.

After completing a new version of the slideshow, you'll extend it to build a multiple-choice trivia app which you can use as a model for building your own trivia games and study guides.

The slideshow you created near the end of Chapter 3 used "if-elseif-else" code to toggle between the pictures. In that app, when the user clicks a button, the code chooses the next picture to display by checking which picture is currently being shown, as shown in Figure 4.1:

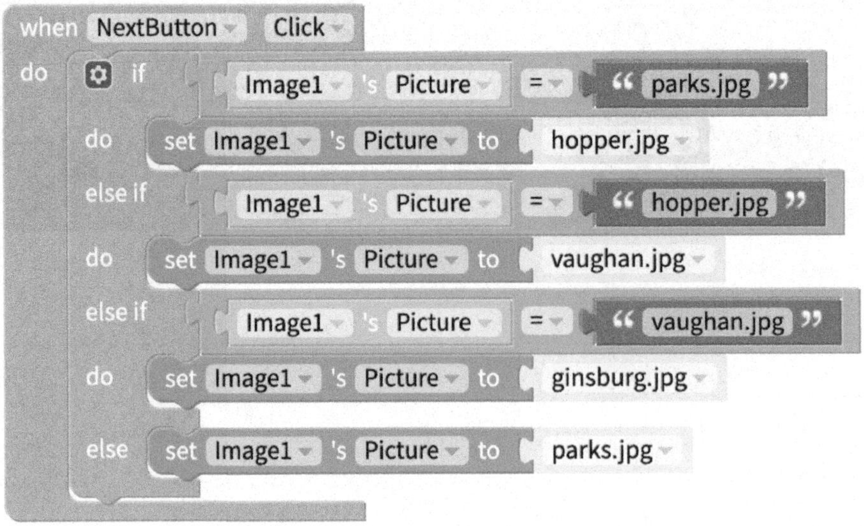

Figure 4.1. "if-elseif" blocks for navigating to the next picture

This solution was used to introduce you to conditional branches. It is a sub-optimal solution because the code explicitly references file names and thus only works for the specific set of pictures embedded in the code ("parks.jpg", "hopper.jpg", etc.). If you decided you wanted to modify the list of pictures shown, you'd have to modify the code to, say, add another "else if" branch. More importantly, this scheme won't work for an app in which the user can upload or use the camera to take new pictures, because in such a case the file names aren't pre-defined. Code should always be designed so that it works generically on any data. In this chapter, you'll learn how to do that.

VARIABLES

You've learned how to work with the hidden memory of an app by viewing and modifying component properties such as Button1's BackgroundColor. Besides component properties, Thunkable also provides another kind of named memory cell called a *variable*. You can think of variables as "free-agent" memory cells because they are not part of a component as are properties such as BackgroundColor.

You create a variable in the Blocks editor by selecting the Variables folder and dragging in the initialize variable to block shown at the top of Figure 4.2.

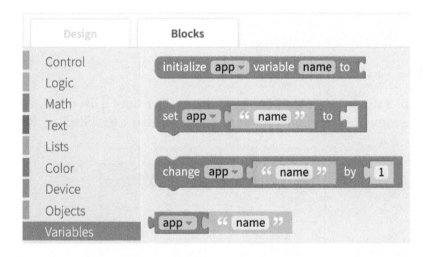

Figure 4.2. The Variables folder provides an "initialize" block.

When you drag in an initialize block, change "name" to something that describes the information that will be stored, e.g., "picList". Once you drag an initialize block in, new blocks for setting and getting the variable appear in the Variables folder. The newly generated blocks allow you to set values into and get values out of the variable you just created. Just like with component properties, "set" means to place something in a memory cell, while "get" means to look at what is in the memory cell. Figure 4.3 shows the Variables folder after the variable picList has been defined.

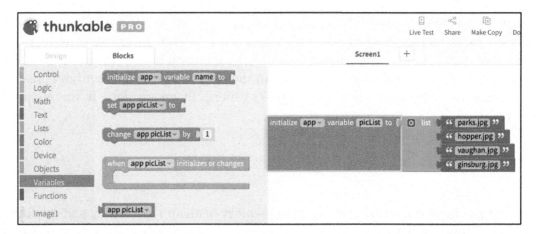

Figure 4.3. "set" and "get" blocks appear when a variable is initialized

The "get" block for the variable picList is at the bottom of Figure 4.3. As with component properties, "get" doesn't appear on the blocks but is implied. The keyword in front of a variable name, in this case, "app", refers to the variable's persistence, and whether the memory cell lives for a single run of the app ("app") or if it is stored in a device or cloud database ("stored", "cloud"). In this chapter, just leave the default setting of "app". You'll learn more about persistent variables in Chapter 12.

LISTS

A variable can store a single value like "Bob" or 34, or it can store a list of information. You define a list by selecting the Lists folder and dragging in either a list block or an empty list block, as shown in Figure 4.4:

Figure 4.4. Blocks for defining lists.

When you drag in a list block, it by default contains the items 1,2, and 3 in it, but you can replace those numbers with any items you'd like. You can also select the blue mutator icon to modify the number of items in the list. For instance, for the slideshow app, you could drag in a list block, use the blue mutator to give it four slots, then fill the slots with the names of the picture files, as shown in Figure 4.5:

initialize app variable picList to
list
" parks.jpg "
" hopper.jpg "
" vaughan.jpg "
" ginsburg.jpg "

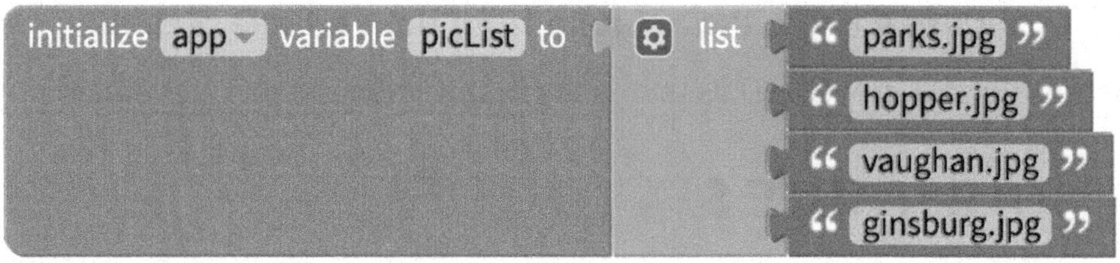

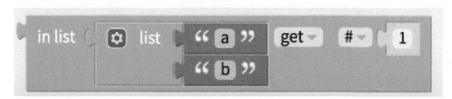

Figure 4.5. A list variable with the image file names as items

With list variables, the variable name refers not to a single memory cell, but to a set of memory cells. Each of the cells is referred to with an index number, starting with 1, as shown in Figure 4.6.

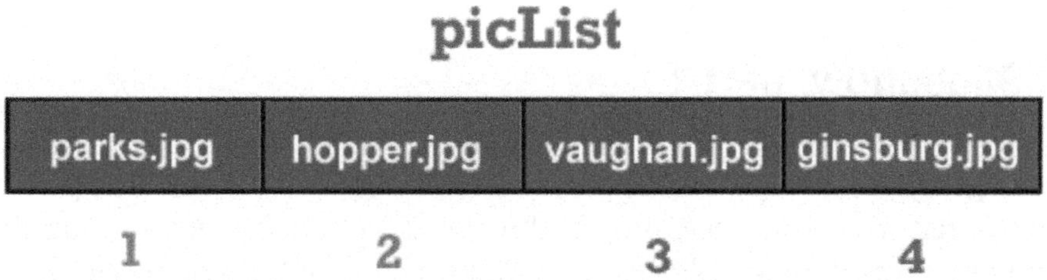

picList
parks.jpg
hopper.jpg
vaughan.jpg
ginsburg.jpg
1
2
3
4

Figure 4.6. List variables have multiple memory slots identified by slot number.

In some programming languages, you select a particular list element with syntax of the form, "picList[1]" ("syntax" is the grammar of a coding language). With Thunkable, you use the in list get block found in the "Lists" folder, as shown in Figure 4.7:

in list
list
" a "
" b "
get
#
1

Figure 4.7. The "in list get" block selects an item from a list.

The in list get block appears with a default list and index. The default block results in "a" being selected from the list because the first item in the list ["a","b"] is "a".

Typically, you'll replace the default list with a reference to a list variable. For instance, the blocks in Figure 4.8 select the first item from the variable picList:

Figure 4.8. get the 1st item from the variable picList.

The result of this block is "parks.jpg" as that is the first item in the picList defined in Figure 4.5.

INDEX VARIABLES

Besides the picList variable, you need a second one named "index". An index is a variable for keeping track of your current position in a list or text string, and is perhaps the most commonly used variable. In this case, you need it to track the position of the currently displayed picture as the user navigates through the slideshow. The index variable will start at 1 and you'll increment it each time the user clicks the NextButton.

Build the Slideshow, part 1

To begin, first open your "Slideshow" app from Chapter 3, the one with the pictures of the inspirational women. You won't use most of the blocks in the app, but you can re-use the user interface components and media files from it. Make a copy of the app by choosing the "…" in the top-right menu and "Duplicate project". Rename your copy, "SlideshowList" and open it for editing. If you haven't yet created a slideshow, just create a new project, add in a few image files of your own, and add Image and Button components onto the Screen.

In the Designer, modify Image1's Picture property so that it is blank to start instead of "parks.jpg". You will show "parks.jpg" as the first picture, but you'll specify that in blocks by abstractly referring to the first picture in the list. That way if you change your list, the code will still show the first picture.

In the Blocks Editor, remove the "if" code from the when NextButton click event handler because you are going to recode how the NextButton is handled.

From the Variables folder, drag in two initialize app variable blocks. Name one variable "picList" and the other "index". Initialize index to 1 and initialize picList with a list of the image file names, as shown in Figure 4.9:

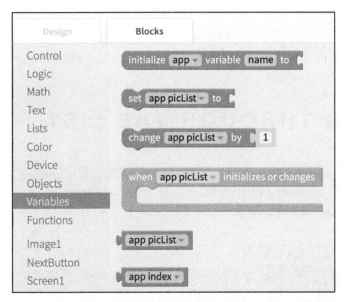

Figure 4.9. Variables for the list and the index

After initializing these variables, open the "Variables" folder. You'll see that there is a set block for app picList and get blocks for app picList and app index, as illustrated by Figure 4.10:

Figure 4.10. After a variable is initialized, new blocks appear

There isn't a set app index block like the set app picList block. You can get a set app index block, however, by dragging in the set app picList block then clicking on the upside-down triangle next to the name and choosing "app index".

Next, code the when Screen Opens event handler as shown in Figure 4.11:

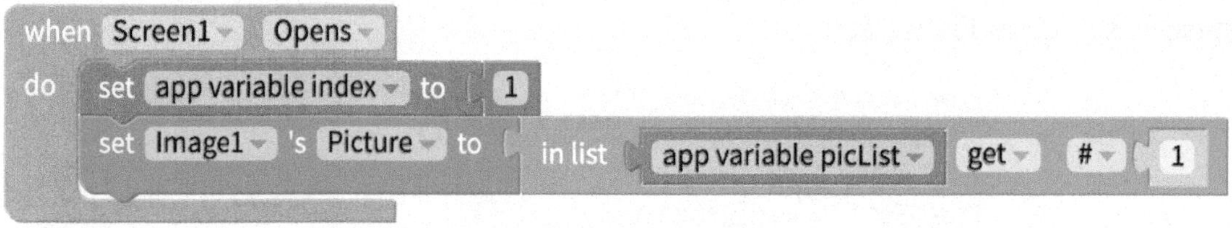

Figure 4.11. When the screen opens, set index to 1 and show first picture

The when Screen1 Opens event handler is triggered when the app launches the first time. The index is set to the starting position 1. The bottom row of the code gets the first item from piclist, which is "parks.jpg", and sets it as the image being displayed.

Test the App

Continually test your apps as you build them, after every few blocks you code. Open Thunkable Live on your phone or tablet, then click the device icon in the Thunkable Menu. Does the picture of Rosa Parks appear?

ITERATING THROUGH THE LIST

Now that your app shows the first picture from the list when it launches, the next step is to define the behavior for when the button is clicked. A naive approach would be to code it to show the *2nd* picture, as shown in Figure 4.12.

Figure 4.12. When "Next" is clicked, get the 2nd picture.

The code will indeed show the 2nd picture, "hopper.jpg", when NextButton is clicked the first time, but what will happen on the second click? If you answered that the picture will stay as "hopper.jpg" no matter how many times you click, you are correct! To test this, add the blocks of Figure 4.12 and test the app.

Clearly, a more abstract approach is needed for the when NextButton.Click behavior. When the button is clicked, the *next* picture in the list should appear, not the 2nd picture. If the first picture is showing, switch to the second. If the second is showing, switch to the third, and so on.

This is where the variable index comes into play. Its purpose is to keep track of the current position as the user navigates through the list. Each time the NextButton is clicked, the code should increment the index variable and then display the "indexth" picture. Figure 4.13 shows the blocks:

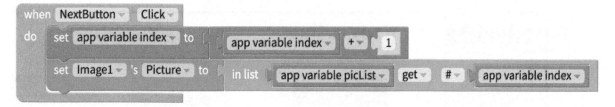

Figure 4.13. Increment index then display the *indexth* item.

When the app executes these blocks, it first adds one to index, then uses the updated value of index when it gets the item from the picList. In this way, the picture is set not to the 2nd or 3rd item, but to the *indexth* item, whichever that might be.

Modify your blocks to appear like those in Figure 4.13, then test the app on your phone/tablet. Rosa Parks should appear when the app launches. Hopper should appear on the first click, Vaughan on the second, and Ginsburg on the third.

But what happens when you click the picture of Ginsburg, the last picture in the list? Try it and see. You'll find that you have a bug—no picture appears! You may have an idea why the error is happening, but first take a moment to learn about a technique called tracing which can help you debug your apps.

TRACING CODE

Tracing code means to play the role of the app and use your finger to step through each block, jotting down with pencil and paper how the properties and variables change as each block is executed.

To begin, take out a piece of paper and draw each of the pertinent properties and variables with lines underneath them. Underneath the lines, show what data is in that memory cell.

When an app is launched, the initial properties in the Designer are put into memory, the variables are initialized, and then the blocks in the when Screen.Opens event handler are executed. If you trace those blocks for this app, the hidden memory will appear as shown in Figure 4.14:

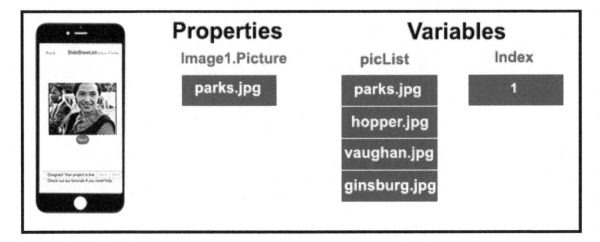

Figure 4.14. The app and its hidden memory.

The next step in tracing is to imagine a user scenario—what the user might do. In this case, the scenario you care about is the user clicking the button a number of times.

When the user clicks the NextButton the first time, the first row of blocks in Figure 4.15 is executed.

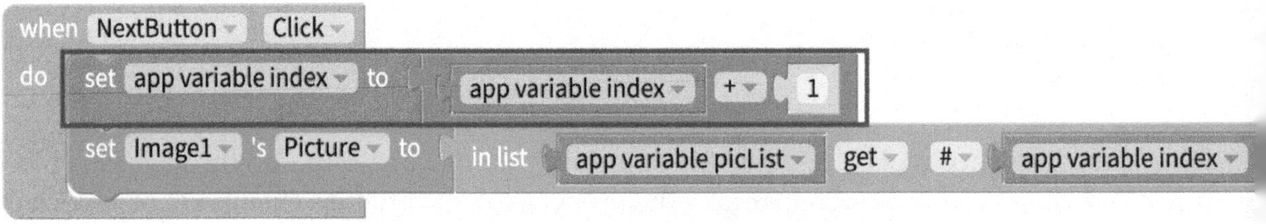

Figure 4.15. Increment the index.

The index variable changes from 1 to 2. Then the second row of blocks is executed, as shown in Figure 4.16:

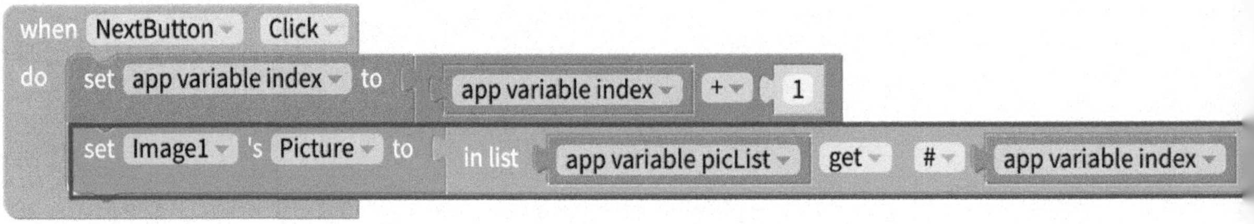

Figure 4.16. The picture is modified to show the 2nd picture (hopper.jpg).

The set block on the left isn't performed until the blocks in the "to" slot are evaluated. The app first gets the value of index from memory. Because it is now 2, the get operation accesses the second item in picList ("hopper.jpg"). Finally, the set is executed, the Image1.Picture property is set to "hopper.jpg", and the user interface changes to show the picture of Grace Hopper. The new state of the UI and hidden memory is shown in Figure 4.17

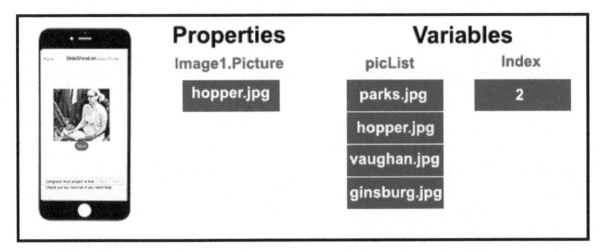

Figure 4.17. Hidden variables after "when NextButton.Click" completes

If you continue tracing through a second click, you'll see that index will change to 3 and the third picture, "vaughan.jpg", will appear. After yet another click, index will be 4 and the fourth picture, "ginsburg.jpg", will appear.

Now envision what happens if the NextButton is clicked one more time.

The first row of blocks will change index from 4 to 5. The second row of blocks will then attempt to get the fifth item from the list, because 5 is the value of index. As there are only four items in the list, the in list get function can't execute correctly and the app fails.

Tracing buggy code in this fashion can help you find a solution. Can you determine how to fix this code?

One solution is to add an if block to handle the case when the index variable gets too big. Figure 4.18 shows blocks for doing this:

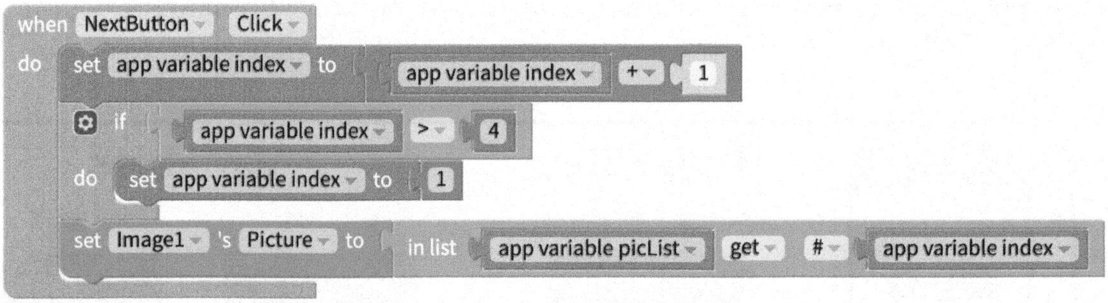

Figure 4.18. When the index is larger than the number of items, set it to 1

When index gets too big (>4), the code sets index back to 1 so that the first item in the list is displayed. The Slideshow in effect, "wraps around" when the end is reached.

Modify your blocks so that they look like those in Figure 4.18. You'll need to drag in an if block from the "Control" folder, and a ">" comparison from the "Logic" folder.

Test the App

Test the app. When you click through the pictures, what happens when you get to the picture of Justice Ginsburg and click the NextButton? Does it "wrap around" and show Rosa Parks?

How the Blocks Work

To understand this solution, first consider the case when the value of index is 1. When NextButton is clicked, index is set to 2. The "if app index> 4" condition is false, since 2 is less than 4, so index is not set back to 1. The final row in the event handler is then executed, as it is not part of the "if" branch, and Image1's Picture is set to the *indexth* (2nd) picture, hopper.jpg.

Now envision that the button has been clicked three times. At that point index is 4 and "ginsburg.jpg" is being displayed. When the button is clicked again, index is set to 5. The "if app index> 4" condition now evaluates to true, since 5 is greater than 4, so index is set to 1 and the first picture, "parks.jpg" is displayed.

You might wonder, "index was 5 for a bit, why didn't that cause an error?" The answer is that index being set to 5 isn't in itself cause for an error. Because of the if block, index is set back to a valid number, 1, before the final row of blocks is executed and an attempt is made to get the 5th item from a 4-element list. It is the in list get operation in the bottom row that has the potential for error. Because of the if block, this code will never attempt to get an item with an index larger than 4.

EXPLICIT VS. ABSTRACT REFERENCES

This list-based solution for the Slideshow is improved from the "if-elseif-else" branching solution of Chapter 3 because the data is not referred to in the event handlers. The event handlers don't refer to file names like "parks.jpg" explicitly, but instead refer abstractly to items in the list variable. Because the code is more abstract, it is easy to change the app so that it works on different lists.

The solution shown in Figure 4.18 is still too explicit, however. Can you tell what the issue is?

The issue is that the code would stop working if there weren't exactly 4 items in the list. Try adding another image to the app by placing a fifth file name in picList, then test to see if the app still works.

You'll find that the app doesn't fail, but it only toggles through the first four pictures—the fifth picture never appears. The problem is that the code is too specific in one place—the reference to 4 within when NextButton.Click.

For your code to work with a list of any size, you need to abstractly refer to the length of the list as opposed to specifically referring to the given list's length of 4. Instead of asking if index is greater than 4, the code should ask if index is greater than the *length of the list*. The List folder provides a length of block for this purpose.

Drag a length of block in, plug an app pictureList block into it, then replace the 4 with these blocks. Your modified code should appear as shown in Figure 4.19:

Figure 4.19. Refer abstractly to the length of picList instead of "4"

With this modification, you can add or remove items from the picList and the app will still work!

SYNCHRONIZED LISTS

Suppose you wanted to show the name of each leader along with the picture, as shown in Figure 4.20:

Figure 4.20. Show the name along with the picture

This addition can be made by creating a second list variable for the women's names and having the name items correlate with the items of picList, e.g., the 1st name corresponds to the 1st picture, the 2nd name corresponds to the 2nd picture, and so on.

You don't need an additional index variable to code this because the one index variable will serve as the current position for both of the lists.

Perform the following steps:

- In the Designer, add a new Label and name it NameLabel. Set its Font Size to 32. Set its Text to "" but realize the blocks will modify this setting.

- In the Blocks Editor, initialize another list variable, nameList, with the names of the women. Your variable should appear as shown in Figure 4.21.

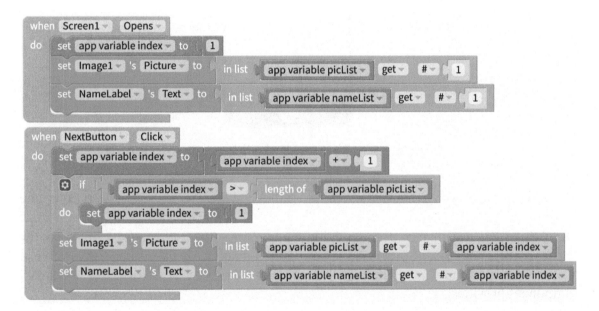

Figure 4.21. Add a list variable for the names

- Add blocks to set the NameLabel as the user navigates through the slideshow. Modify the **when Screen.Start** and **when NextButton Click** event handlers so that they update NameLabel's Text property along with updating the picture. Figure 4.22 shows the updated blocks:

Figure 4.22. Updated blocks set the NameLabel corresponding to the image

Test your updated app: does the correct name appear with each picture?

LISTVIEWER AND A GUESSING GAME

Now let's flip the script. Instead of showing the user the name when the picture appears, convert the app into a quiz app in which the user is prompted to guess the name of each woman. Such a quiz app is shown in Figure 4.23.

Figure 4.23. Convert the Slideshow into a quiz

To build this game, you'll display the entire nameList at once using a ListViewer component.

Recall that variables are part of an app's hidden memory—the user can't see what is in them. The ListViewer component provides the antidote—it displays the items in a list variable and allows the user to choose an item from it. Figure 4.24 shows the key blocks that the ListViewer component provides:

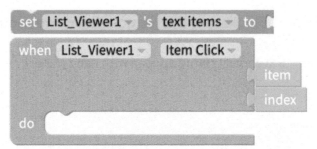

Figure 4.24. Key ListViewer blocks

The set ListViewer's text items block is used to specify the list variable that should be displayed. In this app, you'll display the nameList variable in the ListViewer.

The when ListViewer.ItemClick event handler is triggered when the user selects one of the items in the ListViewer. Two green blocks appear on the right-side of the event handler, item and index. These are *event parameters* and they specify information about the event. The parameters for this particular event specify which item the user selected along with the index of that item in the list. For instance, if the user chose the third name in nameList, the item would be "Dorothy Vaughan" and the index would be 3.

Build the Guessing Game

Make a copy of the "Slideshow" app and name it, "GuessingGame". Then make the following changes to the app:

In the Designer:

- Drag in a ListViewer component and place it below the NextButton.

- Rename the NameLabel to QuestionResponseLabel and change its Text to "Who is this woman?" Here, you're repurposing the Label to ask the question and let the user know if a guess is right or wrong.

In the Blocks,

- In the when Screen Opens event handler, add blocks to display the nameList in the ListViewer by setting ListViewer's text items property.

- In both when Screen Opens and when NextButton.Click, remove the blocks that set what was the NameLabel to an item in the list.

- Drag in a when ListViewer ItemClick event handler and code it to check if the user chose the name of the woman whose picture is showing.

Figure 4.25 shows how the blocks should appear:

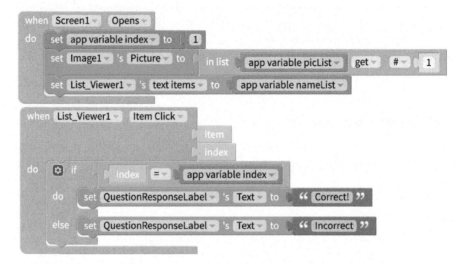

Figure 4.25. Blocks for the Guessing Game App

The "if" condition within the when ListViewer ItemClick event handler checks to see if the user's answer is correct. In English, you'd say "if the user's answer is the same as the name of the current picture then the answer is correct". In blocks, you check if the position of the item chosen (the green index block) is equal to the index of the current picture being displayed (the orange app variable index block).

The fact that both are named "index" is a bit confusing. The green index is the event parameter specifying the position of the item the user chose, and the orange app index refers to the variable being used to keep track of the current picture being shown.

Test the App

Test the app. Try to guess who the first picture is. Does the app respond correctly?

Try clicking the NextButton as well. You should notice a bug—the QuestionResponseLabel needs to be reset to the question, "Who is this woman?" when the user clicks the NextButton.

Add blocks in the when NextButton.Click event handler to fix the problem. Figure 4.26 shows the updated blocks:

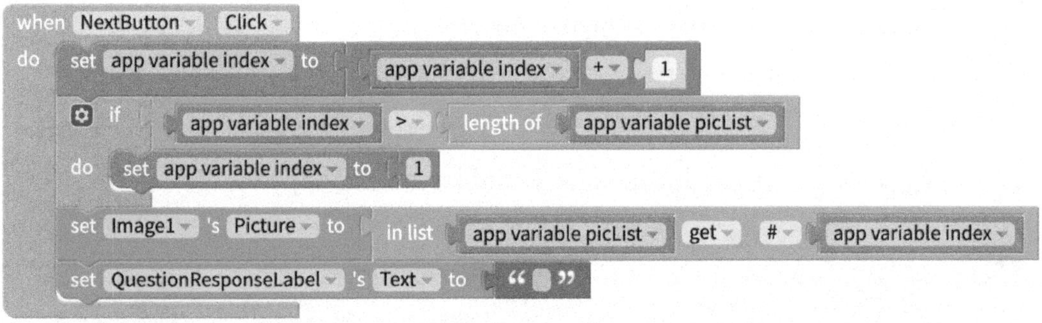

Figure 4.26. Reset QuestionResponseLabel on Next

LISTS OF LISTS AND A TRIVIA APP

The guessing game is relatively simple: the question is always the same, "who is this woman?", and the answer choices are the same for every question. For most trivia apps, each successive question is different and a different list of answer choices are provided for each question. In this section, you'll build such an app.

- Make a copy of the "GuessingGame" app and name it "TriviaApp"

- In the Designer, drag in a new Label and place it below the Image. Name it QuestionLabel and set its Text to "---". Also, set QuestionResponseLabel's Text to blank ("").

- In the Blocks Editor, create new list variables questionList and answerList, with the questions and answers listed below:

Question	Answer
In what city did Rosa Parks famously refuse to give up her seat to a white passenger?	Montgomery, Alabama
Grace Hopper drove the creation of one of the first coding languages. What was it called?	COBOL
Dorothy Vaughan was a mathematician and programmer at which organization?	NASA

Which Ruth Bader Ginsburg case was the first to use the equal protection clause to strike down gender discrimination?	Reed v. Reed

Figure 4.27 shows how the blocks for the new variables should appear.

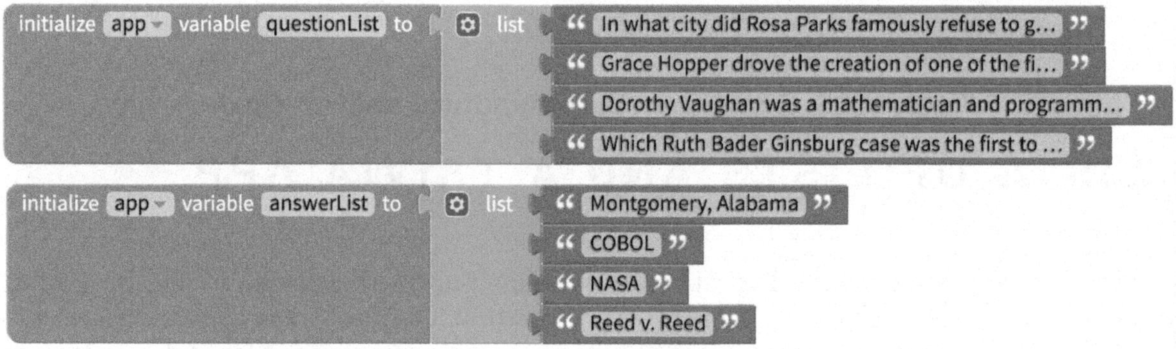

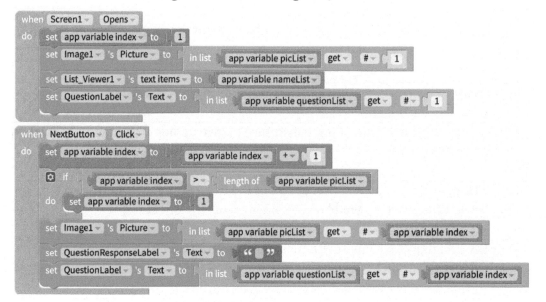

Figure 4.27. Variables for the questions and answers

For long text, Thunkable only displays part of it in red Text blocks and inserts the "...".

- Code when Screen1.Opens so that the first question appears in QuestionLabel.Text on app launch and so that the *indexth* question appears in QuestionLabel.Text when the NextButton is clicked. You should blank out QuestionResponseLabel.Text as well. Try to code this without looking at the blocks in Figure 4.28

Figure 4.28. Change QuestionLabel as the user navigates through the quiz

With these blocks, the QuestionLabel's Text property is set when the app launches or the NextButton is clicked, similarly to how Image1's Picture is set. Note that QuestionLabel's Text is set using an in list get from questionList instead of picList.

Test the App

Test the partially completed app. Does the question matching the image appear when you click the NextButton? If so, the next step is to code the multiple-choice.

Lists of Lists

For a multiple-choice trivia app, you need a list of answer choices corresponding to each question. One of the answers in the choices will match the correct answer, while the others will be incorrect answers.

List items can be of any type, including text, numbers, colors, or true/false values (booleans). List items can also, themselves, be lists. *Lists of lists* are common in software, as are even more complex data structures, such as the decision trees used in AI chess players.

For this app, you'll define a variable, answerChoicesList, as a list of lists. The first item will be the sub-list of answer choices for the first question, the second item will be the sub-list of answer choices for the second question, and so on.

Drag in an initialize variable block and name the variable answerChoicesList. Then plug a list block into the initialize variable block, change it to have four items, and plug list blocks into each of those four items, as shown in Figure 4.29:

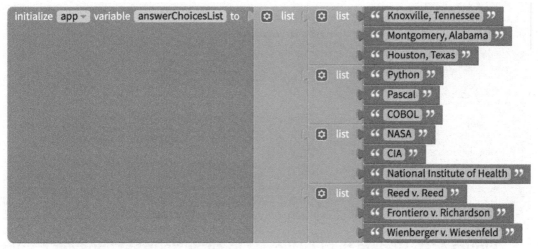

Figure 4.29. A list of lists: answer choices for each question

Recall from Chapter 3 that variables are like named memory cells. If you could see the hidden memory, the variable answerChoicesList would look as shown in Figure 4.30:

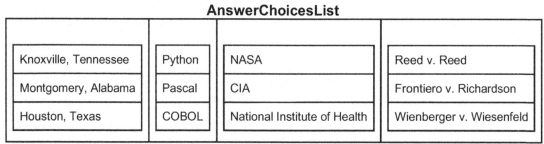

Figure 4.30. The structure of answerChoicesList in the app's memory.

Display the Answer Choices

A different list of answer choices should appear for each question in the trivia app. The List_Viewer's text items property needs to be set both when the app launches and in the when NextButton.Click event handler. When the NextButton is clicked, it should be set to the answer choices for the current question, i.e., the *indexth* sub-list of answerChoicesList. Figure 4.31 shows the changes to the blocks:

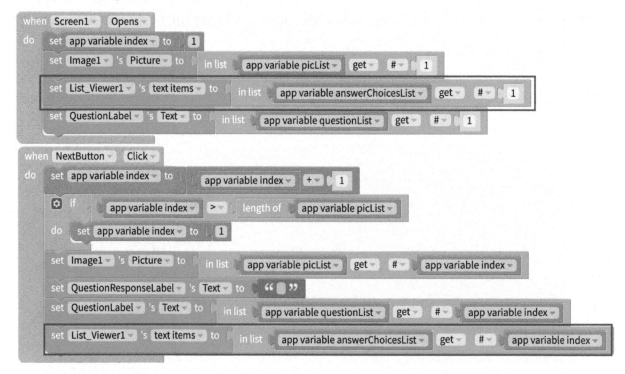

Figure 4.31. Update the ListViewer to show "current" answer choices

Now, when the NextButton is clicked, the Picture, QuestionLabel, and List_Viewer1 are all set to show the data for the *indexth* item of the appropriate list. The *indexth* item of answerChoicesList is itself a list, which makes it appropriate for plugging in to the set List_Viewer1's text items block.

Check the Answer

To check the user's answer, you'll compare the user's selection with the correct answer for that question, which is in answerList. Recall that the when List_Viewer1.Item Click event handler has two event parameters, item and index. In the previous guessing game, you used index, which tells you the position of the item the user has chosen.

For this app, use the item parameter, which specifies the actual text of the item the user has chosen. Compare it with the correct answer from the variable answerList. Code the blocks as shown in Figure 4.32:

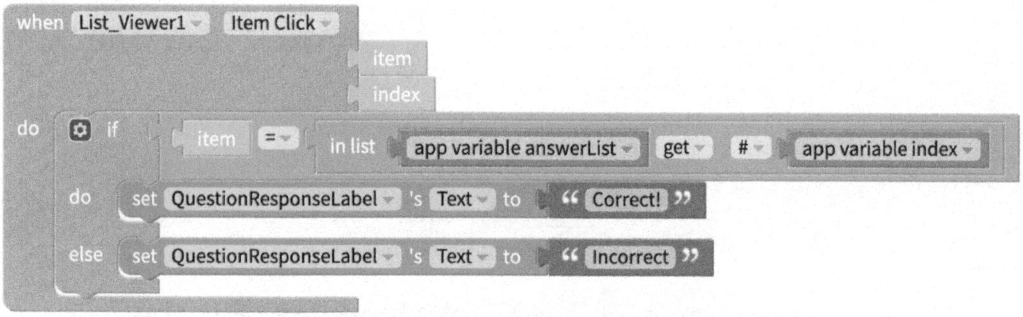

Figure 4.32. Check the user's answer

Note that the item chosen by the user is compared to the indexth item in answerList, which holds the correct answers, and not answerChoicesList, which holds right and wrong answers.

Test the App

Test the app. Does the app check your answers correctly?

All the Blocks

Figure 4.33 shows all of the blocks for the quiz app, together for your viewing pleasure:

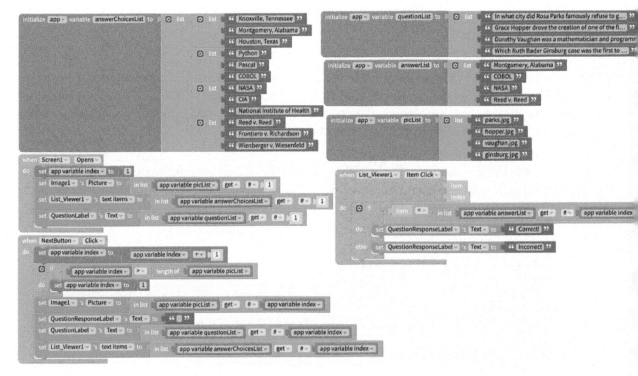

Figure 4.33. The Blocks for entire Quiz app

SUMMARY

In previous chapters you learned about event handlers, hidden memory, and "if" conditionals. This chapter added variables to the discussion—you can define named memory cells to store data besides what is stored in component properties. You also learned about lists and techniques for using an index variable to walk through a list. The code you learned for iterating through a list, like checking an "if" condition to see if the end of a list has been reached, is fundamental and something experienced programmers end up coding thousands of times.

The separation of data and code is another concept featured in this chapter. It is important to define your data, like the picture file names, in a list variable and not within the event handler code of your app. The code in the when NextButton.Click should refer only abstractly to the list and shouldn't refer to data like "parks.jpg" directly. If your code abstractly refers to items in the list, the app can easily be customized for different media and uses—you can remix to make all kinds of quizzes! It also makes it so the code can work even if the list of pictures is dynamic, e.g., an app in which the user can take or upload pictures into the slide show.

You are now building sophisticated apps with abstract references and most certainly running into coding bugs. Do not fret—you are not alone! There is a community of "Thunkers" with whom you can collaborate and get help. Check out Appendix C for more info on how to collaborate with other Thunkers.

RAFIKI BREAKS IT DOWN

Data is the blood and muscle of modern computing. If only ten people could connect with you on social media, that wouldn't make for a very exciting experience, would it? It's the manipulation of data that makes it possible to have tens of thousands of followers, or to have feeds filled with posts from a wide array of different persons. The more savvy you become at manipulating data through your app design, the more impressive will be the experiences that your apps will deliver. Thunkable is a powerful resource in this regard, because it sets you up for data success.

To Abstract is the Upward Tract

If you want your genie powers to grow, *separate your data from your code*. One big lesson you learned in chapter 4 is abstraction, which helps you think more "big picture" about your app strategy and design.

You created storing instructions and logic for general entities (lists) and not a specific data set (the four images of women leaders). In doing so, you developed some coding muscle that empowers you to easily remix your apps for different scenarios. For those of you who are budding musicians, an analogy is the difference between learning to play, "Twinkle, Twinkle" and learning to read sheet music. With the latter skill in hand you can play hundreds of songs and eventually write your own that even other musicians can play. Combining variables and lists is the beginning of your learning to read "app sheet music". Who doesn't love a genie that can make beautiful music?

VOCABULARY VIBE

VARIABLE

A variable is a named memory cell or cells, whether it is a single point or collection of many points. Designing how your app will remember things and recall them is a critical element to effective app design and delivery of a great user experience. Any good app has to call forth and manipulate data at the speed of light and variables are an essential power in their ability to do so.

Varying types of data flowing through an app, and even between apps, constantly or upon request, is much like an orchestra. The melody of it all depends on precision, not approximations or guessing. Harmony and rhythm require the same exactness. If coders are the orchestra conductors of the data music in an app, then variables are the tools they use to ensure that the data notes end up where they belong and in the correct measure.

CONCEPTUALIZE

1. In processing a list, you use an index to keep track of the current position. In determining when you've reached the end, it is better to compare the index to the length of the list as opposed to a fixed number like 4, even if your list has 4 items. Explain why.

2. Explain why the code for the "Slideshow" in this chapter, using a list variable, is a better solution than the "if-elseif-else" solution in Chapter 3.

3. Consider the following blocks and assume the picList has the same items as in the sample of this chapter:

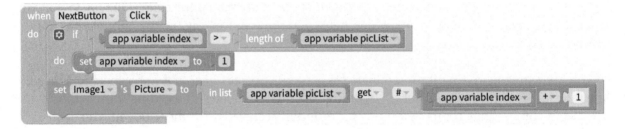

The blocks here are different from the correct solution (Figure 4.19) and don't successfully allow the user to navigate through the pictures. Explain what does happen when the NextButton is clicked the first time, and what happens on successive clicks.

CUSTOMIZE

1. Incorporate video into the slideshow or trivia app by 1) finding a video clip of each of the inspirational women leaders, then 2) adding a Video component to replace the Image on the Screen. The video clips must be .mp3 files and you can either upload them into the app, or reference a URL. You can't reference a YouTube link: it has to be a URL with a ".mp3" extension at the end.

Hint: you'll need another variable for the list of video clips.

2. Add a StartButton to the "Slideshow" app that, when clicked, auto-plays the slides, i.e., every few seconds the next picture appears. While the slides are playing, disable the NextButton and the StartButton. Stop the show and re-enable the buttons when the last picture appears.

Hint: use a Timer component.

3. Add a PreviousButton to the "Slideshow" app such that the user can navigate backward through the pictures.

As with the NextButton, the slideshow should "wrap around" when the endpoint is reached, i.e., when the first picture (Parks) is showing and the user clicks PreviousButton, the last picture in the list (Ginsburg) should appear.

4. Rewrite the "Slideshow" app so that it doesn't "wrap around", but instead disables the NextButton when the last item appears, and disables the PreviousButton when the first item appears. You can set the Enabled property of a Button to true to enable it, and false when you want it disabled. When a button's Enabled property is set to false, it is grayed out. Hint: Be sure to take care of re-enabling the buttons when appropriate.

CREATE

1. Create your own trivia or study guide app, but one with both pictures and sound clips. Find your own media on the Internet. Begin by making a copy of the "Trivia" app and removing the media files already in it, then adding your own.

2. Create a "Name that tune" app.

Share your creative apps with your authors and other *Drag and Drop* coders:

- Use #DragAndDropCode and #MadeWithThunkable on your social media platforms.

- @ us at @DragAndDropCode on Twitter and Instagram.

Chapter Resources: draganddropcode.com/bookCh4

CHAPTER 5. APPS WITH DATA

App: "MeetMyClassmates"

Today, there is a world of data at our fingertips. In every walk of life people are exploring how to use data to make better decisions. In this chapter, you'll learn how to "appify" a spreadsheet by loading its data into your app and displaying it in convenient ways for your users. You'll build a "MeetMyClassmates" app which you can use as a template for any informational apps you want to create. More importantly, you'll take the first step toward building apps that aren't closed silos, but connected to the outside world.

INTRODUCTION

Consider a "MeetMyClassmates" app which displays the pictures and names of all of the students in a class. When you click on a picture, it opens a new screen showing additional information for the particular student.

As a teacher, you can distribute the app the first day of class so everyone can learn each other's names quickly. If you're teaching coding, you can also distribute the source code for the app and assign a project of adding features or remixing the app, e.g., make it into a guessing game where the student's name doesn't appear until you click a "reveal" button.

"MeetMyClassmates" is illustrative of apps with dynamic, persistent data. Such apps are challenging with traditional programming tools because you have to configure and connect to a database, use a separate language like SQL to access the data, and then perform some sophisticated code to display the data and interact with users. Such database programming typically requires advanced coding knowledge and most beginning coding courses don't go there.

Thunkable makes it easy to access and display data from a spreadsheet or database, and it generates blocks for your particular data that make it easy to access and add to it. Thunkable provides an abstraction, the Data Source, that allows you to code your app the same exact way no matter what type of data you connect to. You can connect to a Google Sheet, Airtable or Webflow, tables, or Thunkable's own spreadsheets. Once you connect, the coding is the same.

CREATE A SPREADSHEET

Create a new Google sheet. You can open up the class roster at https://bit.ly/thunkClassRoster and choose File | Make a Copy, or create your own from scratch. If you create your own sheet, add column headings in the first row of the sheet for "name", "pic", and "description" and add some sample data so that your sheet looks similar to Figure 5.1:

	A	B	C
1	name	pic	description
2	David Wolber	https://sites.google.com/site/davewolber/_/rsrc/1472843875095/	USF Professor and Author
3	Tara Chklovski	https://enterprisersproject.com/sites/default/files/styles/large/pub	Technovation CEO
4	Rafiki Cai	https://0.academia-photos.com/277254/941463/1179307/s200_r	Digital Doctor
5	Tomas Wolber	https://lh3.google.com/u/0/d/1rGgcCNSCJDEiZLYOO0DWWeLL	Dime Hoopster
6	Ralph Morelli	https://res.cloudinary.com/dlox0soom/image/upload/v165066238	Professor and Blues Afficianado
7	Jen Rosato	https://res.cloudinary.com/dlox0soom/image/upload/v165066252	Director of National Center for Computing Education

Figure 5.1. A Google Sheet for "MeetMyClassmates"

The "name" and "description" fields are just text. The "pic" column contains URLs referring directly to .png or .jpg image files on the web. For your pictures, be careful to add URLs that refer directly to images and not to the web page containing the images.

CONNECT SPREADSHEET TO YOUR APP

Create a new app in Thunkable named "MeetMyClassmates". To map your app to a spreadsheet, select the "Data" icon in the left menu of the Designer and create a new Data Source. Any Data Sources you've used previously will appear, along with a button to create a new one. Choose the "Create New" button, select "Google Sheet" as the spreadsheet type, then select the sheet you created above.

Be sure you are logged into Thunkable with the same account from which you created your Google sheet.

DISPLAY DATA

Thunkable's Data Viewer Grid and Data Viewer List components makes it easy to display data from the rows of a spreadsheet. You set the Data Source property of those components to the particular spreadsheet to be displayed, and map the columns of the sheet to specific user interface components in the display.

Drag a Data Viewer Grid into your screen, then set its Data Source property to your sheet. You can select the layout type for the items in the grid by clicking the image icon with the "Title" box on it, as shown in Figure 5.2.

Figure 5.2. Map the Data_Viewer_Grid to the Data Source

The items (rows) of the sheet can be displayed with just a title, a title and an image, or a more complex configuration.

When you connect to a data source, Thunkable analyzes the data and determines its column names (e.g., "name", "pic", and "description"). These appear as choices when you choose what will appear in the labels/images of each item in the Data Viewer Grid. In Figure 5.2, the "Picture" to be displayed is mapped to the "pic" column, and the "Text" for the title is mapped to the "name" column.

Without adding any code blocks, you should now have an app which displays your spreadsheet data. Test your app. Does the name and picture of each person in your sheet appear, as in the picture at the top of this chapter? *Note: as of summer 2022, it was necessary to test spreadsheet apps on a device, at least on the first test.*

Note that the "description" data from the sheet does not appear in the Data Viewer Grid, as that column wasn't mapped to the user interface. It is normal that only some of the data appears in the listing. In the next section, you'll add a "ProfileScreen" which shows all of a particular person's data, including the description.

CREATE A PROFILE SCREEN

Click on the "+" near the word "Screens" on the left-side of the designer in order to create a second screen. Name it "ProfileScreen". Drag an Image component into it, increase its size as you like, and set its Picture Resize Mode to "contain". Then add two Labels below the Image. Name the first Label, "NameLabel" and the second "DescriptionLabel".

Before coding the ProfileScreen, modify Screen1 so that, when the user chooses a particular student, the ProfileScreen appears, and has access to the chosen student. You'll use a variable to share the chosen student's id between screens. Variables in Thunkable are global--available to all screens and functions—so they can be used as shared memory between screens.

Each row in a spreadsheet has an auto-generated identifier assigned to it. The id is not the row number--it is a unique identifier generated for each row. For instance, Figure 5.3 shows the identifiers for the first few rows of my version of the ClassRoster2022 sheet:

Figure 5.3. Each spreadsheet row has a hidden auto-generated id

The ProfileScreeen needs to know the id of the row that was clicked, so in Screen1 define a variable, personId, and when the user clicks on a picture place the chosen person's id into that variable. In the when Data_Viewer_Grid1.Item Click event handler, set the personId to the row id of the clicked item, then drag in a navigate to block to specify that the ProfileScreen should be opened, as shown in Figure 5.4:

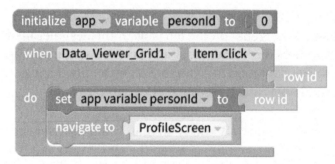

Figure 5.4. Screen1 blocks to navigate to Profile screen"

Next, code the blocks for the ProfileScreen. In the when ProfileScreen.Opens event, you want to display the data for the "current" person. You can access data from the spreadsheet using the **get value from** block found in the "Data Sources" folder, as shown in Figure 5.5:

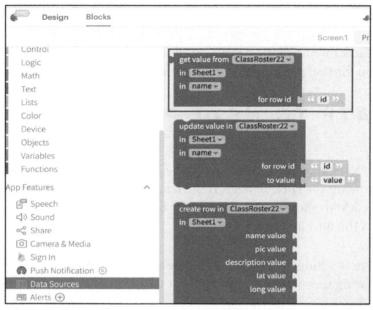

Figure 5.5. Data Source blocks, including "get value from"

The blocks in "Data Sources" were automatically generated by Thunkable when you added your particular data source. In the **get value from** block you identify the spreadsheet (ClassRoster22), the sheet within that spreadsheet (generally Sheet1), and the column you want to access. You also plug in a row id to specify which row of data you want to access. The variable personId was set in Screen1 to the id of the row the user selected, so you'll plug it in as the row id.

Using three **get value from** blocks, place the spreadsheet data into the user interface, as shown in Figure 5.6:

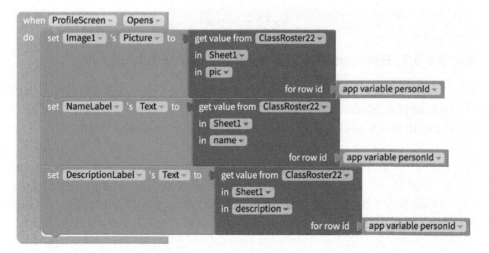

Figure 5.6. Get the data from the spreadsheet and display it

Test the app.

Test the app. Click on one of the people on the home page--does the ProfileScreen appear with the information for that person? Test to make sure it works no matter which person is chosen.

NAVIGATE TO NEXT PERSON

Next, add a Button named "NextButton" in the ProfileScreen so that the user can navigate to the next person (row) in the spreadsheet. If the last row of the spreadsheet is showing when NextButton is clicked, show the student in the first row, using the same "wrap-around" technique as in the quiz app of Chapter 4.

Recall that there is a hidden "ID" for each row in a spreadsheet. For NextButton navigation, you'll need to bring those identifiers into a list variable, as shown in Figure 5.7:

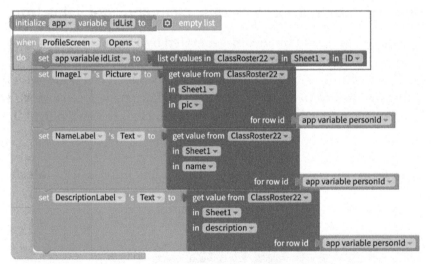

Figure 5.7. Retrieve the ids of all the spreadsheet rows

You'll use the idList you create to code the when NextButton.Click. The code uses an index similar to that used for the "Slideshow" and "Trivia" apps of Chapter 4. However, the code is a bit more complicated in order to deal with the ids, as will be explained below.

The Screen1 blocks for responding to a Data Viewer Grid item being click stored the selected person's id in the variable personId. When the user clicks "Next", you can't just add one to personId as it is not an index number-- it is a long text id autogenerated by the spreadsheet. The ids of the sheet are not sequential, so you can't just add one to get from one row to another.

The algorithm instead involves introducing a variable index, then doing some bookkeeping to grab the index associated with the personId, adding one to that index, then getting the "next" personid from the idList. Figure 5.8 shows the blocks:

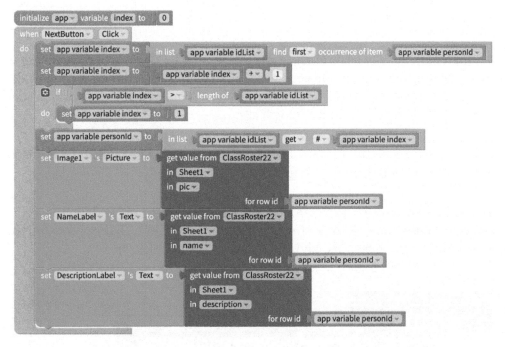

Figure 5.8. Navigating to the next row in the spreadsheet

The find first occurrence of item function returns the index of an item in a list. With personId plugged into it, it returns the index of that id within the idList. Consider the ids shown in Figure 5.3. If personId is "26532...", the second in that list, then the find first occurrence returns 2 and places it in the variable index.

Once the index of the current row is determined, the blocks increment it as normal. Just as with the quiz app, if you reach the end of the list, the index is set back to 1. After the increment, there is still one more necessary operation: in list idList get is called, with the updated index, to reset personid. For the ids in Figure 5.3, the index would now be 3 and the personId would be set to "d1ac72..."

Once the personId of the next person is determined, **get value from** is called three times to access the data from the spreadsheet and place it into Image1 and the Labels.

Test the App

Test the app. Select one of the people in the Data Viewer Grid to view the ProfileScreen, then click NextButton a few times to test if the app navigates through the people as it should.

REFACTOR: DEFINE A FUNCTION

The last three lines of the when NextButton.Click event handler are the same as those in when Screen1.Opens.

Both event handlers display a student's information with three rows of code that are repeated verbatim. It is good software engineering practice to eliminate redundant code by defining a *function* so that the repetitive code is in just one place. That way if a change is needed later, you don't have to change the code in multiple places.

You have *called* many functions built-in to Thunkable, like the **get value from** used in this app. Now you are going to define your own function, then call it.

A function defines a name for a sequence of blocks. You create one by dragging a "do something" block out of the "Functions" folder. Drag one into your app, then change "do something" to a descriptive name, in this case "displayInfo". Then drag the blocks in when Screen1.Opens into the function, as shown in Figure 5.9.

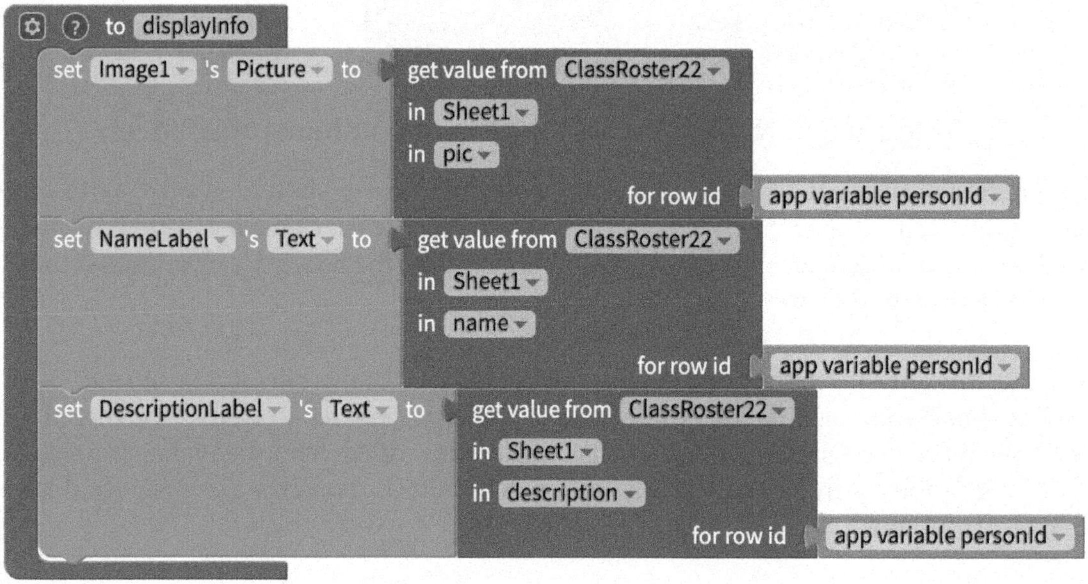

Figure 5.9. The displayInfo function

Once you define the function, a call block for it appears in the "Functions" folder (yes, you can create your own blocks!). Now you can eliminate the redundant code by modifying the two event handlers to call the function as shown in Figure 5.10:

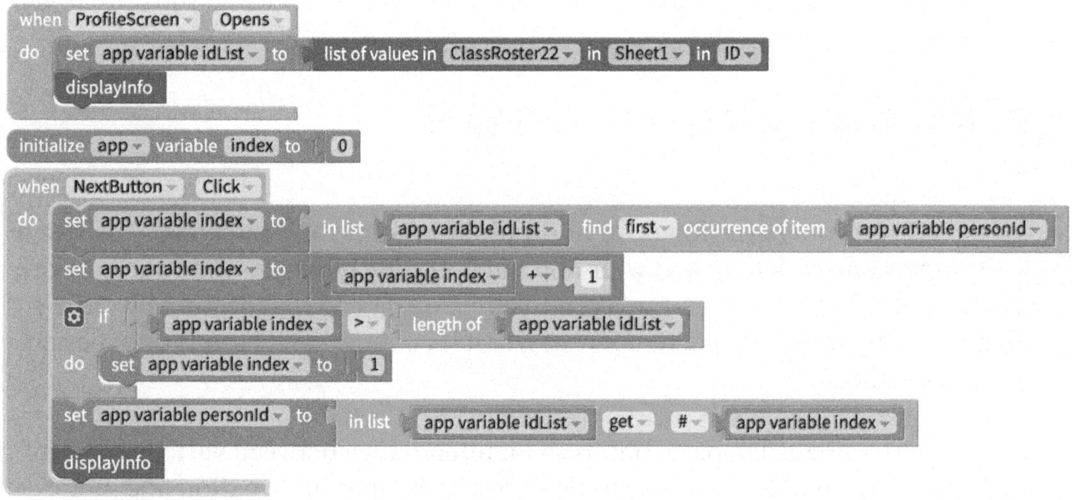

Figure 5.10. Simplify the event handlers by calling a function

The app should work exactly the same from the user's perspective, but the duplicate code is eliminated.

This is a sneak-peek at functions, which are a fundamental building block in coding. To learn more, check out Chapter 13.

SUMMARY

With what you've learned in this chapter you can take any spreadsheet and "appify" it—create a mobile app with an easy-to-use interface for navigating the data. Thunkable's data source feature, along with the Data Viewer Grid and Data Viewer List components, simplify the process compared to traditional development tools.

"MeetMyClassmates" illustrates how to access data and display it. Later, in Chapter 11, you'll build a photo sharing app which not only retrieves data from the spreadsheet, but writes data out to it. You'll also learn how to *process* data once it is in your app, e.g., in Chapter 12 you'll build a "Workout" app that computes the total number of pushups and situps from the columns in a spreadsheet.

A key aspect of this chapter is the separation of code and data. Unlike in Chapter 4, when all of your data (questions and answers) were encoded directly in the blocks, "MeetMyClassmates" takes its data from an external data source, and the code only refers to it abstractly. This separation of code and data provides more flexibility. You could use the app for a different class simply by changing the information in the spreadsheet, and without modifying the code!

It is a data-driven world and you are learning the fundamentals of using software to harness the power of data.

RAFIKI BREAKS IT DOWN

Like oxygen passes through the lungs, in-and-out, in-and-out, and then feeds the rest of your body, so it is the same with data and your app (and one day perhaps even your network of connected apps). The quicker you can learn to circulate data through your apps, the stronger they will be in their capacity to serve up whatever data points, calculations or experiences your app users are seeking.

And not just from a single database, but from an interchange between various kinds of databases. The data you need in order to provide a rich set of information may not exist all in one place. What if you were designing an app to look at the overall quality of life in a community? You might include an analysis of health data, financial data, education data and housing data, so your app would need to pull in and maintain data from various sources.

Right now you're mastering the basic maneuvers of this craft. Now you know how to flow data in from a spreadsheet, and later you'll learn how to record it out. Let the data flow!

CONCEPTUALIZE

1. Could you reuse "MeetMyClassmates" for a different course without modifying the code? Could you reuse the trivia app of Chapter 4 for a different quiz without modifying the code? Explain your answer, and explain the importance of separating code from data in general.

2. The spreadsheet used in this chapter had columns for name, description, and pic, but one could argue that the sheet has 4, not 3, columns. Explain.

3. Why doesn't it make sense to add 1 to a row id from the spreadsheet?

CUSTOMIZE

1. Add a column, "website" to the spreadsheet and provide a profile or some other web page about each person. Modify the app so that this field is displayed on the "ProfileScreen". You can also make it linkable by using the open link block in the "Control" folder, or show it in an in-app browser using the WebViewer component.

2. Modify the app so that the name doesn't appear immediately on the ProfileScreen, giving users a chance to test themselves on knowing their classmates' names. Add a Button or Timer so that the name appears eventually.

CREATE

1. Create a trivia app with the questions and answers in a spreadsheet. Recode the Trivia app from Chapter 4 using a spreadsheet instead of list variables to hold your questions and answers. First, just get a slideshow showing each question to work.

The more challenging part is for the multiple choice. For the answer choices, put all the choices for a question into a single cell, separating the choices with a delimiter like "%". Then use blocks from the "Text" folder to separate those choices after accessing them from the spreadsheet.

2. Create an informational app for your school or organization. Create a spreadsheet of information, or find an interesting one on the web, and "appify" it.

Share your creative apps with your authors and other *Drag and Drop* coders:

- Use #DragAndDropCode and #MadeWithThunkable on your social media platforms.

- @ us at @DragAndDropCode on Twitter and Instagram.

Chapter Resources: draganddropcode.com/bookCh5/

CHAPTER 6. CALLING FUNCTIONS

Apps: "TranslateCatDog" and "DescribeMyPicture"

 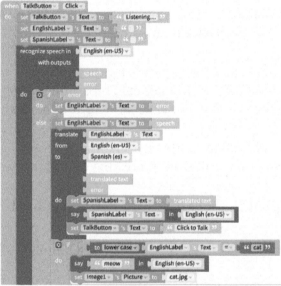

Want to build a Siri-like app that recognizes speech? Or an app that translates text from one language to another? How about an app that uses image recognition to describe, aloud, the pictures you take? Thunkable provides functions to do all of these things and much more. In this chapter, you'll learn how to call functions, and you'll build a translation app and an image processing app, with a little "Siri" built in.

INTRODUCTION

Today's phones are like Swiss army knives in that they provide a variety of functionality through their cameras, sensors, microphones, speakers and web connections. Thunkable provides some powerful functions and components to allow your apps to tap into the great features on the device. For example, you can use the **recognize speech** function to turn on the microphone and transcribe a user's words, the **say** function to have your app talk, and the **translate** function to translate text into a different language. You can also use the **photo from camera** function to turn on the camera from within an app, the **photo from photo library** to allow users to choose a picture from their library, and the **description of image from** function to get a text description of any image. Thunkable has done some heavy-lifting for you and provides some very powerful functionality in simple-to-use blocks!

In this chapter, you'll become familiar with these functions through the development of two apps, the "TranslateCatDog" app, which translates the words the user speaks into another language, and the "DescribeMyPicture" app, which uses image recognition to describe pictures the user takes or chooses. These are fun and dynamic apps which will help you become familiar with Thunkable's capabilities.

More importantly, you'll learn the general technique for calling functions to perform tasks for your app. You'll learn how to specify the input data (parameters) the functions need to perform their job and the output data that is returned from them. Once you learn the fundamentals of calling functions, you can apply that knowledge to access all the incredible tools available.

FUNCTION INPUTS AND OUTPUTS

In the "I Have a Dream 2022" app of Chapter 2, you called functions to play and stop sound clips, as shown in Figure 6.1:

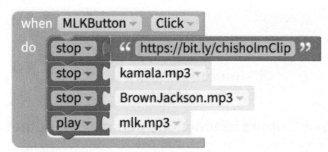

Figure 6.1. Four function calls in the event handler

Function call blocks name the function, e.g., "play" and have slots for parameters. You call a function to ask the phone or other entity in your app to perform an action The parameter(s) specify information needed for the function to do its job. When you call "play", the app needs to know what file to play (e.g., "mlk.mp3").

Some functions have advanced versions. You can convert a function call block to its advanced version by control-clicking on it and choosing "Show advanced block". Figure 6.2 shows the advanced version of the **play** block:

Figure 6.2. The advanced version of the "play" block.

The advanced version of **play** returns an output parameter, error, and it provides a "do" slot for blocks to be executed after the **play** block completes. In the app of Chapter 2, the output parameter error was ignored and the "then do" slot was not used, but you could have coded some blocks so that the app reported an error if there was one, or performed actions you wanted to happen at the end of a clip.

In general, functions are input-output machines, as illustrated in Figure 6.3

1. call with input parameters

| caller | ──────────▶ | function |

**2. on completion,
return outputs**

Figure 6.3. Send inputs to functions and receive outputs.

The "caller" is just some code in the app, either an event handler or function, that calls another function. When you call some functions, you are required to send input parameters, that is, information the function needs to do its job. The function performs its task, then sends results (outputs) back to the caller. The caller then processes the outputs in the "do" area of the call.

Figure 6.4. shows a call to **translate**, a function with both input and output parameters:

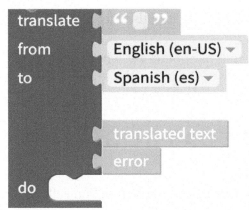

Figure 6.4. Translate has three input parameters and two output parameters.

To use this call block, you must replace the default pink "" in the first input parameter slot with some text you'd like to be translated. You can also choose different languages for the "from" and "to" input parameters. When **translate** finishes its job, it returns the output parameters translated text and error. The parameter translated text holds the result of the translation. error is either null, if the translation was successfully completed, or has an explanation for why the translate was unable to proceed.

Figure 6.5 shows a **translate** function call with its input data filled in and some code added in the "do" slot:

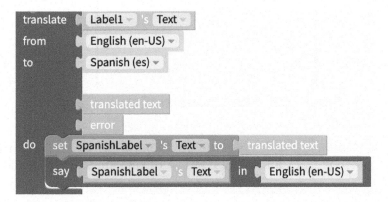

Figure 6.5. A filled-in call to translate

This **translate** call gets the text to be translated from a Label as the first parameter. When the function completes, it returns outputs translated text and error. In this case the code ignores error, assuming things worked, and displays and speaks the translated text in the "do" slot.

You click and drag on an output parameter to get a copy of it. In this sample, the output parameter translated text was copied and plugged into the set SpanishLabel's Text to block

The "do" slots in function calls are similar to those in if blocks. Put code in the "do" slot for processing the output data that the function sends after completing. Sometimes processing the output data just means displaying it in the user interface, as in the blocks of Figure 6.5.

You can only refer to output parameters of a function within the "do" slot and not below. If you plug an output like translated text into a slot outside of the function call's "do" slot, Thunkable will flag it as an error and the block won't have the data returned from the function call.

"TRANSLATECATDOG" APP

Now that you have been introduced to the function call mechanism, it is time to build an app. The "TranslateCatDog" app, shown in Figure 6.6, lets the user speak words in English and automatically translates them into Spanish.

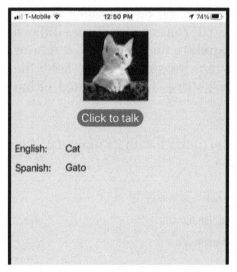

Figure 6.6. The "TranslateCatDog" app.

As a very rudimentary example of Siri-like command processing, the app also displays a picture of a cat if the word spoken is "cat", and a dog if the word spoken is "dog". And it barks and woofs!

Design the App

Design the "TranslateCatDog" app using Figure 6.7. and the instructions below it:

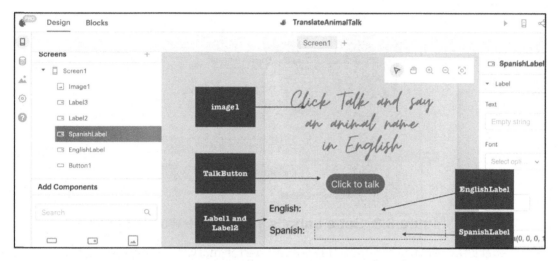

Figure 6.7. The "TranslateCatDog" app in the Designer.

Perform the following steps in the Designer:

- Drag in an Image component and set its Picture to an image like the one in Figure 6.7 (you can download the one shown at draganddropcode.com/bookCh6.)

- Add a Button below the image named TalkButton and set its Text to "Click to talk".

- Add two Labels, one with text "English:" and one with text "Spanish".

- Add two more Labels, one named EnglishLabel and one named SpanishLabel. Set their Text to blank: "". These labels will be set in the blocks.

- Download a picture of a dog and a cat from the Internet or use the ones at draganddropcode.com/bookCh6.). Of course, you can add other animal pictures as well.

Code the Interactive Behavior

Code this app in stages. Begin by exploring the **recognize speech in** function. When this function is called, the user is prompted to speak. After the user pauses, the function transcribes the words into text.

To try it out, drag in a when TalkButton.Click block and a **recognize speech in** from the Speech folder. Control-click the function call block and choose "show advanced block", then place the block in when TalkButton.Click. In the "do" slot of the function call, check if there is an error. If so, place the error in EnglishLabel's Text. Otherwise, set EnglishLabel's Text property to the output parameter, speech, as shown in Figure 6.8:

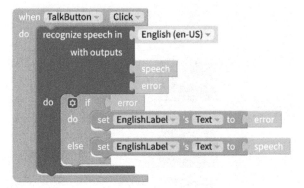

Figure 6.8. Set a Label's Text to the words spoken

The code to check the error in Figure 6.8 is common—for many functions you'll want to assure that a result was returned. For instance, if the microphone was disabled, you might receive an error for **recognize speech in**.

Test the App

Test the app on your device to try out the app you've built so far. Click on the TalkButton and say a few words, then pause. The microphone comes on as soon as you click, though the app currently doesn't signify this (later you can add a Label that temporarily says, "recording").

Translate the Words

The next step is to translate the words that are spoken and place the result into SpanishLabel. Drag in a **translate** call, choose to use the advanced version and place it below the blocks that set **EnglishLabel**. Plug EnglishLabel's Text into the slot for **Translate's** first input parameter "translate".

Then, in the then do slot of the **translate** call, set the SpanishLabel's Text to translated text which is the output of the **translate** call, as shown in Figure 6.9:

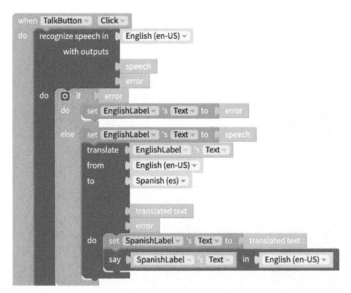

Figure 6.9. Translate the words spoken by the user

Test the App

Test the app again and click on the TalkButton and speak some words. You should see the Spanish translation appear in SpanishLabel as you speak.

Note that the call to **translate** must be within the "do" of **recognize speech in** because it should only happen once that function has completed and returned its speech output, which holds the text of the words spoken. If you tried to use speech outside the "do" of **recognize speech in**, your app wouldn't work.

Refine the User Interface

When the user clicks the TalkButton, the app's user interface should signify that the user's speech is being recorded. One way to do this is to change the Text of the TalkButton to "Listening...." when it is clicked, and then change it back when the translation completes.

The app should also blank out the EnglishLabel and SpanishLabel when the user clicks the TalkButton. Figure 6.10 shows the updated blocks:

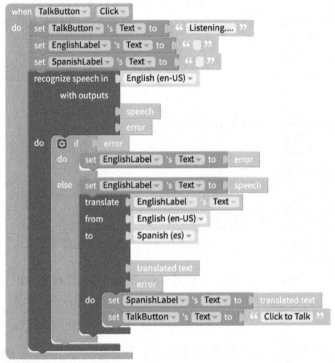

Figure 6.10. An app that translates the words spoken

Add the Animal Pictures

You probably know a child or adult who loves animals. By adding a couple of conditional "if" blocks, you can transform the translation app into a game that shows the picture of either a cat or a dog, depending on what the user speaks, and even meows and woofs.

Figure 6.11 shows the blocks for such an app.

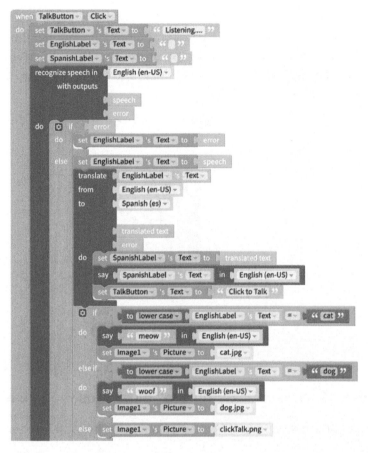

Figure 6.11. Change the picture if the user speaks "cat" or "dog"

The added blocks near the bottom convert the EnglishLabel's Text to lower-case then compare it to the text literals "cat" and "dog". If one of the conditions is true, the corresponding animal picture is displayed in Image1 and the app meows or barks.

You can add some additional animals and "else-if" branches to turn this into a nice game. It may not be the most sophisticated Siri/Alexa behavior ever, but did you ever think you would be building your own voice command processor?

Test the App

Once you have added the blocks as in Figure 6.11, test the app. Click the TalkButton and say a few words. Does the app type out the words you speak? Try saying "cat". Does a cat appear? Does it meow?

DESCRIBE MY PICTURE APP

In this section, you'll build the "DescribeMyPicture" app which illustrates use of the camera, photo library, and image recognition capabilities. In "DescribeMyPicture", the user takes a picture or chooses one from the photo gallery, and the app displays a textual description of the picture. Figure 6.12 shows the app.

Figure 6.12. "DescribeMyPicture" illustrates the use of image recognition.

The user has chosen a picture of Stephen Curry and the app has generated the description, "Stephen Curry jumping up in the air".

Design the App

Perform the following steps to design the app:

- Drag in an Image component.

- Drag in a Label below the Image and name it DescriptionLabel. Remove its default text so it appears blank to begin. Change its Font Size to 18.

- Drag in two Buttons below DescriptionLabel. Name the first TakePictureButton and set its Text to "Take a Picture". Name the second ChoosePhotoButton and set its Text to "Choose Picture".

Your app should appear something like the one in Figure 6.13:

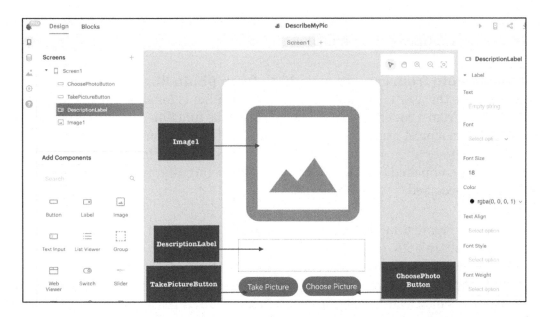

Figure 6.13. "DescribeMyPicture" in the Designer.

Code the Interactive Behavior

The app provides buttons for choosing a picture from the device's photo library and for taking a picture with the camera, so there are two event handlers. In the Blocks editor, configure the blocks like those in Figure 6.14:

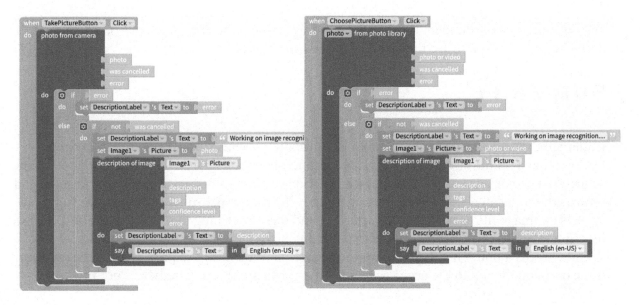

Figure 6.14. The Blocks for "Describe My Picture".

photo from camera and **description of image from** are found in the "Camera" folder. **photo from photo library** is in the "Files" folder.

The functions **photo from camera** and **photo from photo library** are similar, but different. One lets the user take a new picture and the other is for choosing an image from existing photos. From a coder's perspective, however, the function calls are similar as they return output data almost exactly in the same form. Both return an output parameter for the photo (either photo or photo or video, one for was cancelled, which is true or false based on whether the user completed the operation without canceling, and error, which describes issues that might have occurred.

As you can see in Figure 6.14, the code is the same in the two event handlers other than the initial function call. In both, the app checks error and was cancelled, and if neither is true it displays the picture in the Image1 component, displays the text, "working on description...", then makes the call to the **description of image from** function. This function takes the photo that was just taken or selected as an input parameter and returns a number of parameters, including description, which is placed in DescriptionLabel and spoken aloud.

The function also returns tags, which has keywords regarding the image, and confidenceLevel which is, a percentage between 0 and 100, related to how certain the image recognizer is about its result.

Test the App

Test the app. Walk around and take some pictures through the app, or choose one from your photo library. It is fun to see the text that the image recognizer generates!

SUMMARY

Understanding how to call a function is a key to coding because it opens up the many great features that a phone or tablet provides. Each function expects particular input parameters and returns particular outputs. The **translate** function expects some text as input to translate, and returns the translated text and an error message. The **description of image from** function expects an image file as input and returns text and tags describing that image as output. The **say** function takes in a single input, the text to be spoken, but doesn't return any outputs—it just says the words aloud. The **photo from camera** function doesn't require any inputs, but return three outputs: the photo the user has taken, an error (status), and whether or not the user cancelled the operation.

Once you understand how to call functions, your power to build apps is virtually unlimited. The Thunkable code block library doesn't provide every function you might imagine. But it does provide many powerful components, and the tool is evolving and adding more components and functionality to its code blocks library every day.

RAFIKI BREAKS IT DOWN

As a genie your app is at the command of your users. Their request is the app's command. In turn your app has the resources of a mobile device for fulfilling such requests, primarily through the strength of components. You issue instructions to device components via their built-in functions.

Effective instructions provide not only what needs to be done, but also the necessary information required to carry out a particular command. How can you, as the coder, proclaim "Do this and do it now.", if "this" is unclear? In coding, the information clarifying a command is called a "parameter". As code-commander, you supply an input parameter and your soldier-function fulfills the orders, returning the results as output parameters.

Digitization and Miniaturization: Your Power to Command

Consider the history of these things: Maps. Phone Books. Rolodexes. Encyclopedias. Desk Calendars. Photo Albums. Calculators. Radios. Recorders. Sony Walkmans. iPods. Cameras. Polaroids.

All of them used to be actual physical items that were relied upon and used daily. Imagine them sitting on a desk, or shelf, or carried around in everyone's backpacks. They have all magically vanished, at least in their physical forms, and have reappeared as resources inside your mobile device. In terms of coding, each of them is now at your command with a function call, or set of function calls, to add depth and value to your apps.

Moral of the story: if you master your functions, you master a universe of resources. You'll be able to create value for your users that will make them reach for your apps time and time again, just as consumers once reached for the *vanquished items*.

VOCABULARY VIBE

FUNCTION CALL

"Hey, Sound Card, you're needed to play the audio of Kamala Harris's vice-presidential acceptance speech." This is an example of a function call, a request by your app to a component of your mobile device to get involved with helping to fulfill a user's wish.

With Thunkable, such genie-power is as easy as pulling the appropriate block onto the screen.

CONCEPTUALIZE

1. **timed recording** records an audio file of the user speaking. Name the input parameter(s) and the output parameter(s) for the function call:

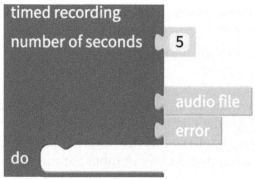

2. What is the purpose of an input parameter?

3. What is the purpose of an output parameter?

4. The following blocks are supposed to place the translated text into SpanishLabel, but there is an issue. Explain why the code doesn't work.

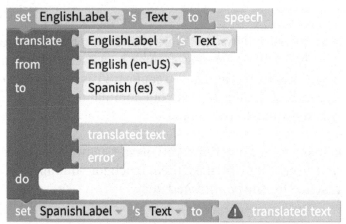

CUSTOMIZE

1. Modify the "TranslateCatDog" app by letting the user choose the language that the user speaks along with the language to which it is translated. Add an options screen with two ListViewer components.

2. Make a copy of the "TranslateCatDog" app, name it "TranslateAnimal" and turn it into a fun game for kids. In the new version, include several animal pictures and show a picture of whichever animal the user speaks. Code it so the animal appears if the user says the name of the animal or makes the animal's sound (e.g., "meow").

CREATE

1. Create a Scavenger Hunt game in which the player must take pictures of a given set of things in order to win. You'll need image recognition and you'll need to check if the text recognized contains a word of one of the things being searched for. The Text folder contains helpful blocks, including a find block.

2. Create a trivia game in which the user answers verbally.

Share your creative apps with your authors and other *Drag and Drop* coders:

- Use #DragAndDropCode and #MadeWithThunkable on your social media platforms.

- @ us at @DragAndDropCode on Twitter and Instagram.

Chapter Resources: draganddropcode.com/bookCh6/

CHAPTER 7. PROCESSING TEXT

App: "American Sign Language (ASL)"

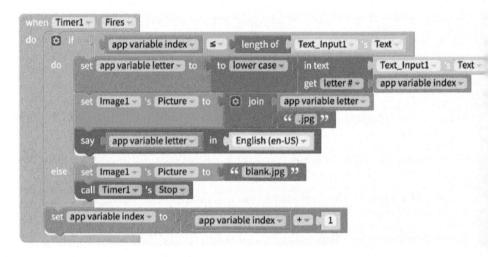

In this chapter, you'll build an American Sign Language (ASL) app that finger spells words in an animated fashion.
You'll learn the fundamentals of natural language processing—how an app processes text. And you'll gain some additional experience navigating information using an index, and working with a Timer.

INTRODUCTION

Just like humans, apps process lots of text. Think of the natural language processing (NLP) that tools like Siri do to interpret your words or the work Google does to parse your searches.

In coding, a *text string* is defined to be a sequence of *characters*, where a character is a letter, digit, symbol, or control character like a tab or carriage return. The terms *"text" and "string"* are used synonymously with "text string"—all are sequences of characters.

Thunkable provides many functions for processing text, including functions to select an individual character from a text string, find the length of a text string, join two text strings together, and find one string within another.

In this chapter, you'll explore the text operations available in Thunkable and algorithms for processing text. You'll then build the American Sign Language ("ASL") app—an app that signs and speaks the words typed in by the user.

The ASL app "finger signs" each letter of the word entered by the user. Figure 7.1 shows the ASL app in action.

Figure 7.1. The ASL App displaying the first letter in "Democracy".

In Figure 7.1, the user has entered the text "Democracy". When the user clicks "Sign It", the app steps through the letters in "Democracy", shows the finger-spelling for each letter, and speaks each letter aloud.

Finger-spelling is just one small part of ASL. When you get done building this app, you might explore adding additional ASL features to it.

To build the app you'll need to iterate through the characters in a text string similarly to how you iterated through the items of a list in the "SlideShow" app of Chapter 4. You'll also need to use a Timer component to animate the app and trigger the display of the successive letters each second.

But first, take a look at the text operations you'll need.

TEXT STRINGS, CHARACTERS, AND TYPES

In textual programming languages like Python and Java, text strings are denoted within quotes, e.g., "dog" is a text string consisting of three characters. In Thunkable, red text blocks with surrounding quotation marks are used, like the ones on the left of Figure 7.2:

Figure 7.2. Text ("24"), number (24), Text ("abc") and variable "get" abc

Text strings are just one of the many data types that apps store. Other data types include integers (whole numbers), floats (decimal numbers), booleans (true/false values), and lists.

The blocks on the top row of Figure 7.2 include a text string "24" (left) and an integer 24 (right) If you plan to use a value in mathematical equations, you should use the numeric 24.

The blocks on the bottom row of Figure 7.2 include the text literal "abc" (left) and a "get" reference to the variable named "abc" (right). The variable reference refers to the value stored in the memory cell named "abc", not the literal value "abc".

SELECTING A CHARACTER FROM A STRING

One of the fundamental text operations is selecting an individual character from the text. The in text get block, found in the "Text" folder, provides this functionality, as shown in Figure 7.3.

Figure 7.3. The "get" operation selects an individual character from a string

The block has slots for the text string you want to select from, and for the letter# you want to select. The label "letter#" should really be called "index#", or "character#" as the text being referred to might not consist of just letters and could include digits and symbols. When you drag the in text get block in it has a default text, "abc", and default letter# of 1. The block in Figure 7.3 would select "a" because the first character of "abc" is "a".

You'll typically replace the default, "abc", with a variable or the text the user has entered in a TextInput. In the ASL app, the user types the words to be signed into the component TextInput1, so you'll replace "abc" with the TextInput1's Text block that gets that text. You'll change the value in the letter# from 1 to select each successive letter of the word.

The blocks in Figure 7.3 specify a 1 as the letter#. Often, you will not refer to a specific number as the letter#. Instead, you'll define an index variable for your app, similar to that used in a slideshow or quiz app, and you'll refer to that index as the letter#. In this case, the index will keep track of the current character position in the text being examined. Consider the blocks in Figure 7.4.

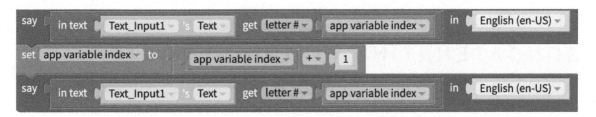

Figure 7.4. An index variable can be used to walk through text.

If "abcdefghi" were typed into TextInput1, and the variable index was set to 1, what letters would the blocks in Figure 7.4 speak?

If you answered, "a" then "b", you are correct. The value of the variable index is used as the "letter#" in the get operation. Since index starts out as 1, the first letter, "a", is selected from

TextInput1. The second row of blocks increments index to 2, and the second get returns the 2nd character, "b".

LENGTH OF TEXT

Another important text operation returns the length of a text string, as shown in Figure 7.5:

Figure 7.5. The "length of" block.

For the default string, "abc", the block returns 3 as "abc" has three characters.

The length of block is often used in conjunction with an index to determine when you've come to the end of processing a text string. When index becomes larger than the length of the string, you are done processing it.

Typically, you'll use blocks that check if the index variable is within range, as shown in Figure 7.6.

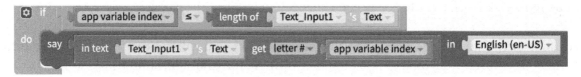

Figure 7.6. Check to see if the index is within range

These blocks check if the index is less than or equal to the length of the text. If it is, the get operation can proceed and the *indexth* letter is spoken.

CONCATENATING (JOINING) TEXT

Whereas the get block selects an individual character from a text string, the join block *concatenates* (attaches) two or more text pieces together. The blocks shown in Figure 7.7 appear when you drag a join into your code.

Figure 7.7. The join block concatenates text

The result of the block is a single piece of text, "helloworld".

You can use the blue mutator in the top-left of the join to add more slots, just as you do with lists or if blocks. Often, you'll use join to concatenate fixed text with the values in properties or variables. For instance, if you wanted to speak the letter in a word along with its position in that word, e.g., "letter 1 is a", you could use the join block to concatenate the parts, as shown in Figure 7.8:

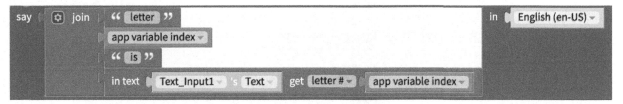

Figure 7.8. join often concatenates fixed and dynamic elements.

The first slot has a fixed, string literal, "letter ", with a space at the end. The second slot has the variable index. If the value of index is 3, this block will result in 3 concatenated to "letter ", giving "letter 3". The third slot of the join is the string literal, " is ", with a space in the front and at the end. The fourth slot selects the *indexth* letter from TextInput1's Text property.

If TextInput's Text property contains "abcdefghi" and the index variable is set to 3, the join block will result in "letter 3 is c" being spoken, as illustrated in Figure 7.9.

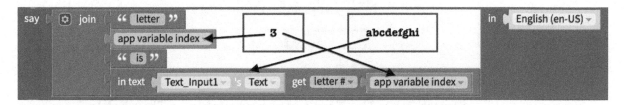

Figure 7.9. For the given data, this join results in "letter 3 is c" being spoken

OTHER TEXT OPERATIONS

Figure 7.10 shows the Text operations provided by Thunkable:

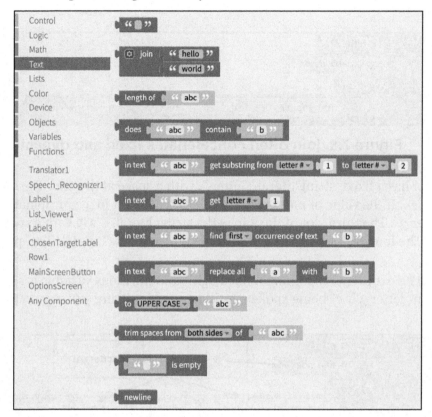

Figure 7.10. The Text blocks available in Thunkable.

Besides the blocks you've already seen, there are blocks for checking if a character is contained in a larger piece of text, for selecting a substring from a larger piece of text, for finding and replacing text, for changing the case of text, for trimming spaces from the front or end of text, and for checking if a text variable is empty.

BUILD THE ASL APP

Now that you have a better understanding of the text operations available to you, you're ready to build the "ASL" app. To begin, create a new Thunkable project and name it "ASL".

Load the Media

The app needs 26 image files which contain the ASL sign for each of the twenty-six letters in the English alphabet. The files are in a zip file at: https://draganddropcode.com/bookCh7/ Download the zip file, then in your Finder app (Mac) or File Manager (Windows), double-click on the file to unzip it. When you unzip the file, you'll get a folder with 26 image files in it. You don't need to upload the files into your app one-by-one. Instead, double-click on the folder to open it, then select all the files in the folder and drag them all at once into the Files area of the Designer in your Thunkable app.

The image files are named with the letter and an extension of ".jpg", so "a.jpg" for the letter 'a', "b.jpg" for the letter 'b', and so on. You'll make use of this naming uniformity when you code the blocks for this app.

Design the User Interface

Figure 7.11 shows the Design View of the "ASL" app:

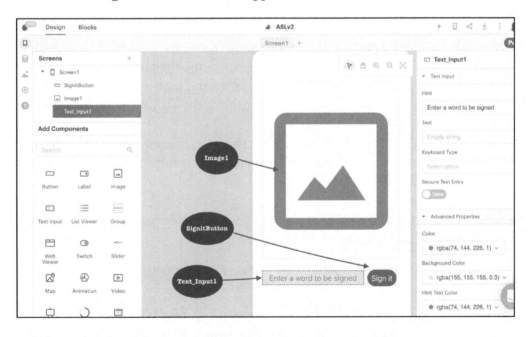

Figure 7.11. The ASL App in the Designer with TextInput1 selected.

Create the "ASL" design using Figure 7.11 and the following instructions.

- Drag in an Image component, set its Picture property to "blank.jpg" and size it as you would like. As the app signs the letters of a word, Image1's Picture property will be changed to the file name for the current letter being signed.

- Drag in a TextInput component and place it below the Image. Set its Text property to blank and its Hint to "Enter a word to be signed". The Hint is the prompt for the user and appears when TextInput's Text is blank. Set the TextInput's Color to blue and its Hint Text Color to blue.

- Drag in a Button component and place it to the right of the TextInput. Set its Text property to "Sign it" and name the button SignitButton.

Code the Behavior

From the user's perspective, the app should work as follows: the user types a word in the TextInput, then clicks the SignitButton. When the button is clicked, the app steps through an animation that "signs" the word. It does this by changing the image file being displayed every two seconds. Here is a pseudo-code algorithm for the app's behavior:

> When the button is clicked, the index should be set to 1 and the Timer enabled so that the when Timer.Fires event begins triggering and displaying images. when Timer.Fires should display the image for the current letter and increment the index. If the index has become larger than the length of the input text, the Timer should be stopped.

A letter's image file is displayed by selecting the indexth character from the text input by the user, switching it to lower-case, then attaching the ".jpg" extension to it. This provides the file name for the image that should be shown.

In the Blocks Editor, begin by defining two app variables, one named index and one named letter. Configure the blocks as shown in Figure 7.12.

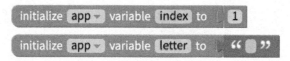

Figure 7.12. The variables for the ASL App

Next, create a Timer by clicking on the "+" near the "Timer" area in the lower-left panel of the Blocks Editor. Set the Timer's Interval to 2 seconds and Loops to true. Keep the Enabled property as false.

Finally, code the blocks for the when SignButton.Click and when Timer1.Fires event handlers. Clicking the button should only initialize the index and start the timer. The repetitive action—showing the picture and incrementing the index--should occur in when Timer1.Fires Figure 7.13 shows the blocks:

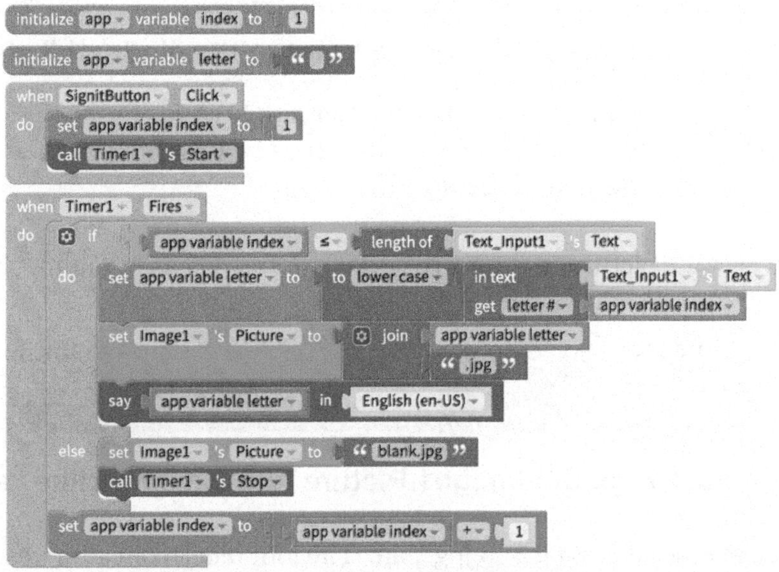

Figure 7.13. Blocks for ASL App

Test the App

Test the app. Enter a word in the TextInput, the click the SignItButton. The image for the first letter you entered should appear, and then each two seconds a new image should appear for each letter.

How the Blocks Work

The variable index is used in a similarly to how its used in the "Slideshow" app. In this case, the index variable keeps track of the current character position as the app steps through a text string entered by the user.

The when SignButton.Click event handler initializes the index to 1 and starts the Timer. Starting the Timer enables when Timer1.Fires to begin triggering, and that event handler has the repetitive action of displaying a letter image.

The when Timer.Fires event handler first checks if the index is too big. If not, the current letter is selected from TextInput1 with the blocks shown in Figure 7.14:

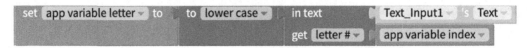

Figure 7.14. Set the letter to the "indexth" character

To understand these blocks, envision that the user has entered "Democracy" in TextInput1.Text. Because the index is 1, the get block selects, "D". The lower case block then transforms it into "d", and finally the variable letter is set to "d".

The code then sets the picture to the correct file with the blocks in Figure 7.15.

Figure 7.15. Set Image1.Picture to a file name like "a.jpg"

The media files are named "a.jpg", "b.jpg", etc. The join block concatenates the current letter with the extension ".jpg" to form the file name. Image1's Picture is then set to display that file.

After the picture is displayed, the **say** function is called to speak the letter.

The "else" branch of the blocks in Figure 7.13 handle the case when the index is larger than the length of the text entered—this will happen when all the letters have been processed and the word has been completely signed. In this case, the "else" branch blanks out the picture and stops the Timer so that the when Timer.Fires event stops triggering (at least until the SignitButton is clicked again).

SUMMARY

Text processing is an important and common task in coding. In this chapter, you explored Thunkable's text processing functions and explored an algorithm for stepping through the characters in a string over time. You also gained more experience with using an index to process each item of a list, in this case a text string (which is a list of characters).

You also worked with the Timer component and animation. This experience will come in handy as you build games in Chapter 8.

RAFIKI BREAKS IT DOWN

In this chapter you were introduced to one of the principle computing developments of the present and future: Natural Language Processing (NLP). NLP is the ability of computers to process text and respond to prompts given in everyday language, like the way you supplied the "Sign It" app a word and it then proceeded to sign that word.

It may come as a surprise to you, but interacting with computers has not always been as easy as simply typing or speaking words. Trust me, it was far more complex not that long ago. The images in Figure 7.16 document how we've gone from instructing computers through stacks of cards, to keyboard and monitors, to now simply our voice.

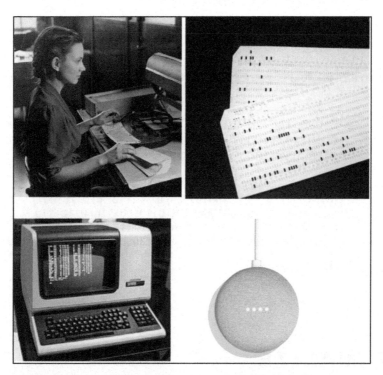

Figure 7.16. The evolution of user interfaces

The Google Home device in the bottom-right is a smart speaker that requires no keyboard or screen, but is able to respond to thousands of commands, all triggered by nothing more than your voice. This trend toward ubiquitous computing is powered in large part by NLP. Keep an eye on this space, with an open mind as to how your increasing programming skills can be an active part of what is rapidly unfolding in our world.

VOCABULARY VIBE

STRING AND CHARACTER

As an English-speaker, your command of language involves primarily the twenty-six letters of the alphabet and the ten numeric digits. There are also the various punctuation marks you see on your keyboard.

In a computer's memory, there aren't really any letters or digits. Instead, each letter, digit, and punctuation mark is represented as a number. The set of 128 characters is known as the American Standard Code for Information Interchange, or ASCII for short. It forms the basis for Unicode, which is the internationalized form of ASCII.

Recall that computers really only understand 1s and 0s. Each 1 or 0 is stored in a bit, and each character is stored in an 8- or 16-bit package called a byte. You then combine a sequence of ASCII characters to store a text string like "Genie in an app". The table below illustrates this:

Binary	01000111011001010110111001101001011001010010000001101001011011100001000000011000010110111000100000011000010110000011100000011100000101110
ASCII Bytes	(G) 01000111 (e) 01100101 (n) 01101110 (i) 01101001 (e) 01100101 (sp) 00100000 (i) 01101001 (n) 01101110 (sp) 00100000 (a) 01100001 (n) 01101110 (sp) 00100000 (a) 01100001 (p) 01110000 (p) 01110000 (period) 00101110
English Text	Genie in an app.

CONCEPTUALIZE

1.What do variables named "index" typically represent?

2.What is the difference between the terms, "letter" and "character".

3. Describe the difference between a red "abc" block and an orange "app abc" block.

4. What should you first check before selecting an individual character from a text string?

5. Consider the following blocks. What will the variable letter be set to if TextInput's Text is "AbCdEfGh" and index is 5:

CUSTOMIZE

1. Make a copy of the "ASL" app and name it "ASLAllLetters". In the new version, instead of animating the letters, display the images all at once in separate Image components. You'll need to place a number of Image components onto the screen. With Thunkable, you must specify a fixed number of Image components in the user interface, so you'll need to limit the number of letters the user can enter.

2. Add a button to the "ASL" app that, when clicked, allows the user to speak the word to be signed instead of typing it. You can use the **recognized speech** block found in the "Speech" folder of the Blocks Editor.

CREATE

Finger spelling just touches the surface of ASL communication, and is used most often to ask someone the proper sign for a particular word. Most words and phrases have their own signs and there are also signs to indicate present/past tense, etc.

Do some research to learn more about ASL and explore the app store to see what tools already exist for communication and learning. Then design some new features to extend the "ASL" app with more sophisticated tools. You need not restrict your ideas to English—you might explore the sign languages and tools available in other languages as well.

Share your creative apps with your authors and other *Drag and Drop* coders:

- Use #DragAndDropCode and #MadeWithThunkable on your social media platforms.

- @ us at @DragAndDropCode on Twitter and Instagram.

Chapter Resources: draganddropcode.com/bookCh7/

CHAPTER 8. BUILD ANIMATED GAMES

Apps: "ThunkableMash" and "Asteroids"

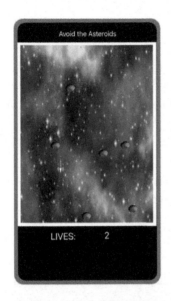

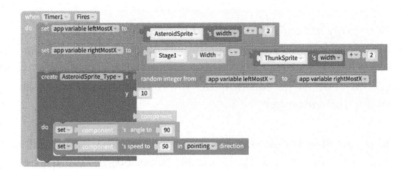

You can build games and other animated apps with Thunkable! In this chapter you'll learn how to set up a canvas with sprites that can be animated using the Timer component and coding techniques you're familiar with from previous chapters. You'll build two classic games, Asteroids and Whack-a-Mole.

INTRODUCTION

You can build games with Thunkable! The apps you've built thus far have had user interfaces with standard components like buttons, labels, and text inputs. In this chapter, you'll learn how to create more free-form user interfaces like those found in games and animations. You'll learn about the the Canvas , SpriteType , and Spritecomponents, and you'll incorporate the Timer to code the animated activity.

A Canvas is just a sub-panel within the screen set aside for user drawing or animated sprites. It is defined as an x-y grid of pixels, where a pixel is a single dot of color that can appear on the screen.

Apps draw by either coloring a particular pixel or placing a sprite (image) at a particular pixel location. A location on the Canvas is defined by x-y coordinates. x defines the placement on the horizontal plane, starting at 0 on the far left and increasing as you move to the right. y defines a location on the vertical plane, starting at 0 at the top and increasing as you move down the screen. The coordinate (x=5, y=6), for example, locates a sprite's center 5 pixels from the left-side, and 6 pixels down from the top, as shown in Figure 8.1:

x\y	0	1	2	3	4	5	6	7	8	9
0	x=0,y=0	x=1,y=0								x=9,y=0
1										
2										
3										
4										
5										
6						x=5, y=6				
7										
8										
9	x=0,y=9									x=9,y=9

Figure 8.1. A 10x10 Canvas Grid. Actual canvas grids have hundreds of slots.

The Canvas grids in Thunkable are different than the grids used in Math. In Math the center of the grid is the coordinate (x=0,y=0) and the grid has both positive and negative numbers. The x-coordinate gets bigger as you go right, and the y-coordinate gets larger as you move up the grid.

With Thunkable's grids, the coordinate (x=0,y=0) is the top-left corner, not the middle. As with the Math grid, the x-coordinate increases as you move right. But the y-coordinate works in the opposite direction—it gets larger as you move down.

For example, the cell to the immediate right of the top-left corner is (x=1,y=0). The upper-right corner has an x coordinate equal to the width of the Canvas minus 1. So if the Canvas is 10 pixels in width, the top-right corner is at coordinate (x=9,y=0). If the Canvas also has a height of 10 pixels, the bottom right corner is at (x=9,y=9) and the bottom left corner is at (x=0,y=9).

SPRITETYPE AND SPRITES

A sprite is an image that appears on a Canvas, with an image file property that defines its appearance, and x and y-coordinates that define its location.

To build an animated app, you'll use the SpriteType and Sprite components. To understand the difference between these components, consider cookie cutters and cookies. Cookie cutters are metal objects shaped in the form of some object, like the snowman cutter shown to the left in Figure 8.2.

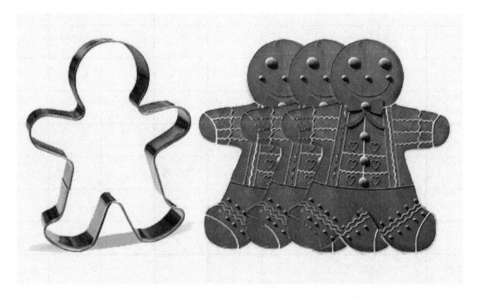

Figure 8.2. A cookie cutter and cookies

To make cookies, you lay out some dough and then stamp the cookie cutter down to carve out actual cookies, which after some baking and frosting look something like those to the right in Figure 8.2.

The cookie cutter defines how each cookie will appear.

In Thunkable, the SpriteType component is like a cookie cutter, only you use it to create sprites, not cookies. For instance, in a game like Asteroids, you'll have an AsteroidSpriteType component and use it to create the asteroids that appear as the game is played.

PLACING SPRITES

Before building a complete game, try the following exercises to get a feel for how the Canvas, SpriteType, and Sprite components work.

1. **Add a Canvas to your app.** Create a new project and name it "ExploreAnimaton". In the Designer, drag a Canvas component onto the screen. When you drag in a Canvas, it by default has a Stage, a SpriteType named Sprite_Type1 and a Sprite named Sprite1. The default image for the SpriteType is the Thunkable icon.

A new tab named "Canvas" also appears at the top of the Designer next to "Design" and "Blocks". You can select the "Canvas" tab to set the initial properties for the Canvas and Stage, and to add any additional SpriteTypes and Sprites you want to appear when the app launches.

For now, select the Stage and set its BackgroundColor to a color of your choice.

2. **Set the location of the sprite in the Designer**. Drag the Thunkable icon that appears on the Stage, Sprite1, to where you want it to appear when the app begins. Test the app.

3. **Set the location of the sprite in blocks.** Drag in the when Canvas1.loads event handler from the "Events" folder under the "Canvas Blocks". Any blocks you put in this event handler are executed after the when Screen.Starts and when Screen.Opens event handlers, if you have those in your app. Don't place blocks related to a Canvas or Sprite in Screen.Starts or Screen.Opens, as they will be ignored. Put them instead in the when Canvas.loads event handler.

Add the blocks in Figure 8.3 to place the sprite in the top-left corner when the app launches. You'll find the set blocks in the "Motion" folder under "Canvas Blocks".

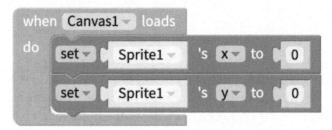

Figure 8.3. Initialize your Canvas and Sprites in "when Canvas1.loads"

Test the app. Does the sprite appear in the top-left corner?

4. **Change the location of a sprite in response to a user action.** Add a Button to your app below the Canvas and name it, CenterSpriteButton. Then add blocks so that when the button is clicked, the sprite moves from wherever it is to the middle of the stage, as shown in Figure 8.4.

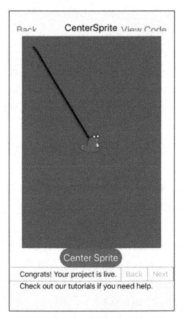

Figure 8.4. When the Button is clicked, move the sprite to the middle

To calculate the center of the Stage, you could look at the Stage's properties in the Designer and divide its Width and Height by two, i.e., if the Width is 400 and Height is 300, you want Sprite1's x property to be 200 and its y property to be 150.

It is always better, however, to avoid referring to fixed numbers. If you instead refer *formulaically* to properties, your app will work even if you change the size of your components. In this case, your code should refer to the Stage's Width and the Stage's Height. That way, if the Stage changes size, the code will still work. Code your blocks as in Figure 8.5, which uses such a formulaic approach. The Stage's Width and Height blocks don't appear in the "Stage" folder, so just drag in any other get block in that folder, then use the upside-down triangle to choose Width and Height.

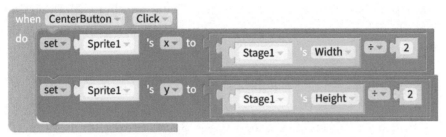

Figure 8.5 Move Sprite1 to center of stage

BUILD A THUNKABLE MASH GAME

In this section you'll build the game "ThunkableMash", an offshoot of the old MoleMash and Whack-a-Mole™ games found in carnival arcades. Figure 8.6 shows my son Tomas playing the game on the left, and the app you're going to build on the right:

 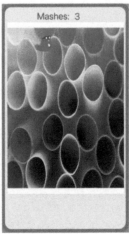

Figure 8.6. Whack-a-Mole arcade game

In "ThunkableMash", the Thunkable beaver jumps around the stage and the user gets a point for touching it. To build it, you'll use Canvas and SpriteType, as well as a Timer and when Timer.Fires event handler to make the sprite jump to a random spot periodically.

- Create a new Project named "ThunkableMash"

- Drag in a Canvas and set the Stage's BackgroundColor to a color of your choice. You can also set the Stage's Background to an image file like that at https://draganddropcode.com/bookCh8/, Set the name of the SpriteType that comes with the Canvas to ThunkSpriteType and the Sprite's name to ThunkSprite.

- Drag in one Label and set its text to "Mashes"", and another with the name "ScoreLabel". Set ScoreLabel's Text to 0. Don't forget to set its Text to 0 or the app will not work.

Switch to the Blocks Editor to code the app's behavior.

- Click on the + near "Timer" to create a Timer. Set its properties as follows:

Loops: true, so it will fire more than once

Enabled: true

Interval: 500 milliseconds (so it will fire every ½ second)

- Drag in a when Timer1.Fires event handler, and configure the blocks as shown in Figure 8.7:

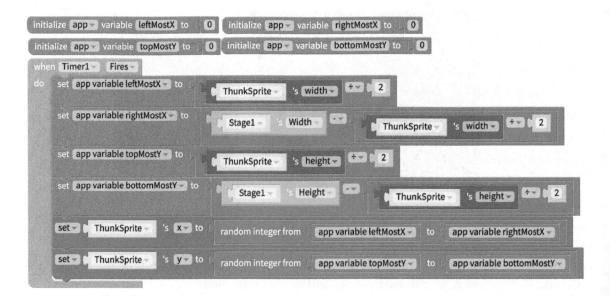

Figure 8.7. Place ThunkSprite in a random position

The when Timer.Fires event will trigger with a frequency defined by Timer's Interval property. Since it is set to 500 milliseconds, the event will trigger every ½ second.

The blocks within the when Timer.Fires event handler change the location of the ThunkSprite by setting its x and y properties to random numbers within a range. The left-most x position is determined using the **ThunkSprite's Width** divided by 2, while its right-most x position is determined by subtracting ½ of **ThunkSprite's Width** from the width of the Stage. Can you determine why?

The answer involves the fact that a Sprite's x and y properties specify its center. If you set a sprite's x value to 0, its center is on the left edge of the stage, and half of it is off stage to the left. An x value equal to ½ of the Sprite's width places it's left edge on the Stage's left edge.

Similarly, if the Sprite's x coordinate is set to too large a number, part of it will be off the right edge of the stage. The largest value of x should thus be Stage.Width-(**ThunkSprite.Width**/2)

The minimum and maximum values for the y property are set using the same logic, but using the Height instead of Width.

Next, code blocks so that touching the sprite adds a point. Drag in a when ThunkSpriteType is clicked event handler, and add blocks to increment the ScoreLabel within it. The blocks should appear as shown in Figure 8.8:

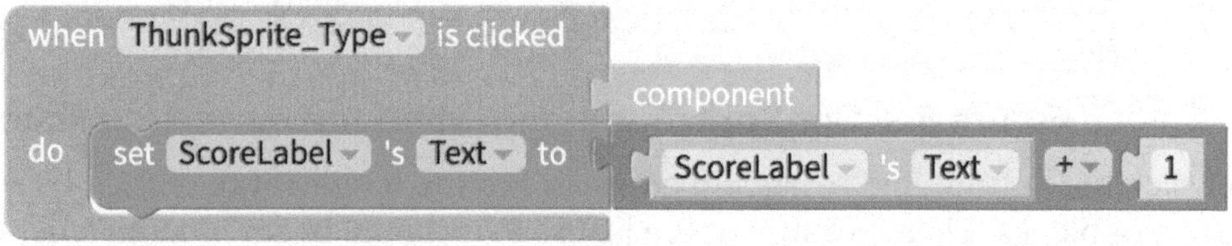

Figure 8.8. Add one to the score when sprite is clicked

ThunkSprite_Type is referred to in the event handler, instead of ThunkSprite, so that the code will work even if you decide to allow new sprite instances to appear as the game is played.

Test the App

Test the app. Does the ThunkSprite jump around the screen? When you touch the ThunkSprite, does the score increase?

The app is pretty bare bones, so take some time to add some bells and whistles. Change the character you're trying to mash to an image of someone you know, maybe your little brother or sister? Add sound effects for when the sprite is touched, add some blocks so that the player wins when a certain score is reached, and add a restart button so the user can start a new game.

SMOOTH ANIMATION

The "ThunkableMash" app *transports* the Sprite. The Sprite is in one spot and then every ½ second it appears in another. Besides transporting sprites, you can also code them to move *smoothly* across the screen. Sprites have speed and angle properties for defining smooth animation. A Sprite's speed is defined in pixels per second—if you set the speed to 50 the Sprite will move 50 pixels every second. The angle property defines the direction of the movement and is in degrees, a number between 0 and 360.

Explore Movement

Open the "ExploreAnimation" app you built earlier, and add blocks to the when CenterButton.Click event handler so that Sprite1's speed is set to 50, as shown in Figure 8.9

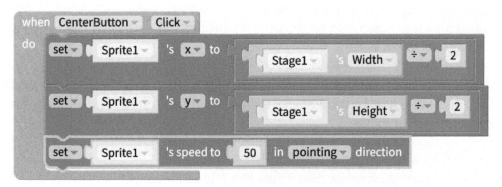

Figure 8.9. Set Sprite1 moving when the button is clicked

When you click the button, Sprite1 should *transport* to the middle of the Stage based on the first two rows of blocks. Then, because of the last row, it should begin *moving smoothly* in the direction it is pointing. It should stop when it hits the edge of the Stage.

You can modify the Sprite's pointing direction by setting its angle property. By default, angle is set to 0, which means it will travel to the right. Try setting angle to different values between 0 and 360 to see how Sprite1's direction changes. Figure 8.10 shows the direction a sprite will move for various settings of angle.

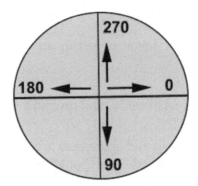

Figure 8.10. The angle of various directions

Bounce

In the tests above, the sprite stops moving when it hits an edge. The reason for this is that Sprite has a property, bounce, which is set to 0 by default. You can cause a Sprite to bounce off edges by setting bounce to a non-zero value.

The bounce property is a percentage 0-100 and determines how the speed of the sprite is affected by hitting an edge. A setting of 100 means the speed will remain the same after a sprite bounces off the edge. A speed of 50 means the speed will be reduced by ½ when the sprite hits an edge.

In the Designer, set Sprite1's bounce property to 50. The Sprite should now bounce off each edge it hits and slow down.

BUILD AN ASTEROIDS GAME

In this section, you'll build a game in which the player maneuvers one sprite to keep it from being hit by other sprites falling from the top of the Stage. The game, shown in the top figure of this chapter, will start with a single asteroid. More asteroids will appear as the game goes on. The player will drag the main character sprite around the screen trying to avoid the falling asteroids, and lose a "life" each time a collision occurs.

In building the game, you'll learn how to:

- create sprites that appear dynamically over time.

- work with collision events.

- specify that the user can drag a sprite.

Build the app iteratively. In iteration 1, focus on getting an asteroid to fall from the top of the screen. In the Designer:

- Create a new project named "Asteroids" and drag in a Canvas component.

- Upload images for of an asteroid and space background into the app. You can use the samples at https://draganddropcode.com/bookCh8/

- Click on the "Canvas" tab and set the Stage's Background Picture to the background image you uploaded. If you downloaded the samples, the file will be named "skyImage.jpg". Set its Background Picture Resize Mode to "stretch".

- The Canvas comes with a single SpriteType and Sprite. Rename the SpriteType to "ThunkSpriteType" and the Sprite to "ThunkSprite". This is the sprite the user will move so it doesn't get hit.

- Add a second SpriteType. You can add a SpriteType by choosing the Canvas tab in the Designer and then clicking on the "Add Sprite Type" button in the left panel. Name the new SpriteType "AsteroidSpriteType" then drag in an initial sprite from it and name it "AsteroidSprite.

- Add the image file of the asteroid to AsteroidSpriteType's pictureList ("asteroidgif.gif" if you used the provided sample). A SpriteType's pictureList contains the images that *may* appear for a sprite, with the one on the left the initial image. Remove the default Thunkable icon image from the list.

- Set the AsteroidSpriteType's passesThrough property to "true". When you add multiple asteroids later, this will keep them from bunching up together if they come in contact with each other.

- Place AsteroidSprite near the top of the Stage.

- In the Blocks Editor, add the blocks shown in Figure 8.11:

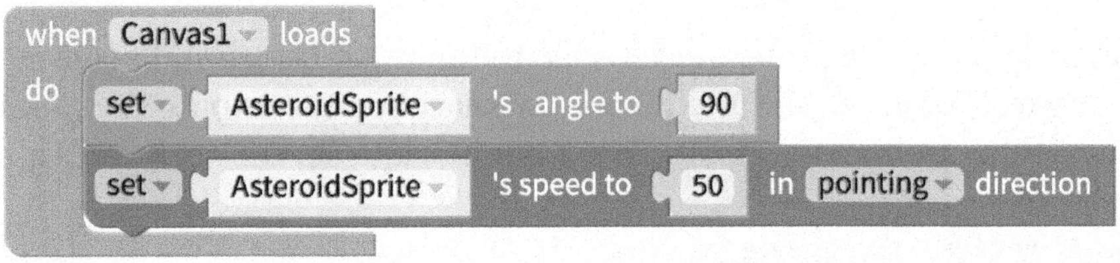

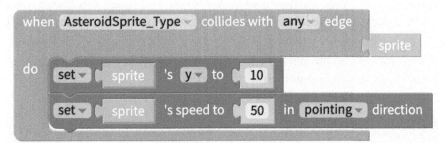

Figure 8.11. The AsteroidSprite should move down on app launch

Test the App

Test the app. Because of the angle and speed settings, the asteroid should move smoothly down the screen and stop when it hits the bottom edge.

Move the Asteroid Back to the top

Code blocks so that, when the asteroid hits the bottom edge, it reappears at the top of the stage at a random location on the horizontal axis. Drag in a when collides with edge event handler from the "Events" folder under "Canvas Blocks". Set the object being collided with to AsteroidSpriteType and put blocks within it as shown in Figure 8.12:

Figure 8.12 When an AsteroidSprite hits bottom, place it back on top

Choose AsteroidSpriteType, not AsteroidSprite, in the "when" slot, because you want all the AsteroidSprites that are created to respond the same to hitting the bottom edge. You haven't yet coded the part where new AsteroidSprites are generated, but you will.

For the same reason, use the event parameter sprite, not AsteroidSprite, in setting the y and speed properties. The event parameter sprite is the particular one that hit the edge.

Test the App

Test your app. Each time the AsteroidSprite hits the bottom, it should reappear at the top of the Stage and come down again.

Randomize the Asteroid Placement

The blocks in Figure 8.12 always move the asteroid to the same horizontal place (x-coordinate) at the top of the screen. To randomize the horizontal placement, compute the minimum and maximum x values, then use the random integer from block to set the sprite's x value. Figure 8.13 shows the blocks:

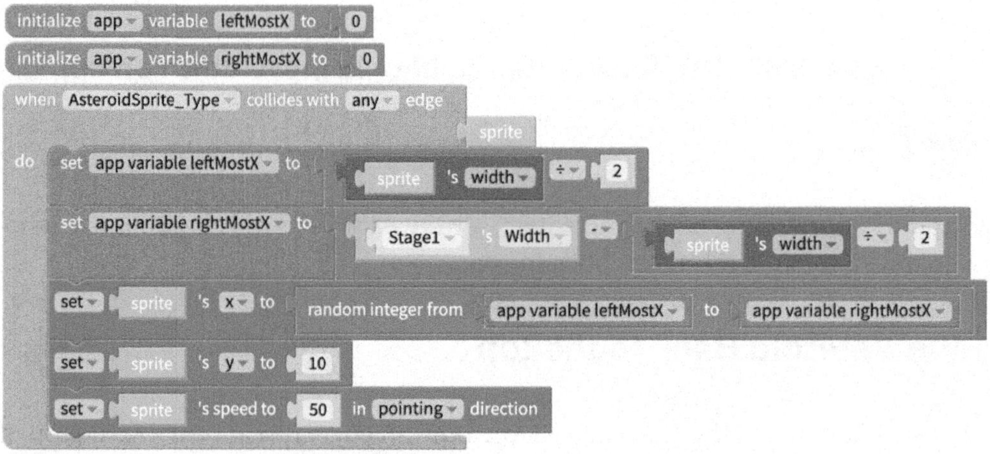

Figure 8.13. Randomize the x-location of asteroids moved to the top.

The variables leftMostX and rightMostX variables are defined to store the minimum and maximum values that are plugged into the random integer from function, similarly to what was done in the "ThunkMash" app. Using these variables, the smallest number generated places the asteroid on the left-edge and the largest random number places the asteroid on the right-edge.

You don't need to change the blocks for changing the y property as you always want the asteroids to re-appear 10 pixels down from the top.

Test the App

Test the app. When the AsteroidSprite hits the bottom edge, it should reappear at the top, but at a random horizontal location each time.

Code the User Interaction and Collision Reaction

The next steps are to code it so that the user can drag the ThunkSprite to avoid the AsteroidSprite, and so that the user loses a "life" each time the AsteroidSprite hits the ThunkSprite.

- In the Designer, set the ThunkSpriteType's isDraggable property to true. This setting allows the user to drag ThunkSpriteType sprites around the Stage.

- Add a Label under the Canvas named LivesLabel. Set its Text to "10".

- In the Blocks Editor, drag in a when AndroidSpriteType.collides with block. Set the "when" slots of the block so that it checks for AsteroidSpriteType instances hitting ThunkSpriteType instances. When such a collision takes place, subtract one from the LivesLabel. Figure 8.14 shows the blocks:

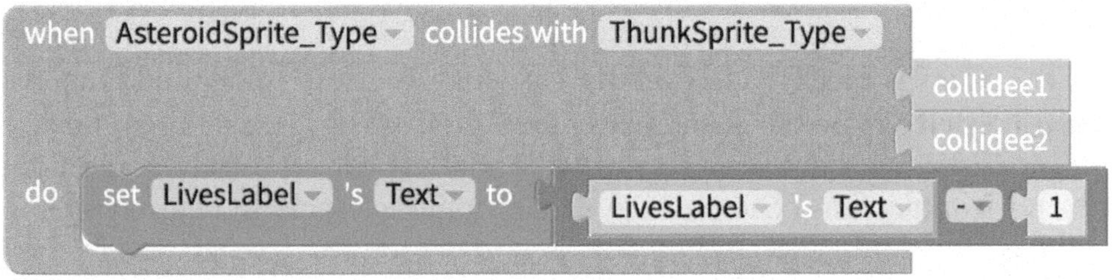

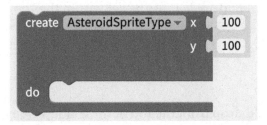

Figure 8.14. Subtract a "life" when an asteroid hits the ThunkSprite

Test the App

Test the app. An asteroid should drop from the top of the Stage when the app launches. Use your finger to move the ThunkSprite so it is either hit or not by each asteroid. Each time it is hit, one should be subtracted from LivesLabel.

Code the Dynamic Creation of Asteroids

The previous apps you've built had a fixed, pre-defined set of components that appeared on screen, which you specified in the Designer by dragging them in. Some apps, like the "Asteroids" game, need to create objects dynamically, i.e., *on the fly as the app executes*. SpriteType is the one Thunkable component that allows for the dynamic creation of components. Its **create** block, shown in Figure 8.15, allows Sprite components to be created dynamically from SpriteTypes (just as cookies are created from cookie cutters).

Figure 8.15. A block to create a sprite dynamically

Use the **create** block to code it so that new instances of AsteroidSpriteType are created every ten seconds.

- In the Blocks Editor, drag in a Timer component and set its properties as follows:

  Interval: 10 seconds
  Loops: true, so it will fire more than once
  Enabled: true

- Drag in a when Timer.Fires block.

- From the "Canvas Blocks", click on the "Add and Remove" folder and drag in a **create AsteroidSpriteType** block and place it within the when Timer fires block. Set the x and y properties so that the newly created Sprite appears at the top and randomly located on the horizontal plane (you can copy-paste from the blocks in Figure 8.13).

- When the **create** function completes, the newly created Sprite is in the component parameter. Set its angle to 90 and its speed to 50.

The blocks should appear as in Figure 8.16:

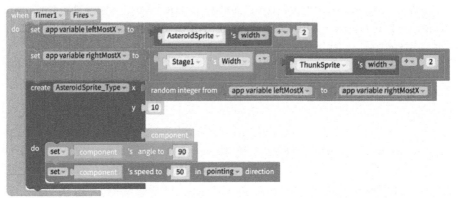

Figure 8.16. Create a new asteroid every 10 seconds

Recall that you can only use the output parameters of a function call within the block's "do" slot Thus, the new component speed and angle must be set within the "do" slot, and not below the entire **create** block.

Test the App

Test the app. An asteroid should drop from the top of the Stage when the app launches. After ten seconds, a second asteroid should appear and new asteroids should appear every ten seconds thereafter. Be sure and test that a collision between the ThunkSprite and *any* asteroid results in a life being lost.

SUMMARY

The Canvas, SpriteType and Sprite components allow you to build animated 2D games and apps. The coding is similar to other apps you've built—you still respond to events and set properties—but you are setting properties like speed and angle which allow the objects on the Screen to come alive.

The SpriteType component also has a special block, **create**, which allows for Sprites to be created dynamically. With this block, you are no longer restricted to pre-defining all the objects that will appear in your app, but can code blocks that create them dynamically.

RAFIKI BREAKS IT DOWN

Until this chapter, the components you've been coding have been static—locked in place. Now you have motion in your arsenal. This can help you bring a liveliness to your apps, so that they have a dynamic and modern feel.

Besides using animation to build games, you can also use it to visualize changes in data. Envision a goal-tracking app that helps you keep tabs on your consistency with a particular task. Let's say the goal was to build your technology vocabulary, by learning two new words or concepts each week. Each time you typed in a new definition, or voice-recorded it, that would earn you a point. With each point, you could code a sun to grow bigger or rise higher on the vertical axis of the screen.

Your own creativity could lead you in many directions. You could depict a rock moving up a hill, starting out small and growing larger You might even take on the challenge of figuring out how to have the sun, or rock, reverse the process if you don't make an entry after a four-day period. You might code your app to show a competition with your friends—see whose sun is growing the fastest! This could lead to more and more complex animations and the input actions needed to trigger then. That's what coding is all about, learning a basic technique and then figuring out how to grow muscle with it.

CONCEPTUALIZE

1.The speed property is not measured in miles per hour (MPH). How is it represented?

2.What does it mean for a sprite's angle property to be set to 270? Which direction will it move?

3. Why would you typically not set a Sprite's x and y property to 0? What do the x and y properties represent?

4. Sprites can be *created dynamically*. Explain what this means.

CUSTOMIZE

1. Add sound effects to the "ThunkMash" app and code it so the player wins when 10 points are scored.

2. Add a second SpriteType to the "ThunkMash" app, with a different image, and code it so the player loses a point if the sprite of that type is touched.

3. Modify "Asteroids" so that the asteroids appear from anywhere on the screen, not just the top, and so that they move in a randomly chosen direction, not just down.

4. Add an Accelerometer to "Asteroids" and code it so the player moves the Thunkable character by tilting the phone/tablet. You'll find the Accelerometer in the "Sensors" folder of the Blocks Editor.

CREATE

1. Create an app that helps the user record accomplishments toward some goal and use the creation or transformation of sprites to show progress towards that goal, e.g., an app in which the user records each time he or she walks to school/work instead of driving, with a tree that grows each time that occurs.

2. Build one of your favorite video games, or make a game up and build that!

Share your creative apps with your authors and other *Drag and Drop* coders:

- Use #DragAndDropCode and #MadeWithThunkable on your social media platforms.

- @ us at @DragAndDropCode on Twitter and Instagram

Chapter Resources: draganddropcode.com/bookCh8/

.

CHAPTER 9. REPEAT LOOPS

App: "MathBlaster"

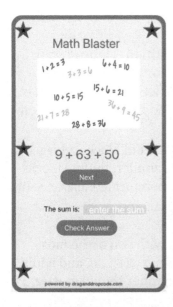

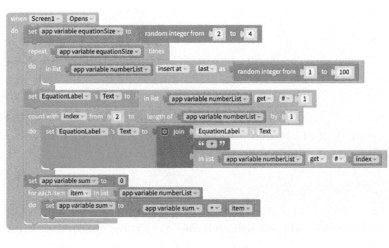

In this chapter, you'll learn how to code repetitive operations with repeat loops, you'll learn how to instruct an app to add up numbers, and you'll build a Khan-Academy-like app for practicing arithmetic.

INTRODUCTION

In this chapter, you'll learn how to add up a list of numbers. Not too exciting? You learned that in kindergarten? Well, coding an app to add is more challenging than actually adding numbers in your head or on paper! You have to examine how your brain works and turn a second-nature, subconscious process into blocks! To do this, you will learn to use *repeat loops*: blocks that cause other blocks to be repeated over and over.

Adding a list of numbers is just one operation that requires repetition. Think of your social media app visiting all your friends' posts to present a list for you, or banking software processing all of its accounts to add interest (or charge fees!). Computation is often about repeating tasks. The fancy code term for this repeated behavior is iteration.

You've learned how to use a conditional if block to specify that a set of blocks, plugged within it, should be *conditionally* performed. *Repeat* blocks are similar, but the blocks plugged into them are repeated over and over, instead of being pereformed just once or not at all.

Repeat blocks are used for many app behaviors, but you'll start with two of the most common beginning coding problems: adding the first n numbers, 1+2+3...n, and adding up a list of numbers. These are coding milestones that every beginner should master.

After mastering the arithmetic, you'll apply your knowledge to build a more complex app, a Khan-Academy-like Math blaster app that quizzes students with randomly generated arithmetic problems.

ADDING UP NUMBERS

Add the first n numbers (1+2+...n) challenge: In this section, you'll be challenged to create an app that adds up the first *n* numbers, where *n* is a number the user enters in a TextInput. Figure 9.1 shows the app:

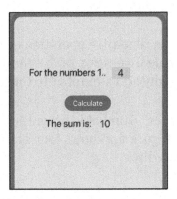

Figure 9.1. The user has entered a "4", so 1+2+3+4=10 is displayed.

Adding up numbers is second nature to many of us. Coding the "artificial intelligence" to add numbers is challenging because our brains seemingly do it automatically. You have to take a pause and observe your brain at work, which isn't easy to do.

Before you begin coding, give yourself the task of adding up the first four numbers (1+2+3+4) in your head. As you do it, try to observe your brain as it fulfills the task, including the steps and "memory cells" you use.

If you are like me, you start with 1 and add 2 to it to get a *running sum* of 3. You then add the next number 3 and get a running sum of 6. You then add the next number 4 and get a running sum of 10.

On reflection, you'll find that your brain is using three memory cells: one to keep track of the number you're on, one to keep track of the continually changing sum, and one which stores the limit number n for knowing when you're done (4 in the example).

To code the app, you'll define variables for two of the memory cells, one named number, which is a counter variable similar to the index used in the "Slideshow" app, and another named sum to keep track of the "running sum". The limit number n will be input by the user, so you don't need a variable for it—the memory cell for it is the TextInput1.Text property (where the user has entered a "4" in Figure 9.1).

REPEAT BLOCKS

In the "Slideshow" app of Chapter 4, the app repeats something—showing the next slide—but it only performs the repeated action once each time the NextButton is clicked.

The user must click multiple times to repeat the operation, and the app itself doesn't repeat any blocks within an event handler.

For the "AddNNumbers" app, a repetitive operation occurs each time the user clicks the CalculateButton. Within a single invocation of the when CalculateButton.Click event handler, the app must repeatedly add a number to the running sum.

Like all programming languages, Thunkable provides multiple ways to specify that a set of blocks are to be repeated. Figure 9.2 shows four Thunkable repeat blocks in the "Control" folder of the Blocks editor.

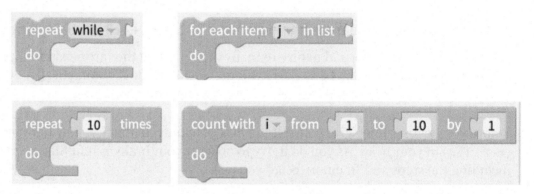

Figure 9.2. Thunkable repeat blocks

The repeat while in the top-left is the most general and can be used to code any type of repeat operation. The others are provided for convenience and make some repetitions easier to code, as you'll see later.

The repeat while is similar to an if block in that it has a slot on the right for a Boolean (true/false) condition, as shown in Figure 9.3.

Figure 9.3. "if" and "repeat while" both conditionally perform operations.

With an if, the condition is checked once and the blocks in the "do" are either performed once or not at all. With the repeat while, the condition is checked initially and the "do" blocks performed if the condition is true, just like with the "if". But after the blocks in the "do" clause are performed, control loops back up and the condition is re-checked. This process is repeated and the "do" blocks executed until the condition becomes false. The blocks within the "do" clause must make progress towards making the condition false, otherwise the code will repeat forever!

THE "ADDNNUMBERS" APP

Try to code the "AddNNumbers" app on your own. Design the user interface using Figure 9.4 as a guide:

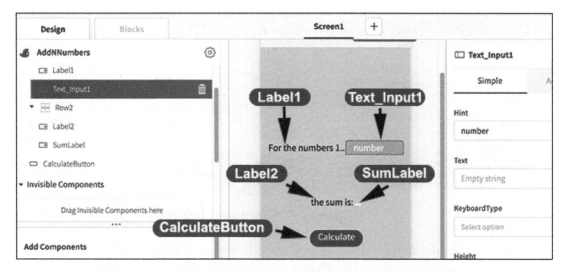

Figure 9.4. The Design of an AddNNumbers app

Label1 displays "for the numbers 1.." and Label2 displays "the sum is:". These labels are fixed and separate components from Text_Input1 and SumLabel. The user will enter the limit number in Text_Input1 and you'll place the result of the calculation in SumLabel.

Once you've designed the screen, code the blocks. The following pseudocode describes how to add up the first n numbers:

    set number to 1, the first number in 1+2+...n
    set sum to 0 to begin
    while number<=n do
        add the new number to the sum
        increment number
    when done, display the sum in a label

The two bolded lines are repeated: adding the current number to the running sum and incrementing the current number. As described earlier, your brain performs this same algorithm when it adds numbers.

See if you can code the blocks using the provided pseudo-code as a guide. If you get stuck, the blocks in Figure 9.5 offer a solution:

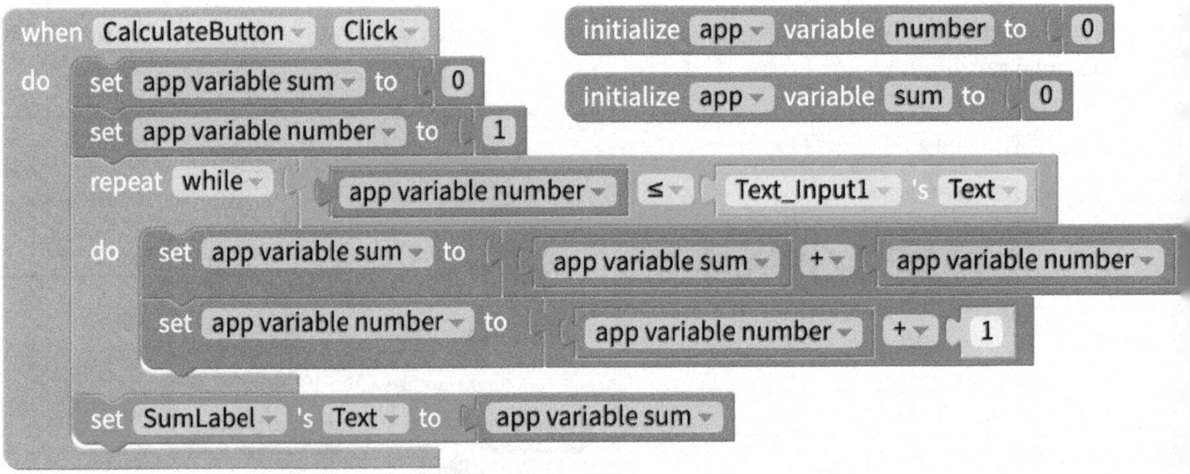

Figure 9.5. Blocks to add up 1+2+...+n.

Variables are defined for number and sum. If the user enters 4 in Textinput1.Text then clicks the CalculateButton, the blocks within the repeat while will be repeated 4 times. The variable number will eventually become 5, causing the while condition to evaluate to false, and the app will *pop out* of the repeat loop. After the loop, SumLabel's Text is set to the computed sum.

Step through and trace the blocks in Figure 9.5 with your finger, and jot down on paper how each property and variable change. Your trace should end up looking like:

number	sum	TextInput.Text	where in code
~~1~~	~~0~~	4	before loop
~~2~~	~~1~~		after first loop iteration
~~3~~	~~3~~		after second loop iteration
~~4~~	6		after third loop iteration
5	10		after fourth loop iteration

Test the App

Test the app and enter 4 in the TextInput. Does the app display 10 as the sum? Try some numbers besides 4 as well.

ADDITIONAL REPEAT BLOCKS

The repeat while is general-purpose and can be used to code any type of repetition. Thunkable, like most languages, provides additional repeat blocks that can make coding certain repeated behaviors more convenient.

"count with" block

The count with repeat block, shown in Figure 9.6, automates some of the bookkeeping required to repeat code, so it is easier to use than the repeat while. count with is similar to the "for" loop in traditional languages like Python and Java.

Figure 9.6. "count with" initializes and increments a counter variable.

The count with block defines a new counter variable, by default named "i". You can rename the variable by clicking on the upside-down triangle near the "i".

You set the "from" slot to initialize the counter variable, the "to" slot to set the limit for when the loop should end, and the "by" slot to specify how much to increment each time (usually 1).

Figure 9.7 shows an alternative solution for the "AddNNumbers" app, using the count with block (the repeat while version is also provided for comparison).

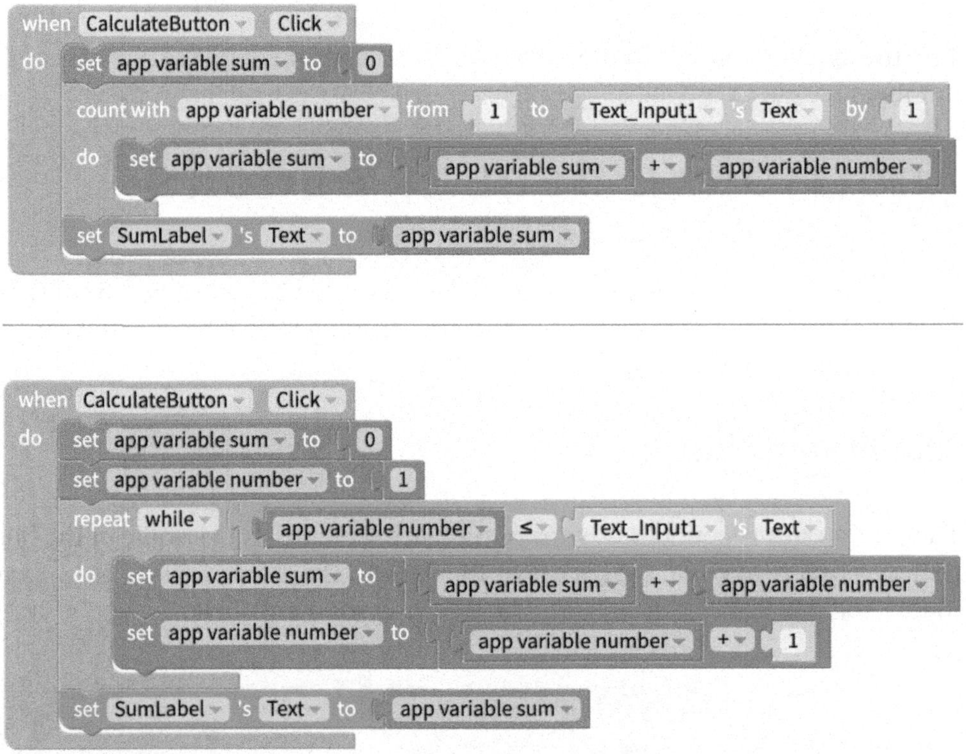

Figure 9.7. The "count with" block (top) automates counting for you

In the count with solution (top), the counter variable number is defined by changing the default name "i". When you use the count with block, you don't need to set the counter variable (number) explicitly—it is automatically initialized and incremented as the repeat loop is executed.

The repeat while solution on the bottom explicitly initializes number to 1 with a set block, and explicitly compares number with TextInput's Text to determine when to stop looping. Inside the loop, it explicitly increments number. All of these operations are performed automatically in the count with solution. The variable number changes from 1 to 2 to 3 to 4, just like in the repeat while solution, and even though it isn't explicitly set.

"for each item in list" block

Another convenient repeat block is the for each item in list block, shown in Figure 9.8. It is used when you need to process every item in a list.

Figure 9.8. The "for each item in list" block.

You specify which list you want to process in the open right slot labeled "in list". The blocks in the "do" clause will be repeated once for each item in the list.

The block also defines a new variable representing the *current item*. By default, this variable is named "j". You can and should rename it, either to "item" or a name descriptive of the items in the list. Just as the count with repeat loop automatically modifies a counter variable, the for each item in list block automatically sets the current item variable on each iteration. The first time the "do" code is performed, the current item variable is set to the first item in the list, the second time it is set to the second item, and so on.

ADD A LIST OF NUMBERS

Add a List of Numbers Challenge. Use the for each item block to create an app that, on launch, displays a list of numbers, then calculates the sum of the numbers and displays that as well. For this challenge, define an app variable, numberList, with some arbitrary values, and add up those numbers.

The algorithm is similar to the "AddNNumbers" example: on each iteration you add a new number to the sum. The difference is the number added on each iteration is not the counter variable, but the current item from the list. Figure 9.9 shows the code:

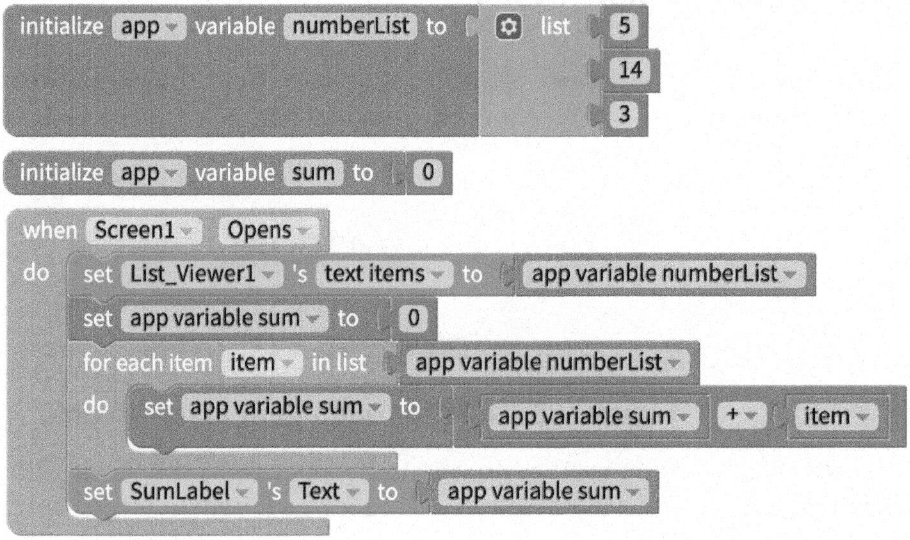

Figure 9.9. Add a list of numbers with "for each"

Trace through these blocks to get a feel for how the for each item works, jotting down how each variable is changed as execution proceeds. Your trace should end up as:

sum	item	SumLabel.Text	Where in Code
~~0~~	5		first loop
5	~~14~~		second loop
~~19~~	3		third loop
22		22	after end of loop

How the Blocks Work

The ListViewer is populated with the list and variable sum is initialized to 0 to begin. When the for each item block is first reached, the first list item, 5, is set into the variable item. The for each item block does this automatically—you don't have to set item explicitly. The "do" code is then performed for the first time. The item, 5, is added to the sum, which was originally 0. Thus, sum is set to 5.

Once the code within the "do" is executed, the app loops back to the top of the for each item and the next item in the list, in this case 14, is automatically placed into the variable item. The blocks within the "do" are then repeated, with sum changing from its current value, 5, to 5+14=19. Execution loops back up again, 3 is placed into item, and the "do" code is executed a final time, setting the sum to 22. As all items in the list have been processed, the for each item loop completes, and the SumLabel is set to display the sum, 22.

As you can see, for each item block automates changing the item variable for you each time through the loop, as well as stopping the loop when the entire list has been processed.

You could add up the list using repeat while instead of for each item, but you'd have to do the bookkeeping work yourself. Figure 9.10 shows the repeat while solution:

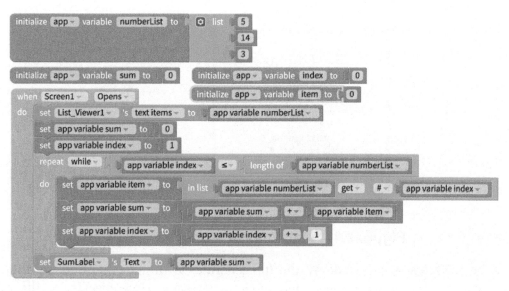

Figure 9.10. The "repeat while" solution must do the bookkeeping explicitly

Compare this solution with the for each item version of Figure 9.9. The repeat while solution in Figure 9.10 explicitly initializes an index variable and checks on each iteration to see if the index is less than or equal to the length of the list of numbers. It also must explicitly set the item each time using the in list get block, and increment the index. All of these operations are performed automatically by the for each item block (Figure 9.9).

MATH BLASTER APP

The "MathBlaster" app is shown in Figure 9.11.

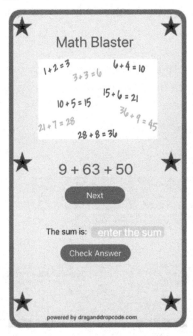

Figure 9.11. MathBlaster App.

Like the quizzes at Khan Academy, the app generates arithmetic questions for the student and checks to see if the student answers correctly. More specifically, the app generates random addition problems consisting of 2-4 numbers, with every number between 0 and 100 (e.g., 9+63+50)

Random Numbers

If you completed the games in Chapter 8, you became familiar with the blocks to generate random numbers, shown in Figure 9.12.

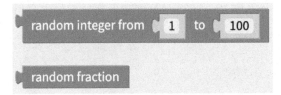

Figure 9.12. Blocks for generating random numbers.

The random fraction block returns a floating point (decimal) number between 0 and 1. The random integer block returns a whole number within a given range. You can change the "from" and "to" numbers to change the range. Each time you call the block it will give you a different random number.

You'll use the random integer block twice for the "MathBlaster" app, both to generate a random count for how many numbers are in each equation, and to generate each of the numbers in each equation.

Create a Dynamic a List

In the "Slideshow" app of Chapter 4, you defined a list containing the names of the image files, and the items were fixed (never changed). In the MathBlaster app, the data is not fixed. Instead, you need to generate a new list of numbers for each addition equation given to the user. Data that changes as the app runs is said to be *dynamic data* as opposed to fixed data.

Figure 9.13 shows the list block used to define a fixed list in the "Slideshow" app:

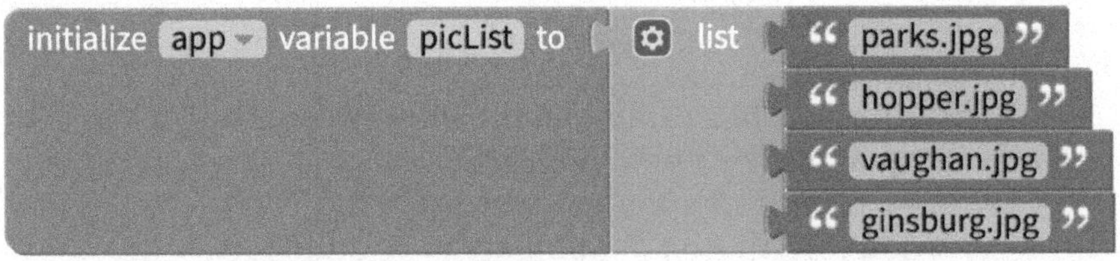

Figure 9.13. The Slideshow app defines a fixed list.

With the MathBlaster app, you'll define a list variable, but the items for the list will be generated randomly for each new question, so you can't pre-define them. For such apps, you use the empty list block to initialize your list, as shown in Figure 9.14:

Figure 9.14. Defining a list as empty to start.

Insert an Item into a List

You can dynamically add items to a list with the in list insert at block, shown in Figure 9.15:

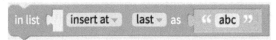

Figure 9.15. Insert items into the list dynamically.

You fill the open slot on the left with a list variable and you replace the "abc" with the item you want added to the list.

With these additional list operations, you are ready to build the "MathBlaster" app. Make a copy of the "Add List of Numbers" app and name it "MathBlaster". Then modify it so that instead of the list always being the same, it is dynamic and loaded with two to four random items.

You'll need a variable equationSize, which will hold a number between 2 and 4. The pseudo code is shown below:

> When the app launches
> > set equationSize to a random number between 2 and 4
> > repeat equationSize number of times
> > > get a random number between 0 and 100
> > > add it to the list of numbers to be added
> > display the list in a ListViewer

Using the pseudocode as a guide, modify the when Screen1.Opens event handler. For now, continue to show the list of numbers in a ListViewer. In the next iteration you'll display the numbers in a Label as an equation, e.g., "3+8+44".

Figure 9.16 shows a solution:

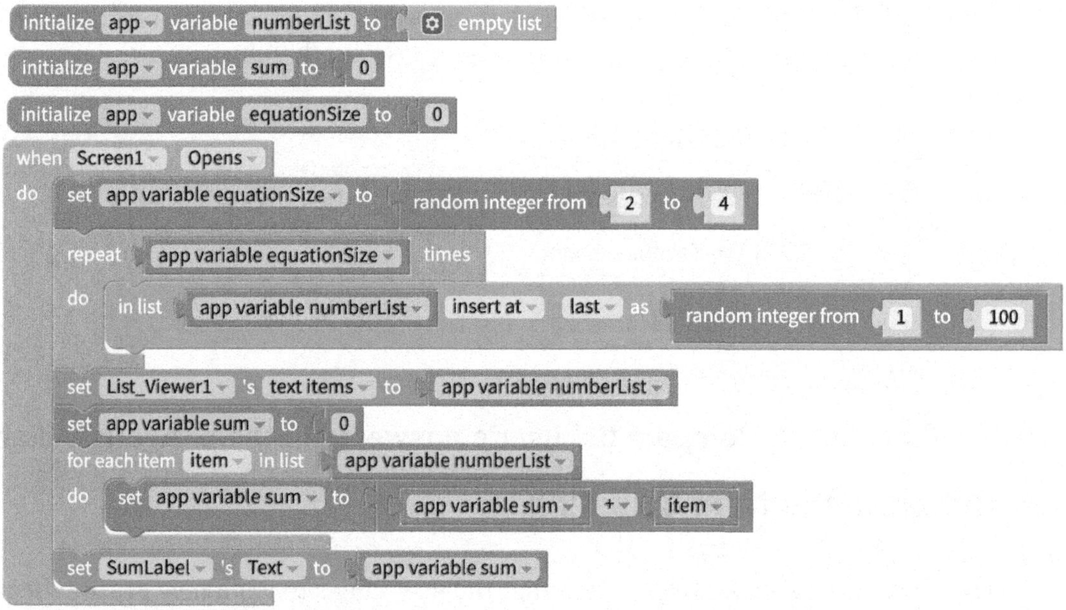

Figure 9.16. Generate a list of random numbers and add them up.

The variable equationSize is first set to a random integer between 2 and 4, the number of values that will be inserted into the list.

A repeat loop is then executed equationSize times. On each iteration, a random number between 1-100 is inserted into numberList.

Once the list is built, it is displayed in the ListViewer and a **for each item** loop is executed to compute the sum of the newly generated list. The app stores the calculated sum in the variable sum. For now, that sum is displayed in SumLabel.Text, but eventually you'll remove that last row of the blocks as you don't want to give away the answer!

Check the User's Answer

The goal is for the user to view the list of numbers, enter an answer in a TextInput, then click a button to check if the answer is correct.

In the Designer, add a TextInput component, a Button named AnswerButton, and a Label named FeedbackLabel. Your app should appear something like the one in Figure 9.11. Then add blocks to check if the entered number is the same as the sum that the app calculates in when Screen.Opens. Figure 9.17 shows the blocks:

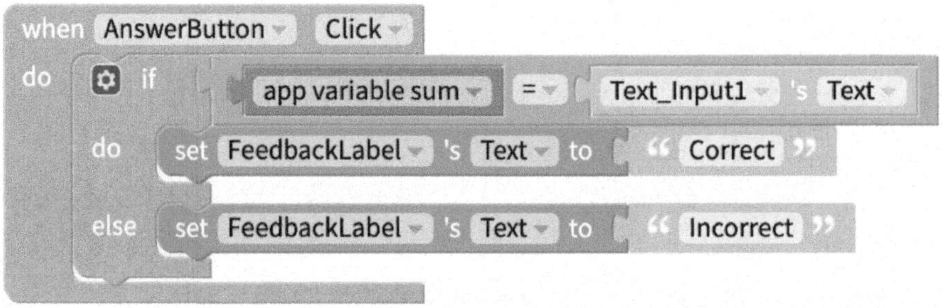

Figure 9.17. Compare the user's answer with the previously computed sum.

Generate the Next Question

The app also provides a NextButton that the user clicks to get a new arithmetic problem. In the Designer, add a button and name it NextButton.

The when NextButton.Click event handler should do what when Screen Opens does— generate a list of numbers and add them up. You can copy-paste the blocks, then add two additional rows to clear the FeedbackLabel and numberList, as shown in Figure 9.18:

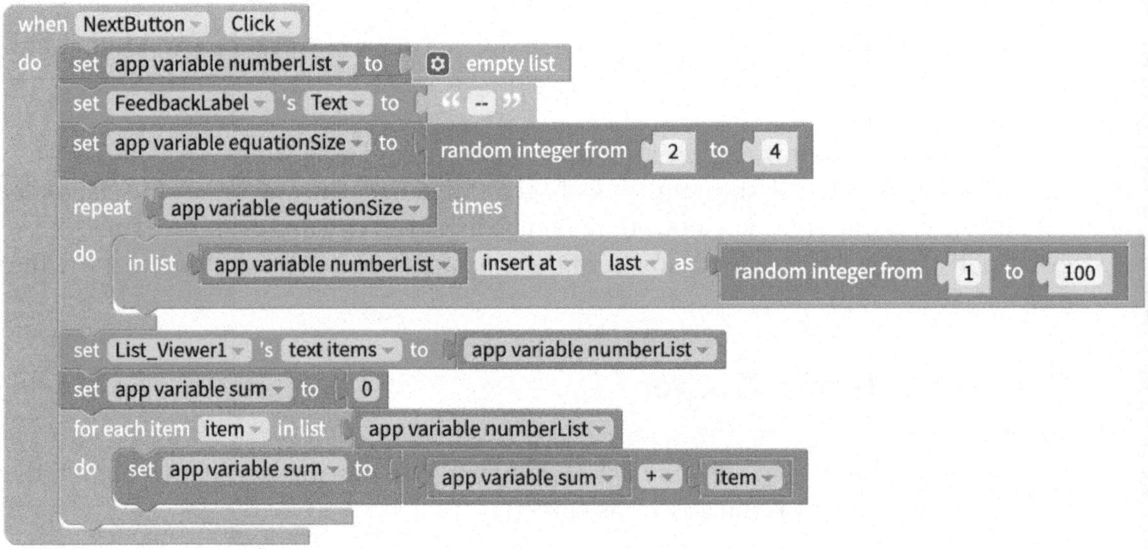

Figure 9.18. Generate a new question when NewQuestionButton is clicked.

Duplicating code as was done here is not the best practice from a software engineering perspective. In Chapter 13, you'll learn how to create *functions* and place such repetitive code in one place, but for now just have the two copies of the code in the two event handlers.

Test the App

Test the app. When you click the NextButton a new equation should appear. Be sure and test that the answer-checking works for newly generated questions.

MATHBLASTER V.2: DISPLAY AN EQUATION

The app built so far displays the numbers in a ListViewer instead of as an equation like "4+83+7". You can rectify this by adding blocks to build a text string equation from a list of numbers.

To begin, copy your project and name the copy, "MathBlasterEq". Then in the Designer, remove the ListViewer and add a Label named EquationLabel, in which you'll display the generated equation.

The code to generate the equation is fairly complex. Just as you build up a list of random numbers using a repeat loop, you can build the equation by repeatedly adding each number in the list to the EquationLabel, along with "+" symbol in between. More specifically, you'll put the first number from the list into the equation, then repeat adding "+" and the next item to it for the rest of the list.

For example, consider the list of numbers [4,83,7]. You'll first add "4" to the EquationLabel. Then you'll repeat twice, adding "+83" the first time to get "4+83", then adding "+7" the second time to get the complete equation "4+83+7". Here is the pseudocode:

> Initialize EquationLabel with the first number in the list
> Repeat for the rest of the list items starting from the second one:
>   join "+" and the current item to the previous value of EquationLabel

Figure 9.19 shows the modified when Screen1.Opens blocks. You'll also need these same changes in the when NextButton.Click event handler.

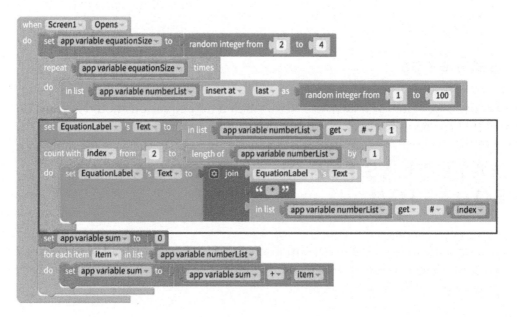

Figure 9.19. Build an equation in an iterative manner.

EquationLabel is now used instead of the ListViewer to display the numbers. The first number in the newly generated numberList is added EquationLabel.Text, and then the count with loop is executed to add the "+" signs and the successive numbers to the equation. The counter variable within the count with has been renamed "index" instead of the default "i". Instead of starting at 1, index is started at 2. In the count with "do" code, EquationLabel's Text is set to *its current value* joined with a "+" and then the current number in numberList. When the count with completes, EquationLabel's Text is in the form exemplified by "4+83+7".

SUMMARY

Repeat blocks allow a few lines of code to perform a large amount of processing. Thunkable provides the repeat while block, which can be used for any repetitive task, as well as other repeat blocks which make various repetitive behaviors more convenient.

In this chapter, you used repeat blocks to code some "milestone" problems, including adding the first n numbers and adding up a list of numbers. You then applied the techniques, along with some new knowledge on generating random numbers and dynamic lists, to build an educational app, "MathBlaster".

RAFIKI BREAKS IT DOWN

"MathBlaster" is one of my favorite examples in this book, in part because its simplicity on the front-end experience is misleading in relation to the power of the computational logic behind it. By grasping the architecture of "MathBlaster", you are actually laying hold of a powerful set of keys. It reminds me of my favorite math teacher, Ms. Hines. She coached us to be two and even three grade levels ahead in our math skills. In part, because she was lively and beautiful; but more so because she was vested in our success as students. She helped us grab the keys of executing math and grow our confidence in handling those keys.

Part of that key-grabbing process was crossing the lake of fire represented by tricky word problems. Oh, the angst and agony! Once we learned to be detail-oriented, to not rush and to listen for the deflections and deceptions in the problems, the rest fell into place. Our strength of deduction and logic grew, as did also our computational skills. It's the very same for you with counting numbers and programming. Once you grasp the flow of it, you will have essential keys right in your hand to program valuable and engaging tools and experiences.

From Addition to Multiplication to Algebra and Onwards

In this chapter you coded for addition only, but with that in place you can easily add both division and multiplication to the app's repertoire. That places you squarely on the doorstep of algebra, which is merely an abstraction of standard mathematics to the inclusion of variables, symbols and the solving of broader equations. These elements should sound familiar to you: abstraction, variables, equations.

Here's the takeaway: the broader your comfort with programming Math, the wider is the canvas of possibility in your hands. By learning the arithmetic of coding and the coding of arithmetic, you are now wielding a mighty genie lamp that can make things happen. Impressive things.

VOCABULARY VIBE

ITERATION

An app often needs to perform an operation or sequence of operations over and over, sometimes thousands or even millions of times. Iteration—also known as looping—is the process of repeating operation(s).

You certainly don't want an unwieldy number of blocks in your app, so all coding languages provide a way to specify iteration. Thunkable provides a number of repeat blocks which, in different ways, say, "perform the blocks within me multiple times".

CONCEPTUALIZE

1. List the tasks that the count with block performs automatically that you'd need to code explicitly if you used a repeat while?

2. List the tasks that the for each item in list block performs automatically that you'd need to code explicitly if you used a repeat while?

3. Trace the code blocks in Figure 9.19, showing how all pertinent properties and variables change. Assume the first random number is 2, the second is 8 and the third is 11.

CUSTOMIZE

1. Modify the "MathBlasterEq" app so that the equations consist of 4-6 numbers with numbers in the range -1000 to 1000

2. Add sound effects to the "MathBlasterEq" app.

3. Recode the "MathBlasterEq" app so that the only repeat block used is the repeat while.

CREATE

1.Create a grade point average calculator. In the when Screen.Opens event handler, define a list of grades (e.g., "A", "C", "B"), display the grades in a ListViewer, and compute and display the GPA. For your first version, assume there are no "+" or "-" in the grades.

2.Create a memory test game which generates and displays sequences of words and asks the user to speak the sequence back to the app. You'll need the **recognized speech** block in the "Speech" folder.

Share your creative apps with your authors and other *Drag and Drop* coders:

- Use #DragAndDropCode and #MadeWithThunkable on your social media platforms.

- @ us at @DragAndDropCode on Twitter and Instagram.

Chapter Resources: draganddropcode.com/bookCh9/

CHAPTER 10. MAPS AND LOCATION

Apps: "MeetMyClassmatesMap" and "SafePlaces"

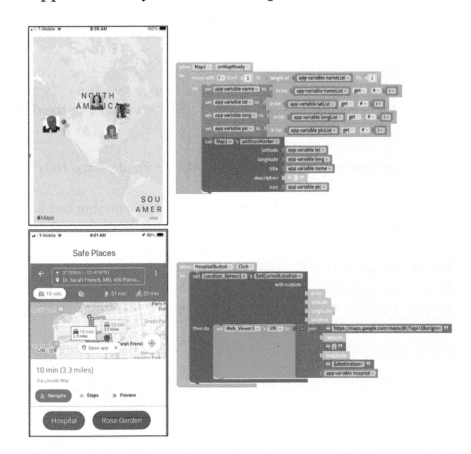

In this chapter, you'll learn how to add maps and location information into your apps. You'll learn about the Global Positioning System (GPS), the Map and LocationSensor components, the WebViewer, and the Google Maps API. You'll add a map showing people in your "MeetMyClassmates" app and you'll build a "Safe Places" app for quick directions to special places

INTRODUCTION

We track our children's locations, point our phone to the sky to learn what stars we're looking at, and find our way to anywhere. All of this is possible because of mobile phones, satellites, and the Global Positioning System (GPS) .

In this chapter you'll learn to use Thunkable's Map component to display a custom map within your app. You'll use the Map component to expand the "MeetMyClassmates" of Chapter 5 with a MapScreen showing pictures of all the people.

You'll also learn about the Google Maps API and an alternative method of displaying a map based on the WebViewer component and the API. You'll learn about Maps URLs and URL parameters, how to display directions on a map, and how to find the current location of the user. You'll use this knowledge to build a "SafePlace" app with buttons for quick-access directions to important places.

LATITUDE AND LONGITUDE

With the GPS system, every location on earth is defined by a latitude and a longitude, a two-number value such as the one for this spot in Quito, Ecuador: 0.06265818945546206, -78.33510546638126. The first number is the latitude and defines the North-South location, so a place near the Equator, like Quito, Ecuador, has a near-zero latitude, as shown in Figure 10.1:

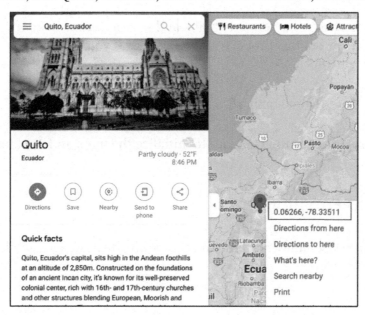

Figure 10.1. Quito, Ecuador has latitudes near 0.0.

The second number is the longitude. It defines how far east or west you are of the Prime Meridian. If you visit the Royal Observatory in Greenwich, England, you can walk on the Prime Meridian "line" and its longitude of 0.0.

Go to maps.google.com to find the latitude and longitude of any place. Just control-click (iOS) or right-click (Windows) on the map and the location numbers will appear as shown in Figure 10.1

THE MAP COMPONENT

Thunkable's Map component provides functionality for displaying a map and adding markers, lines and polygons to it.

Map Component Properties

The key properties in the Map component include:

- Latitude and Longitude. Specify the center of the map that appears.

- Zoom. Specify the zoom level. Thunkable's documentation (https://docs.thunkable.com/map) specifies that the zoom level should be between -15 (most zoomed out) and 15 (most zoomed in). Depending on your need, you'll need to try some values for the zoom level.

- Provider. If you leave this property blank and your app runs in an iPhone, an Apple map will appear. If you set this property to "google", or if you run your app on an Android, a Google map will appear.

- Map Type. Choose from standard, satellite, hybrid, or terrain.

You can set these properties in the Designer to initialize the map, and use blocks to change things dynamically.

Map Events and Functions

The Map component has a number of functions for adding text, images, or shapes to a map, as shown in Figure 10.2:

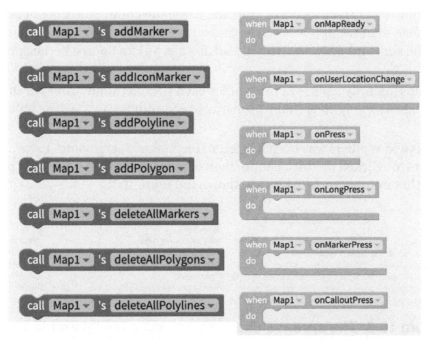

Figure 10.2. The Map component's functions and events.

addMarker displays the default marker at a location. **addIconMarker** lets you specify an image that should appear at the location. You can also draw lines and shapes and delete anything you've added.

when Map.onMapReady is triggered when the map is loaded and ready for your code to place items on the map. It triggers after the Screen's Open event, so always add your markers and other items for the map in the onMapReady event.

when Map.onUserLocationChange is triggered when the phone (user) moves. This event is key for "breadcrumb" apps that record paths. There are also events for when the user presses the map or a marker on the map. With these events and functions, you can provide a rich interactive experience for the user.

ADD A MAP SCREEN TO "MEET MY CLASSMATES"

In this section, you'll remix the "MeetMyClassmates" app of Chapter 5 to include a latitude and longitude of a significant place for each person in the spreadsheet, and you'll code the app to loop through the location information and display a marker for each person on the Map.

To begin, copy your "MeetMyClassmates" app and name the copy "MeetClassmatesMap". Then copy the spreadsheet that the app is based on and add two more columns to it, naming one "lat" and one "long". Be sure and add your new spreadsheet as a Data Source in the app.

Using Google Maps, identify a place of interest for each person (hometown?) in the spreadsheet and add the latitude and longitude in the proper row and column.

For example, I (David Wolber) was born in Mercy Hospital of Sacramento. I searched for that in Google Maps, control-clicked on the location, then copied the latitude/longitude pair that was shown. I copied that into my spreadsheet, as shown in Figure 10.3.

	A	B	C	D	E
1	name	pic	description	lat	long
2	David Wolber	https://sites.google.com/site/davewolber/_/rsrc/1472843875095/	USF Professor and Author	38.57128777	-121.4527806
3	Tara Chklovski	https://enterprisersproject.com/sites/default/files/styles/large/pub	Technovation CEO	37.51296691	-122.2709504
4	Rafiki Cai	https://0.academia-photos.com/277254/941463/1179307/s200_r	Digital Doctor	33.75050745	-84.39452057
5	Tomas Wolber	https://lh3.google.com/u/0/d/1rGgcCNSCJDEIZLYOO0DWWeLL	Dime Hoopster	45.20134546	-123.1992742
6	Ralph Morelli	https://res.cloudinary.com/dlox0soom/image/upload/v16506623f	Professor and Blues Afficianado	44.68340032	-71.77975889
7	Jen Rosato	https://res.cloudinary.com/dlox0soom/image/upload/v1650662525	Director of National Center for Computing Education	48.45309569	-92.41333987

Figure 10.3. The spreadsheet with columns for lat and long.

If you are building this app for your class or organization, you might even share the spreadsheet and allow each person to enter their own data including the latitude and longitude of their hometown.

Next, add a new screen to "MeetMyClassmatesMap" named "MapScreen", and drag a Map component into the new screen. In the Designer, set the latitude and longitude of your Map component to appropriate values in order to center it. You can also set the Zoom property. The people in my spreadsheet are located in the United States, so I centered the map in Kansas, which is in the middle. I set the Zoom property to -10 which resulted in most of the country appearing.

The next step is to provide access to the MapScreen from Screen1. In Screen1, add a button, "MapButton", with the text "map". Then, in the when MapButton.Click event handler, add code to navigate to the new MapScreen.

You need to perform some bookkeeping in your Screen1 as well. The original "MeetMyClassmates" defined one variable, idList, and loaded the ids from the spreadsheet into it. Now you need to define four additional app variables: nameList, picList, latList, and longlist, and load the data from the spreadsheet into them.

Recall from Chapter 5 that the "Data Source" folder has blocks for accessing the data in the spreadsheet. **list of values in** loads an entire column in the spreadsheet. In Screen1.Opens, call that block four additional times (five total) to load in the names, latitudes, longitudes, ids and pics from the spreadsheet into your list variables. It is common to bring the data from the sheet into variables so you can process it. In this case, you'll use the data to add markers to your map. Figure 10.4 shows the blocks for when Screen1.Opens and when MapButton.Click,

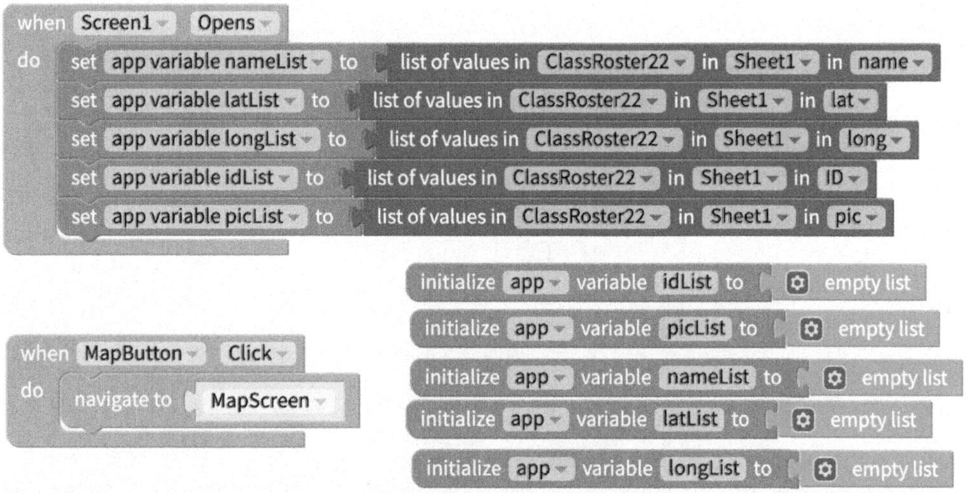

Figure 10.4. The Screen1 blocks for loading data and navigating to the map.

Now you're ready to code the blocks for the MapScreen and add markers to your Map. Be careful here—you want to initialize your map in the when Map1.onMapReady event, not the when MapScreen.Opens event.

The code should loop through the list variables you created in Screen1 and show each person with an icon marker on the map. Figure 10.5 shows the blocks:

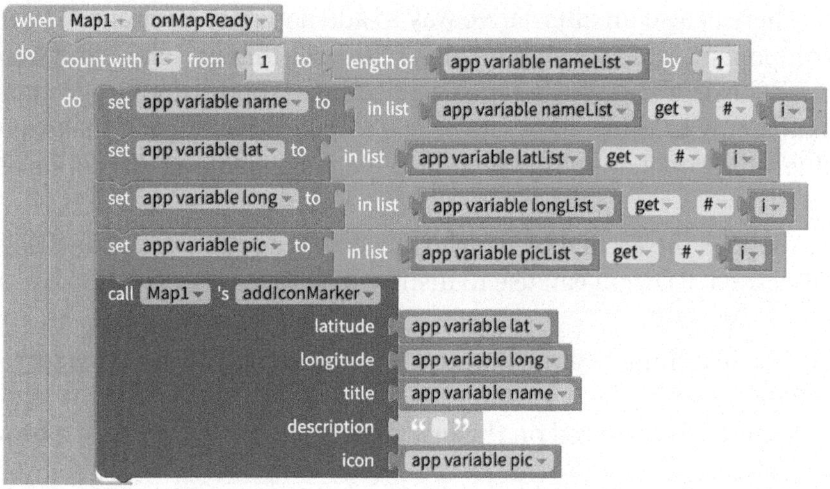

Figure 10.5. When the map loads, add markers for each person.

The count with block is used to loop through the items in the list. The counter variable i begins at 1. The blocks within the count with will be repeated n times, where n is the length of the nameList (which is also the length of the other lists). On each iteration, the person's picture is added as the icon, at the latitude and longitude defined in the spreadsheet, and with a title set to the person's name.

Figure 10.6 shows the MapScreen in action with the locations of the people in my spreadsheet:

Figure 10.6. The MapScreen showing the people in the spreadsheet

WEBVIEWER AND THE GOOGLE MAPS API

Thunkable's Map component is useful and the Thunkable team is continually adding new functionality to it. There is also an alternative way to add a map to your app. The method uses the WebViewer component, which is an embedded browser that can show any website within your app, and it makes use of URLs using the Google Maps Application Programmer Interface (API). This alternative way to show maps allows you to take advantage of the extensive Google Maps API including what you'll do in this section, which is displaying *directions* on a map.

An API, in general, defines the format by which you access functionality. The Google Maps API defines the format of the URLs you can use to display a map.

Google Maps URLs for searching begin with https://www.google.com/maps/search?api=1. For instance, https://www.google.com/maps/search/?api=1&query=Eiffel+Tower shows a map with the Eiffel Tower in Paris centered on the map. Try typing that URL into a browser!

Think of the "maps/search" of the URL as a function, similar to Thunkable's functions you call with blocks. The URL is basically calling a function named "maps/search" on Google's servers. The parameters to the function come after the function name in the URL. The first parameter always appears after a "?" and additional parameters appear after "&"s. For the URL https://www.google.com/maps/search/?api=1&query=Eiffel+Tower, "api" is the name of the first parameter and its value is "1". The "api" parameter just specifies that Google's universal cross-platform API will be used.

The second parameter is named "query" and its value is "Eiffel+Tower". The "+" denotes a space, so the parameter is specifying that the map should show results for the search term "Eiffel Tower". If you put the URL into a browser, the Eiffel Tower in Paris will be centered on it.

A second Maps API function, "maps/@", is used to display a map using GPS coordinates, as in this sample:

> https://www.google.com/maps/@?api=1&map_action=map&center=37.764387990412
> 324,-122.45743679060993

The parameters for the "maps/@" function include "api", "map_action" which should be set to "map", and "center", which is set to a latitude and longitude.

Another Maps API function is "maps/dir", which shows directions from one place to another. For example, the URL:

> "https://www.google.com/maps/dir/?api=1&origin=37.77652094813085,-
> 122.45068669027548&destination=37.77177191867418,-122.47180103813703"

shows directions from the Rose Garden in San Francisco to the University of San Francisco. The parameters for the "maps/dir" function are "api", "origin", and "destination". The documentation for the entire Google Maps API is at "https://developers.google.com/maps/documentation/urls/get-started."

To explore, create a new app and name it "Safe Places". Drag a WebViewer component onto the Screen, and in the Designer set the WebViewer's URL to one of the URLs above. Play around some with URL parameters to show different maps.

The WebViewer is a browser embedded within your app. The user can interact with it without leaving your app, which is an advantage compared to a link that takes them away. In your apps, you can add components around the WebViewer and essentially expand the page's (map's) user interface.

LOCATION SENSING

The LocationSensor component tells you the current location of the phone on which the app is running. The component can be found within the Blocks Editor's "Sensors" folder. The **GetCurrentLocation** function is shown in Figure 10.7.

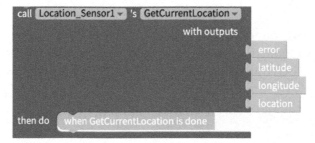

Figure 10.7. GetCurrentLocation reports the GPS location of the phone

The output parameters of the function provide the latitude and longitude of the user's current location. The error parameter will report if there was a problem accessing the GPS data.

CREATE A "SAFE PLACES" APP

Using a WebViewer and LocationSensor, make an app with two buttons. Clicking each button should bring up directions to a safe place for the user. For this sample, make the app specific to you or someone you know personally. Later, you might generalize it to make it useful to any user.

- If you created a "Safe Places" app earlier, use it. Otherwise create a new app and add a WebViewer to it. Then code the when Screen1.Opens so that the user's current location is displayed on the map. Call **LocationSensor.CurrentLocation** and then use the location information returned to build a Google Maps API URL that centers the map at that location. The blocks are shown in Figure 10.8:

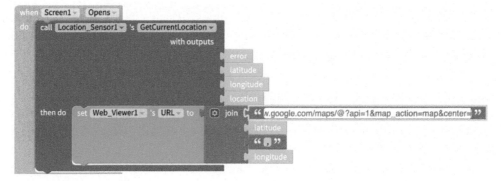

Figure 10.8. Show the user's current location on map

Note that the full text in the block at the top of the join is
"https://www.google.com/maps/@?api=1&map_action=map&center=".

- Consider the user you are building the app for (maybe you?), and determine the latitude and longitude for two significant places. For my sample, I'll use the UCSF hospital in San Francisco, and the Rose Garden in Golden Gate Park, the first being for a physical emergency, the second if my soul is in need of beauty. Go to maps.google.com and determine the latitude and longitude of your two spots.

- Add two buttons to your "SafePlaces" app. Set the text on the buttons to describe them. For me, one button says "Hospital" and the other says "Rose Garden.

- Code the buttons to change the WebViewer's URL when each button is clicked. Using the locations I determined, the blocks for my when HospitableButton.Click appear as in Figure 10.9:

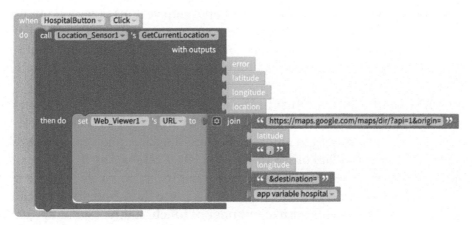

Figure 10.9. When the button is clicked, show directions

SUMMARY

Humans now carry around very powerful computers—our phones-- and there are powerful satellites in the sky that can determine everyone's location. We are only just beginning to figure out how to utilize these phenomena and now you have some super powers to explore it yourself.

Thunkable's Map component and LocationSensor make the process of displaying custom maps and determining the user's location easy. You can also bypass the Map component and use the WebViewer and Google Maps API to take advantage of the rich features available there.

RAFIKI BREAKS IT DOWN

You have no idea how excited I am to write this particular RBID segment. For a long time now, I have understood the power of Application Program Interfaces (APIs) and have longed for ways to put them at the command of novices like yourself. Oftentimes the challenge of being a visionary advocate, is that you have to wait for the everyday landscape to catch up to what you can foresee. Finally, the Land of APIs is being opened up for neophytes. With Thunkable you now have a visa to enter. Welcome!

You just tapped into the richness of Google's Maps API, which offers much more than we had time to describe here. In Chapter 14 you'll explore the Books API and learn about APIs that return JavaScript Object Notation (JSON). Realize, though, that these are just examples of a vast world!

Imagine if teams of experienced developers, seasoned technology leaders and venture capitalists, were to spend years and millions to develop various powerful platforms. Then further imagine that the resources of such developments were made easily available to outsiders who did not help build or did not invest in the heavy lift that built them. That's the world of APIs in a nutshell. Others labor and construct but you get to leverage the fruits of their labor.

How vast is API Land? Consider this: I am constantly invited to API developer conferences such as API World, which draws developers from over 50 different countries. There is such a thing as the API Economy which is written about by Forbes Magazine and driven by multi-billion-dollar entities such as MuleSoft, Plaid or Postman-- the latter catalogs an inventory of 10,200 different APIs built or accessed by developers from every country in the world. There's even a *State of The API Report* released annually. In a word, there's a there there and now you can increasingly tap into it, to bring your apps to life with all manner of functionality. You'll repeatedly look like a Genius Genie, as you leverage the creativity of millions of other developer minds from around the world. API power is Genie power. Make the API do what it do, for you (and those whom your apps will serve).

CONCEPTUALIZE

1. What does a "?" and a "&" denote within a URL?

2. How is a URL involving the Google Maps API like calling a function?

CUSTOMIZE

1. Modify the "MeetMyClassmates" app so that each person's description also appears when touched on the map (currently the name appears). You'll need to load the descriptions in from the spreadsheet.

2. Change the "Safe Places" app so that it shows walking directions instead of driving. You'll need to add an additional parameter to the URLs. Check out the Google Maps API documentation: https://developers.google.com/maps/documentation/urls/get-started.

CREATE

1. Create an "Where's My Car?" app that lets the user record a location and then later shows a map from the user's current location to the saved location.

2. Consider your own life and design and build an app with a map and/or LocationSensor that helps you and/or the world in some way.

- Use #DragAndDropCode and #MadeWithThunkable on your social media platforms.

- @ us at @DragAndDropCode on Twitter and Instagram.

Chapter Resources: draganddropcode.com/bookCh10/

CHAPTER 11. BUILD A PHOTO SHARING APP

App: "PhotoShare"

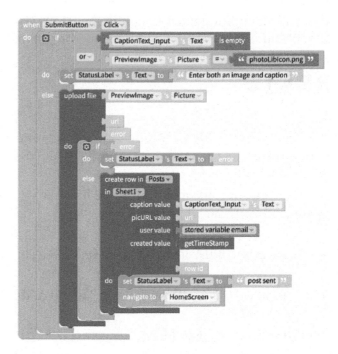

In this chapter, you'll build an Instagram-like posting app with user login and dynamic data stored in a Google sheet. You'll configure a template app for handling registration and login and you'll learn how to build input forms that take user input and add it into a database.

INTRODUCTION

Photo-sharing apps like Instagram are representative of *dynamic data apps*. The user can register and login, can view data stored in a database, and can input data that gets placed in that database. Such apps are sophisticated and have traditionally not been within the realm of the novice coder.

Because of innovations by Thunkable and other visual tools, the power to build dynamic data apps is now solidly within the reach of novices like yourself. How amazing is that? This is a huge development in the history of software development and you have the opportunity to be among some of the earliest benefactors of this shift.

In previous chapters, you worked with an app that displays data from a spreadsheet database ("MeetMyClassmates" in Chapter 5) and one that generates data (the "MathBlaster" app in Chapter 9). In this chapter, you'll take the next step and learn how to manage the users of an app and how to build forms in which the user's entries are stored persistently in a database. With what you learn, you'll be armed with a new super-power in app building.

TRY THE LOGIN-PROFILE APP

You could build registration and login screens from scratch with Thunkable, but since such screens are similar for most apps, you can make use of a template that your author has created.

- Open the "Login and Profile" template app in Thunkable. The link is at https://draganddropcode.com/bookCh11.

- Try the template app. Test the app on your phone-- it must be tested on a device! Click the "Login" button, then the "Sign Up" button in the top-right corner. Provide a real email, as the app will send a verification message.

  Check your email and click on the verification link. Then login to the app and check out the different tabs. You can view all registered users and edit your profile, including adding a photo. It is not an interesting app by itself, but it has some fundamental features with which you want to begin many of your app building projects.

MAKE YOUR OWN LOGIN-PROFILE APP

You can use the template to start any app that needs user registration, login, and profile functionality. Click on "Copy Project" from the template app to get your own copy of the "Login and Profile" app.

The app works with two external tools. Firebase is used to manage user accounts and login, and Cloudinary is used for storing the profile images. You need to create your own account with these tools and configure some settings in the app before your copy of the app will work. Don't be afraid—you can quickly and easily get free accounts at both Firebase and Cloudinary and configure your app.

Once you do that, you'll also need to tweak some blocks so that a Google sheet you create is used instead of the original. The good news is you can complete the work in about 30 minutes following the instructions in this chapter. Once you've set things up, you'll have your own version of the "Login and Profile" app that can be used as a starter for all of your apps requiring user login.

Connect your app to Firebase for User Registration and Login

Firebase is a Google cloud database tool. One service it provides is registration and login management, including storage of user information and email verification for new users. Firebase is not specific to Thunkable-- you can connect web and mobile apps built with any language to it. Thunkable provides an easy-to-use connection to Firebase and blocks to facilitate registration and login.

- If you don't have one, sign up for a free account at Firebase.com

- Create a new Firebase project, you'll be prompted for a name.

- Disable the Google Analytics.

- Firebase provisioning will take a few seconds, just wait.

- Create a Firebase "app" as a web app. Even though you are building a mobile app, you need to create your Firebase project as a web app (Thunkable is actually the web app that makes the connection). The dialog in Figure 11.1 will appear for creating an app within your Firebase project:

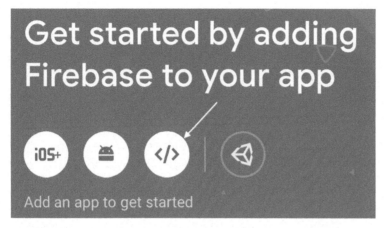

Figure 11.1. Choose the "web" icon on the right.

- Provide Firebase with a nickname for your app (it can be the same as the project name). Do not choose "hosting" option. Click "register app" then continue to console.

- Set up user authentication. Click "Authentication" and "get started". In the "sign-in method" tab, enable "Email/password" but not "email link".

- The final step is to add one Firebase setting, the "ApiKey" into your Thunkable app. At Firebase, choose "Project settings" and copy the API key as shown in Figure 11.2:

Figure 11.2. Copy the ApiKey from your Firebase project (without quotes)

Then paste that ApiKey into your Thunkable app: at Thunkable, choose the settings icon in the left menu, then scroll down to find Thunkable's Firebase setting, as shown in Figure 11.3:

Figure 11.3 Connect your Thunkable App to your Firebase project

That's it—your app is now configured to work with your Firebase project and store user information there.

CONNECT YOUR APP TO CLOUDINARY TO STORE PROFILE IMAGES

Cloudinary is a cloud tool for storing images and sound clips. You as an individual can upload files there and get a URL to access each. Thunkable provides blocks that allow your apps to also store media at Cloudinary. Cloudinary's free accounts provide a decent amount of storage, so it's a great tool to use while you're developing an app. The Photo-sharing app you're building will store all of the images uploaded by the user at Cloudinary.

- Register for a free account at cloudinary.com. That site will store the images that your users post.

- The Cloudinary dashboard has three settings that need to be input as settings in your Thunkable app, the "Cloud name", "API Key" and "API Secret" as shown in Figure 11.4:

Figure 11.4. Copy the Cloudinary properties into your Thunkable app settings.

- At Thunkable, choose project settings in the left panel and scroll down to find the Cloudinary settings. Copy the information from your Cloudinary dashboard into the corresponding settings

That's it—your app is now configured to store images at Cloudinary.

Create A Google Sheet for Profile Info

The template app uses a spreadsheet, UserProfileDD, owned by the template app's creator, yours truly David Wolber. The spreadsheet stores username, email, description, and pic for each user. Since you don't own the sheet—I do--you have to create your own Google sheet and modify your copy of the app to connect to your sheet.

- Create a Google sheet with a single row with the column headings "username", "email", "description" and "pic", as shown in Figure 11.5.

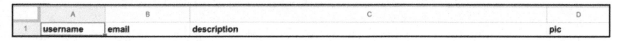

Figure 11.5. Create a Google Sheet with a single row and these exact headings

Your column names must be exact. Name your sheet "UserProfiles".

- In Thunkable, add a new data source and select the spreadsheet you just created. Don't delete the data sources that are already in the project (you'll end up deleting UserProfilesDD and keeping "RecentProfilesFirst" but leave both of them for now).

Modify the Blocks to Use Your sheet

The template app's Login, Registration, and Profile screens all refer to the original spreadsheet, UserProfileDD. You need to change those blocks so that the data source is the new one you just created, instead of the original. **Be careful, this is the super important tricky part of setting up your version.** When you change the data source in the blocks, the parameters get modified and you'll need to fix them. Consider, for instance, the blocks in Figure 11.6

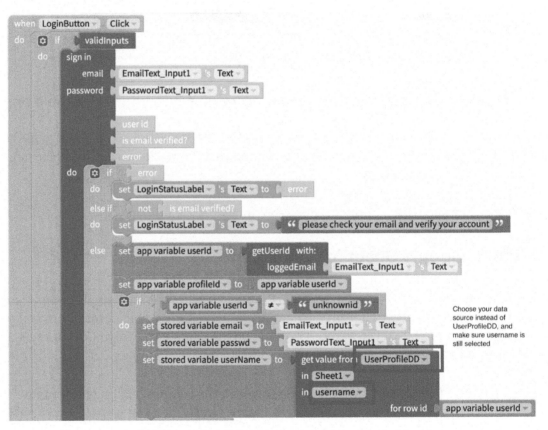

Figure 11.6. Modify the LoginButton.Click blocks

The block to "get value from" refers to "UserProfileDD", the original spreadsheet. Select the triangle next to "UserProfileDD", and choose your spreadsheet (UserProfile). When you make this switch, Thunkable may choose a different column instead of "username. If it does, just re-select "username" as the column.

The **when LoginScreen.Opens** event handler blocks also need to be changed, as shown in Figure 11.7:

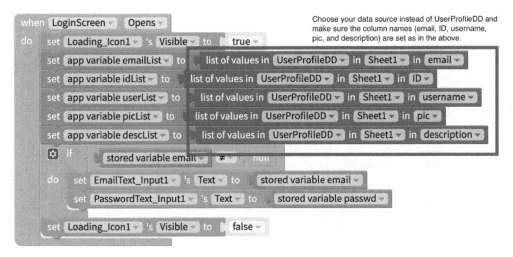

Figure 11.7. Modify the LoginScreen.Opens blocks

Be sure and modify the five rows so that "UserProfiles" is used instead of "UserProfilesDD", and re-select the columns to make sure they are the same as in Figure 11.7.

The RegistrationScreen blocks, shown in Figure 11.8, also need to be changed:

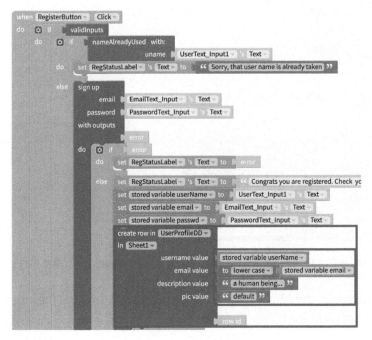

Figure 11.8. Modify the RegistrationScreen blocks

When you change "UserProfileDD" to your spreadsheet, the parameter blocks may pop out of the slots. Just carefully re-plug the blocks so they look exactly like the above (other than replacing "UserProfile" for the "UserProfileDD".

Finally, make two changes in the ProfileScreen, as shown in Figure 11.9:

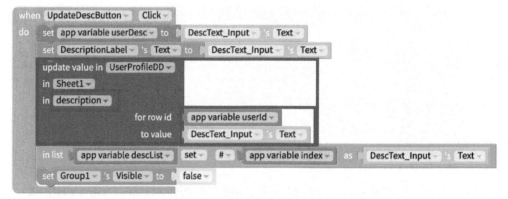

Figure 11.9. Modify the ProfileScreen blocks (1)

and Figure 11.10:

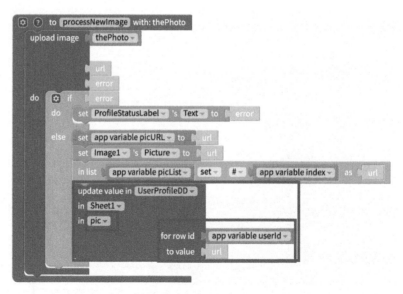

Figure 11.10. Modify the ProfileScreen blocks (2)

In each case, be careful to set the blocks exactly as in the above images (changing only "UserProfileDD" to "UserProfiles").

Test the App

Test your version of the app on your device. Click on "Login" then "Sign Up and enter your email and a password to register. If things are working, you'll receive an email to verify the email. Open the email sent to you, click the link to verify, and then you should be able to login.

If you don't receive a verification email and can't login, trouble shoot by going to your Firebase console and checking if a new user has been added. If not, check the Firebase settings in your Thunkable app—the "ApiKey" must be set correctly.

After registering, there should be a new row in your Google sheet with your information. If a row hasn't been added to the spreadsheet, check that all the blocks in the app refer to your new data source and have the proper column settings as shown in the examples above.

If you have issues, you may need to reset and remove users from Firebase as well as your spreadsheet. Be sure and keep the information at Firebase compatible with that in the spreadsheet--if there is one user at Firebase, there should be one row in the spreadsheet with an email the same as the Firebase user.

Once you successfully register/login, test the Profile screen. If you have trouble setting an image for the profile, check your Cloudinary settings within Thunkable.

When you get the app working, clean up some of the screens in the template that you don't need. Remove the AllUserScreen as you probably don't want that in your app. The LandingScreen is what appears when the app launches. You can either delete it and instead have the LoginScreen appear as that first page, or modify the LandingScreen with your own media and text.

Save the app as your own "Login and Profile" template. You can copy it each time you want to create a new app with login. In the next section, you'll learn how to do that for a photo-sharing app.

CREATE THE POSTS SPREADSHEET

The "Login and Profile" app you just created is a starter app for any project that requires user login. In this section, you'll build an Instagram-like posting app that builds upon the "Login and Profile" app.

You already have a spreadsheet and data source for storing user profile information, but you need a different sheet to store your posts. Different apps allow the user to post different types of information. For this app, focus on simple Instagram-like posts with a single image and a caption. You'll also add columns to identify the user and to timestamp the post.

Create a Google sheet named "Posts" with the first row set as column headings and the second row sample data, as shown in Figure 11.11

	caption	picURL	user	created
1				
2	SF's Cliffhouse	https://res.cloudinary.com/dlox0soom/image/upload/v1618697374/z01yjkspc8ei0ud5tcdg.jpg	wolberd@gmail.com	4-7-2022

Figure 11.11. Create a Google Sheet with a heading row and sample data

The caption can be any text, the picURL should be a URL pointing directly to an image file, the user should be an email of a test user (you), and the date can be any text for now. For the image file, you can manually upload it to your Cloudinary.com account and copy the URL Cloudinary assigns for it (this is how the URL in Figure 11.11 was created).

SHOW POSTS ON HOME PAGE

The template app has a screen named "HomeScreen" that appears once the user logs in. In this section, you'll edit that screen to show the posts from the spreadsheet on it.

In the template, there is a single Label on the screen. Change its text to "Recent Posts" and add a Data Viewer Grid below it. Then add a Data Source and map it to your "Posts" spreadsheet. In the properties for the Data Viewer Grid, choose to show an image, title, and subtitle, and map those to the "picURL", "caption", and "user" columns of the spreadsheet, respectively. The settings should look like those in Figure 11.12.

Figure 11.12. Map the Data Viewer Grid to the Posts sheet

Test your app

Test the app on your device. Does your sample data appear in the Data Viewer Grid?

CREATE AN INPUT FORM FOR POSTING

The input form for your app will consist of an image upload widget, a TextInput for the caption, and a submit button. Create a screen named "PostScreen", add components to it, and place it within the Top_Tab_Navigator1 as shown in Figure 11.13:

Figure 11.13. The PostScreen and where it fits in the Navigator

In the left-side panel of the Designer you can drag screens to place them either at the top-level or as part of a navigator menu that appears at the top of screen to the right of Figure 11.13. "PostScreen" has been dragged into "Top_Tab_Navigator1". Any screens within that will appear as a menu item in the top menu. You can change the text for the menu item in the properties for any screen.

The PostScreen has an Image named PreviewImage for displaying the image chosen by the user, a ChoosePhotoButton to provide access to the photo chooser on the device, a TextInput named CaptionText_Input, and a SubmitButton.

Once you've designed the PostScreen, modify the HomeScreen to provide access to it. Add a button with a "+" on it on the HomeScreen and add blocks so that clicking on the button opens your new PostScreen.

The behavior of the PostScreen form should be as follows: the user should choose a photo and see it previewed in the Image component. The user should then enter a caption and click "Submit". If both an image has been chosen and a caption input, the app should upload the image to Cloudinary, add a new row to the spreadsheet, and navigate back to the HomeScreen.

Thunkable's "File" folder provides blocks for accessing the Photo Chooser and storing files at Cloudinary, as shown in Figure 11.14:

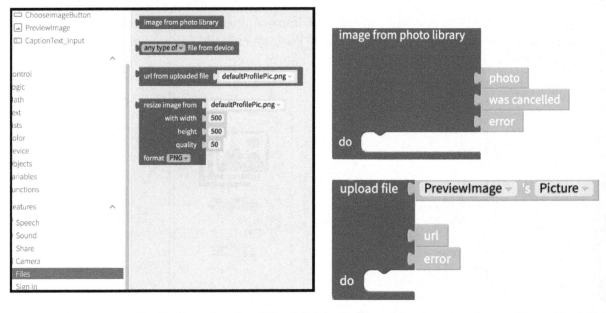

Figure 11.14. Functions in the File folder (left) and advanced versions (right)

The blocks in the left are the ones in the "Files" folder. The two on the right are advanced versions of two of those blocks. Blocks that access system tools come in simple and advanced form—you get the advanced form by control-clicking the block and selecting "Show Advanced Block". You'll generally want the advanced blocks, as they provide information about errors and user cancellations, and they provide a "do" slot so you can specify blocks that should only happen once the function completes.

Consider, for instance, the **image from photo library** block shown in Figure 11.14. That block opens the device's photo chooser and allows the user to pick an image. The advanced block returns three output parameters when the user finishes with the photo library. The photo is the image the user chose, if one was chosen. The was cancelled output parameter returns as true if the user cancelled the photo choosing operation. The error parameter is text that is non-empty if something went wrong.

Figure 11.15 shows the blocks for the when ChooseImageButton.Click event handler that calls the advanced version of **image from photo library**:

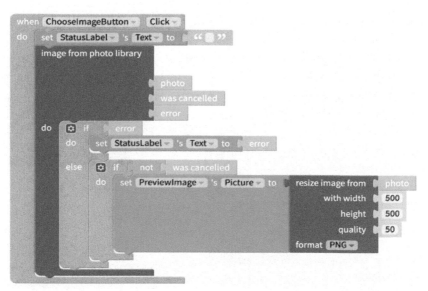

Figure 11.15. Open the Photo Library and store user's choice in PreviewImage

After **image from photo library** is called, the error is checked. If there is one, it is put into a Label so the user knows there was an issue with the Photo Library. Otherwise the "else" branch is taken and the was cancelled is checked with a *nested if*. If the operation wasn't cancelled, the picture is set with the chosen photo. Examine the code in Figure 11.15 closely. "if-else" branches can be nested to arbitrary levels. As your software gets more complicated with more artificial intelligence, you'll define more complex and nested conditional blocks.

The second key event handler for the PostScreen is when SubmitButton.click. You'll once again use an advanced block, the one for **url from uploaded file,** which gets renamed to **uploaded file** in its advanced form. Figure 11.16 shows the blocks:

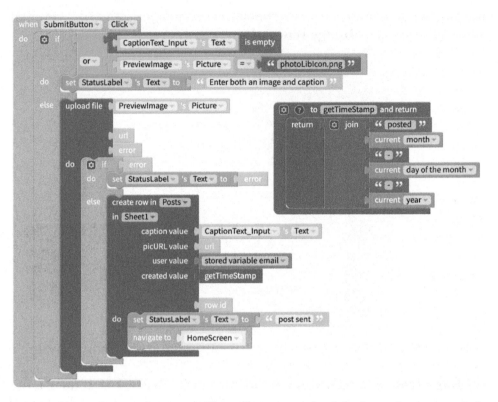

Figure 11.16. Upload the photo to Cloudinary and add a row to spreadsheet

The blocks first perform some *data verification* to make sure the user has indeed entered both a caption and an image. Notice the "or" that is used so that it checks if either of the required inputs is missing. If the user has input the picture and caption, the blocks call **upload file,** which sends the given file to Cloudinary. If you haven't set your app's Cloudinary settings correctly an error will occur, and the blocks display the error in StatusLabel. If the settings are correct, the file is stored at Cloudinary and a URL returned. The blocks then call **create row** to create a new spreadsheet row. The url returned from **upload file** is set as the picURL. The "created" slot is filled with a timestamp generated from calling a function **get time stamp**. That function, which you'll need to define, calls functions from the Device folder to access current date information.

The blocks place a URL from Cloudinary into the picURL column. Placing the data into the cloud and getting a URL for it is key, as local file references, like the photo returned from the photo chooser, have no meaning in a multi-user app—one user can't access files on another user's device. Thus, **upload file** is used to put the image in the cloud and get a URL for it. URLs are universal, so any user, can access the photo using the link.

There are two additional bookkeeping tasks the app must perform. First, the StatusLabel is used to report errors. If the user, for instance, tries to click "Submit" before entering a caption, an error message is placed in that label. Since the message shouldn't appear forever, it needs to be blanked out. This is already done at the top of when ChooseImageButton.Click (see Figure 11.15). You can also make it so that the label is blanked out when the user clicks within the CaptionTextInput, as shown in Figure 11.17:

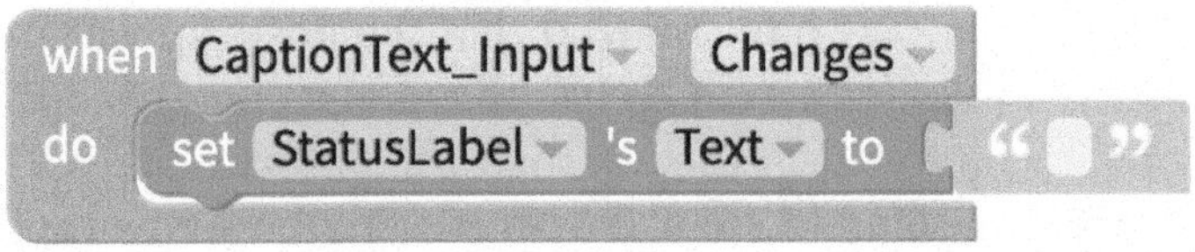

Figure 11.17. Blank out the StatusLabel when the user begins typing a caption

A second bookkeeping task involves the list of posts that appears when the user is returned to the HomeScreen. A new post has been added in the spreadsheet, and you want that extra item to appear in HomeScreen's Data Viewer Grid. To facilitate this, add a call to **Data_Viewer_Grid1.RefreshData** in when HomeScreen.Opens, as shown in Figure 11.18:

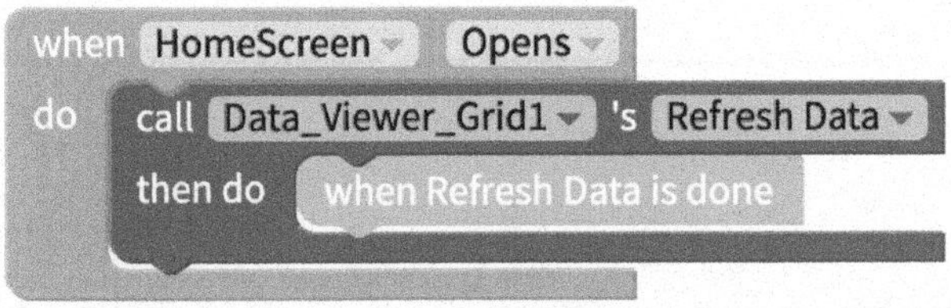

Figure 11.18. Refresh the Data Viewer Grid when HomeScreen (re-) opens

The HomeScreen.Opens is triggered the first time the screen is opened, and also when the user returns to it. When the user returns there after posting something, the blocks in Figure 11.18 result in the updated data appearing.

Test the app

Test your app on a device. Login and then post something. Does your entry appear back on the HomeScreen? Also test that the app works correctly when the user (1) doesn't enter an image or a caption before clicking the SubmitButton, and 2) chooses "Cancel" in the Photo Chooser.

But at this point you really haven't tested anything! Remember, this is a sharing app, and for those you must test the app with multiple devices to see if the sharing is working! Get access to another device (call a friend!) and have them test the app as well. Do you see the posts of the other user?

DISPLAY MOST RECENT FIRST

If you have successfully built a photo-sharing app working, congratulations! But with coding there are always more details. You may have noticed that the posts appear in the Data Viewer Grid in the same order as the spreadsheet, which has the oldest posts at top. For a sharing app, you typically want the most recent posts at the top instead. Unfortunately, Thunkable doesn't provide a property in Data Viewer Grid to change the order that the rows appear (or to filter so that only some rows are shown).

There is a work-around that works for re-ordering and can also be used to filter data (which you'll see later). The work-around involves creating another spreadsheet and copying rows from the original sheet into it. As you copy, you can reorder and filter out rows.

The first step is to create a new spreadsheet. Choose the Data Sources icon in the left panel, select the "+" to add a new one, and "Create New" You'll be given the choices shown in Figure 11.19:

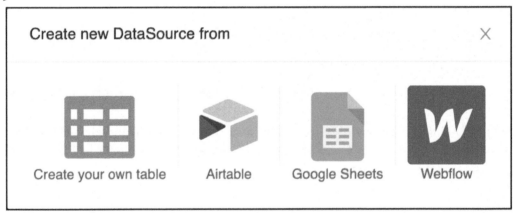

Figure 11.19 Choose "Create your own table" to create a Thunkable sheet

You could create another Google sheet, but in this case choose "Create your own table", which creates a Thunkable-controlled table local to each user's device. Name the table "RecentPostsFirst".

The table will appear with some sample columns. Change the column headings so that they're the same as those in the "Posts" sheet: "caption", "picURL", "user", and "created".

Next, change the mappings for the Data_Viewer_Grid1 on HomeScreen so that it maps to the "RecentPostsFirst" data source instead of "Posts". You'll also need to reset the Title, Image, and Subtitle fields so that they again point to the "caption", "picURL" and "created" columns as before.

The most significant task is to add blocks in when HomeScreen.Opens to copy the rows of the spreadsheet from "Posts" to "RecentPostsFirst", in reverse order

Here is the algorithm: clear all of the rows of the "RecentPostsFirst" sheet each time, copy the columns of "Posts" into list variables, then loop through those lists in reverse order, adding a row to "RecentPostsFirst" each time.

You can bring a column into an app's memory—into a list variable—with the **list of values in** function found in the Data Sources folder. Figure 11.20 shows the blocks:

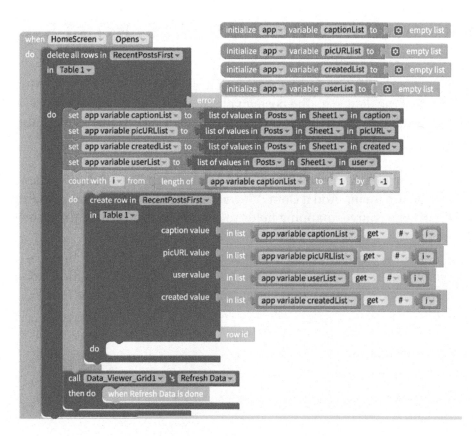

Figure 11.20. Copy the posts in reverse order into the second sheet

The blocks introduce four new list variables, and use **list of values in** to load them with the spreadsheet data. The code then loops through the lists, adding a new row of data into the "RecentPostsFirst" spreadsheet for each item.

The count with loop is different than the ones you saw in the "MathBlaster" app of Chapter 9. The counter variable "i" doesn't start at 1 as usual. Instead, it starts at the length of the captionList and counts downward each time. So if the spreadsheet has 7 items, i will start at 7 and decrement down to 1.

On each iteration, a new row is created in the second sheet. If there are 7 items, the 7th is placed in row 1, then the 6th in row 2, and so on, until the new sheet has all the rows in reverse order.

Test the App

Test the app to see if the HomeScreen now has the most recent posts at the top.

It took some work, but the good news is that the iteration code you used to reorder the data can also be used to filter the sheet and show, for instance, only posts from the logged in user.

FILTER: SHOW ONLY USER'S POSTS

The posting app you've built shows the posts for all users on the HomeScreen. Most apps also show filtered views of the data, e.g., the posts made by a particular user, or the posts for all followers of the logged in user. In this section, you'll build a screen that shows the posts for the logged in user.

Create a new Screen named MyPostsScreen, and add it to the Top_Tab_Navigator1 so it a link to it shows up in the top menu. Add a Data_Viewer_Grid to the screen and map the grid to the "RecentPostsFirst" data source, mapping fields to columns as you did on the HomeScreen.

Open HomeScreen and copy the blocks within its Opens event handler, then paste them into the PostsScreen blocks in when MyPostsScreen.Opens. After pasting the blocks, add an "if" so that only the rows that were posted by the current user are copied over into "RecentPostsFirst".

Figure 11.21 shows the blocks:

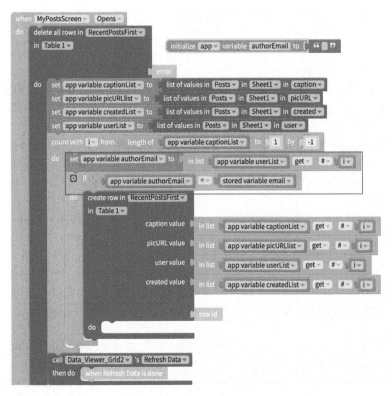

Figure 11.21. Filter out all but the posts from the logged in user.

The blocks use the list variables defined in the HomeScreen, and define an additional variable, "authorEmail", to hold the email of the author of each post. As each post is examined, if its author is the same as the logged in user's email, stored in stored variable email, then the row is created in "RecentPostsFirst" (note that the Login-Profile template, which you started out with, sets the variable email when the user logs in).

SUMMARY

To fully mimic Instagram, there would be hundreds of other details still to be added. But take a moment to contemplate what you did learn in this chapter: you now have the know-how to build a sophisticated app with users and dynamic data!

You should feel empowered to build a whole new class of app, one which few beginner or novice coders have been able to tackle in the past. You also have been exposed to a template, which you customized, that allows you to start with registration and login built-in to any app you create. Go forth and prosper!

RAFIKI BREAKS IT DOWN

When I was growing up, whenever there had been a marked improvement in one's circumstances or the sophistication of resources at one's command, the old folks would say "you're cooking with gas now". It was a cultural reference to a time when families cooked on stoves that were powered by wood or coal. To be 'cooking with gas' was to step into a way of life distinctly more modern and efficient. I'll update the reference a bit, by saying to you: you're cooking with solar now. You have now laid a hold of resources that in the coding life are indisputably cutting edge and magnitudes more efficient than what has been the norm.

Imagine a time when cooking entailed chopping wood, or gathering filthy coal into one's kitchen stove; which itself would have no temperature controls and definitely no timers. What a challenge a meal preparation must have been under such conditions. The ease with which you can now stand up dynamic apps, versus what it would've required before the Thunkable age is akin to our stove scenario. Apps with users and data-- you've jumped right over the wood and coal and essentially went straight to the push button level.

And there's undoubtedly yet more to come. For example, it is common for login processes to involve some form of what is known as Two Factor Authentication (2FA). It is a means by verifying that the person attempting to access an account, is indeed who they say they are. Usually this entails sending a code to the account holder's phone and having them enter that code into the app. But what if such authentication was as simple as a Voice Biometric filter, where the person logging in could speak and their voice print served the same purpose as a fingerprint. Yes, a feature like this could be added to Thunkable and thus provided to you in the form of a block! Keep an eye on the resource page at draganddropcode.com/bookCh11!

CONCEPTUALIZE

1. For the PhotoSharing app, why is it important to store the file of the photo taken at cloudinary?

2. What block is used to add new data into a spreadsheet?

3. Explain why the additional spreadsheet "RecentPostsFirst" is needed in the Photo Sharing App.

4. Describe the purpose of the **list of values in** block used in the code of Figure 11.21. What does it return?

CUSTOMIZE

1. Modify the timestamp attached to each post so that the hour and minute are included, e.g., "5/11/22 at 3:27 pm". You'll need to modify the "getTimeStamp" function shown in Figure 11.16.

2. Allow the user to take the picture to be posted, as an alternative to choosing from Photos. Use the **photo from camera** block in the "Camera" folder, and right-click to use the "Advanced Version". You should still place the picture in the cloud, just as you do when its chosen instead of taken.

CREATE

1. You can now create posting apps with data and input forms. Think of a way to make use of this power in your life by building an app for your class, sports team, or friend group.

2. Add users and a high score list to one of the game apps you built in Chapter 8. You'll need to re-build the app starting with the "Login and Profile" template, and you'll need a spreadsheet to store user's scores.

Share your creative apps with your authors and other *Drag and Drop* coders:

- Use #DragAndDropCode and #MadeWithThunkable on your social media platforms.

- @ us at @DragAndDropCode on Twitter and Instagram.

Chapter Resources: draganddropcode.com/bookCh11/

CHAPTER 12. STORED AND CLOUD VARIABLES

App: "Multi-UserGuessing Game"

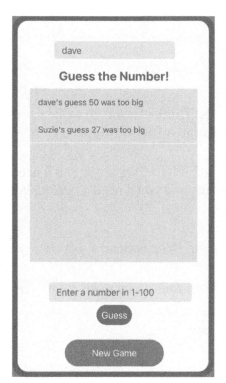

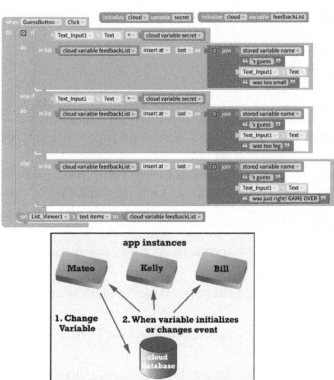

In this chapter, you'll learn about persistent variables, an innovative method for storing data and an alternative to the spreadsheet method presented in Chapters 5 and 11. You'll build a multi-user game in which each player tries to guess a number while tracking feedback on everyone's guesses.

INTRODUCTION

Thunkable's *persistent variables* provide an alternative method to spreadsheets and databases for storing data. Persistent variables allow you to designate whether a variable's data lives only for a single run of the app, is stored persistently in a database on the device, or is stored in the "cloud" and shared with other users.

Persistent variables are a unique, innovative feature of Thunkable and not available in other coding languages. With most languages, your code must explicitly copy data from the app's variables into a database, and bring data from the database back into the app variables as well. The Structured Query Language (SQL) is commonly used for such database coding, and languages like Java and Python provide code libraries for embedding SQL database code into an app. In Chapter 11, you used Thunkable blocks to store photo posts into a Google spreadsheet.

Thunkable's persistent variables ease the task of database coding dramatically: you just mark a variable as "app", "stored" or "cloud", then use normal variable set and get to modify the data, instead of special "database" code. When a "stored" or "cloud" variable is modified, the data is automatically written out to the database. When your code accesses (gets) a variable, the data is automatically retrieved from the database. The simplified database coding afforded by persistent variables significantly lowers the bar with respect to *who* can create apps with data.

To illustrate the use of persistent variables, this chapter will lead you through building a simple game, the kind where you guess a number and the game tells you whether the number is too small or too big. You'll first build the game with no database or persistence. Then you'll add persistence so that the secret number and guesses are stored in a local database on the device. This version will allow the user to close and reopen the app, and resume whatever game was being played previously.

For your grand finale, you'll build a social app in which the guesses posted by each user are stored in the cloud and viewed by all the app's users. This one will be fun to play, as each player has to track the feedback from everyone's guesses.

As with spreadsheet apps, apps using persistent variables are more abstract and challenging to code than apps without dynamic data. The data is not fixed so you don't see it as part of the code itself, like with the "Slideshow" app. Instead, you must imagine data that the user will enter when the app runs.

Taking this leap will be worth it, however, as most real apps involve user-generated, shared data. Want to build the next social network or an interactive game? Complete this app and you will be on your way!

Create a Private Guessing Game

Create a new app named "GuessingGame". In the Designer, add components so that the game appears as in the figure at the top of this chapter. The game should have a Label at the top that says "Guess a number between 1-100", a ListViewer to display all previous guesses, a TextInput for the user to enter guesses with a Hint of "please enter a guess", and two buttons, one for making a guess and one for starting a new game. You should also add a Label to display the secret that the user is trying to guess. Eventually you'll hide or remove it, but it will be helpful as you code and debug the app.

For the private version of the game, define two "app" variables, "feedbackList" and "secret" as shown in Figure 12.1.

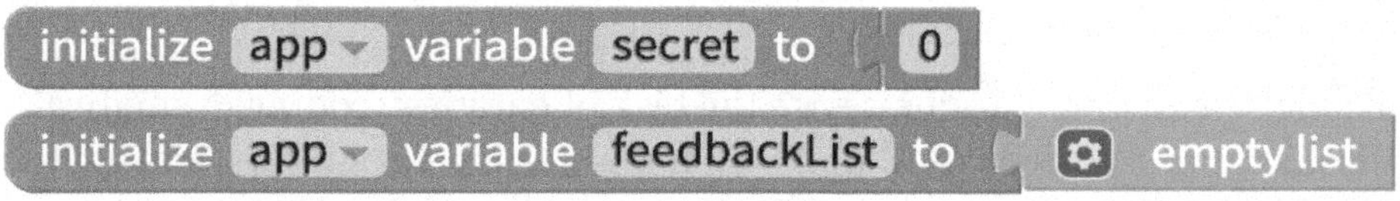

initialize app variable secret to 0

initialize app variable feedbackList to ⚙ empty list

Figure 12.1. Define app variables for the secret code and the feedback list

"app" variables are stored in the local memory of each app. Since this first game you're building is private, this is sufficient.

In the Blocks Editor, add code to generate a random secret code when the app launches. Figure 12.2. shows the blocks:

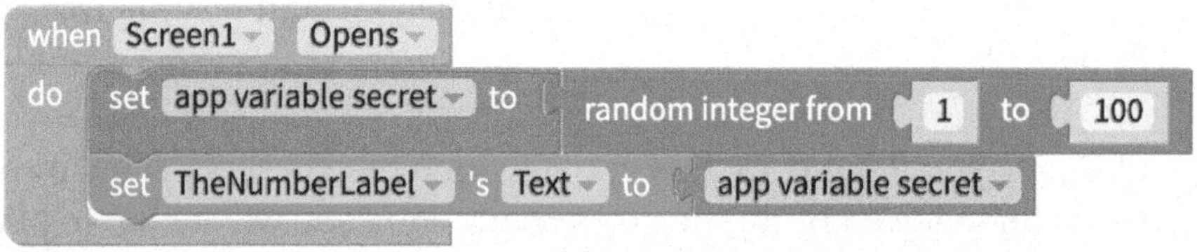

when Screen1 Opens

do set app variable secret to random integer from 1 to 100

set TheNumberLabel 's Text to app variable secret

Figure 12.2. Create a new secret when the app launches

Next, code the blocks for the when SubmitButton.Click event handler. This code should compare the user's guess (Text_Input1.Text) with the secret. There are three possible branches: the guess is bigger, the guess is smaller, or it's the same as the secret. Since there are three branches, use an "if-elseif-else" as shown in Figure 12.3:

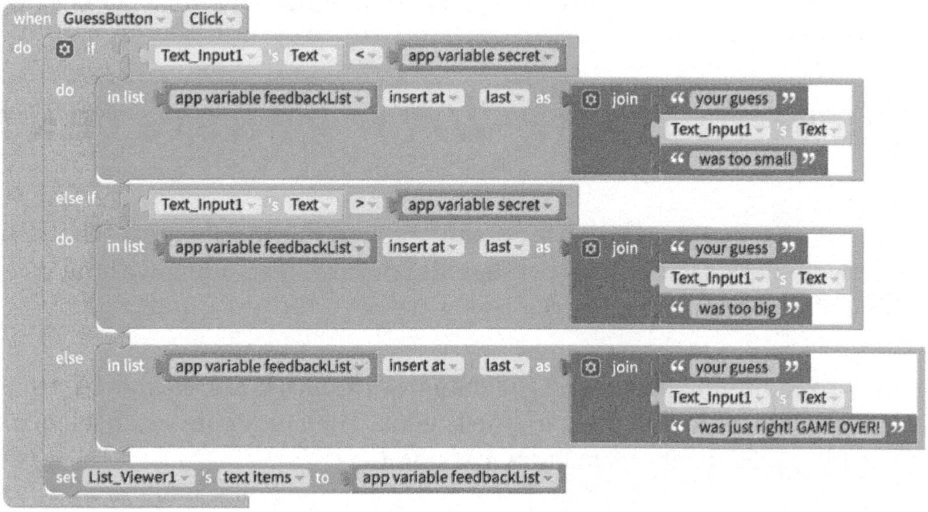

Figure 12.3. Add each guess and feedback to a list

The in list insert at blocks add text such as "your guess 50 was too big" to the feedbackList. The final row of blocks displays the list, updated with the newly added feedback text.

Before testing the app, add one more behavior—code the when NewGameButton.Click event handler. It is fairly straight-forward: just initialize your variables and update the display properties as shown in Figure 12.4:

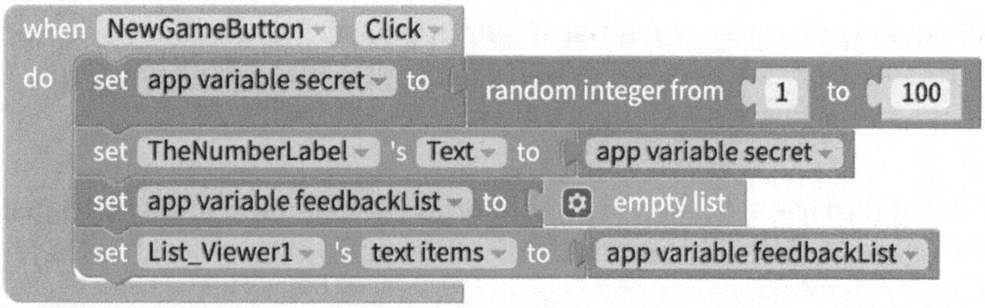

Figure 12.4. Re-initialize your variables when a new game starts

Test the App

Test the app. Enter a guess and click the GuessButton. Does the app provide the correct feedback? Since you're showing the secret you can check this.

Next, click on the Thunkable preview button again to simulate an app re-launch. Because the feedbacklist and secret are "app" variables, the data that was in them is lost when the app restarts. So you should see a new random secret and an empty feedbacklist.

In the following section, you'll modify the app to "remember" previous guesses when the app is closed and relaunched.

A GUESSING GAME WITH PERSISTENT DATA

Data is *persistent* if, when you close the app and reopen it, the data is still there. In this section, you'll learn how to mark a variable as persistent. For now, read along without coding, to get an understanding of how persistence works.

In traditional programming languages, the data in variables is stored short-term and as soon as the app closes the data stored in the variable is gone. The fancy computer science term for short-term memory is *transient* data (also known as *volatile* data).

In the game you just built, the variables are defined as "app" variables. App variables behave like traditional variables—their data is transient. That is why your previous guesses and the secret were gone when you restarted the app.

Thunkable provides two alternative variable types, "stored" and "cloud", both of which are *persistent* variables. With persistent variables, the app takes care of storing the data in a database each time the variable is changed, and retrieving it each time the variable is referenced. The variables don't lose their values when the app closes as with "app" variables.

A "stored" variable is saved in a database on the user's device. Such a variable is meant for apps in which the data is private to each particular app user. Private diary or to-do list apps use "stored" variables. For the guessing game, using a stored variable will allow the user to close the app and resume playing the same game again after re-opening.

Changing the app to use a "stored" variable requires just a few steps. You just designate the variables as "stored", then add some initialization code in the when Screen.Opens event handler.

To begin, make a copy of the "GuessingGame" app and name it "StoredGuessingGame". Then, in the Blocks Editor, select the upside-down triangle on the initialization block for the variables feedbacklist and secret, and choose "stored" instead of "app", as shown in Figure 12.5.

Figure 12.5. "stored" variables are saved in a database

Don't create new variables, just change the designations of the existing variables.

When you choose "stored", you'll notice that the right-hand slot for initializing the variable disappears. You can't initialize "stored" and "cloud" variables like you do "app" variables. Instead, you must initialize such variables in the when Screen.Opens event handler.

For "stored" or "cloud" variables, you must envision two possibilities for app launch. The first time the app is launched, before any data has been entered, the variable will be "null", meaning undefined. On successive app launches, after the user has entered data, the variable will already have data in it.

Drag in a when Screen.Opens event handler. Inside it, check to see if the secret variable is null, as it will be the first time the app is launched. If it is, initialize it to a random number. If secret is not null, it means secret has been initialized in a previous launch of the app and you should leave it as is. Figure 12.6 shows the blocks:

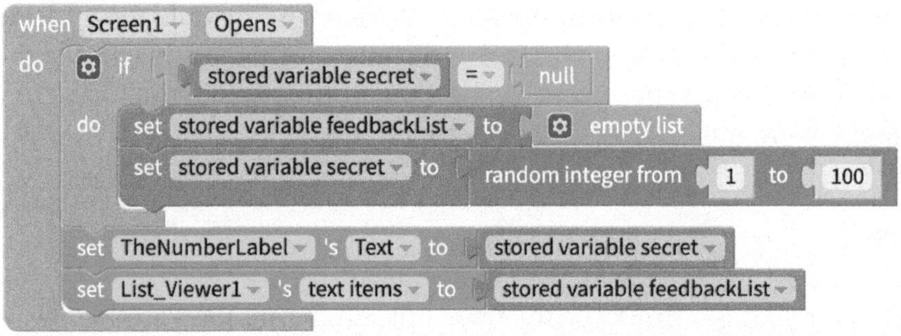

Figure 12.6. initialize persistent variables in "when Screen.Opens"

The when GuessButton.Click remain the same as it was in the first version of the app, though the references to the variables will have the designation, "stored".

Test the App

Test the app. Make a couple of guesses, then click Thunkable's preview button again to mimic a re-launch of the app. Do your previous guesses still appear in the ListViewer? If so, your stored variables are indeed being stored in a database.

A MULTI-USER GAME WITH CLOUD VARIABLES

The game developed thus far is for private use. The app installed by each user will store the secret and feedbacklist in a database directly on that user's device, so each user's guesses and feedback won't be shared with other app users. In this section, you'll create a new app in which the game is a shared experience and each user sees the guesses and feedback of all other users.

To begin, copy your "StoredGuessingGame" app and name it "CloudGuessingGame". Then, in the Blocks Editor for Screen1, modify the secret and feedbacklist variables so that they are set as "cloud" variables instead of "stored" (do not create new variables). After this change, all of the references in the blocks will change automatically from stored to cloud.

With stored variables, there is a secret and a feedbacklist for each app instance, for each user. Variables designated as "cloud" are stored in a web database accessed by all instances of the app. There is only one instance of each variable and anyone who installs the app will see the one and only secret and the one and only feedbacklist. Because of this, users will see the guesses and feedback received from the other users. To be good at the game, you'll have to multi-task and consider not only your guesses but those of others!

Test the App

The app's behavior changes dramatically by simply changing the variable designations to "cloud", but you can't test the change on a single device. To test it, you need to run the app on two devices (don't use the web preview for this testing).

Find two devices, maybe asking a friend to help. Try the following:

- Player1 opens the app

- Player 1 makes a guess

- Player 2 opens the app

What do you think will happen with this scenario?

The answer is that Player2 should see the guess and feedback that Player1 made, because when the app opens, it displays the feedbacklist, and there is only one such list living in the cloud.

Now that both players have the app open, have Player2 make a guess. Does Player1 instantly see the guess? The answer is "no". Yes, the feedbacklist has changed due to Player2's guess, but Player1's display—the ListViewer—hadn't been updated. Player2's guess will only appear when Player1 closes and reopens the app.

You want immediate updates, of course, so you'll need to add code so that the apps of both players—all players—are immediately updated when anyone makes a guess.

Notifying App Instances of a Change

When a cloud variable changes, all other *app instances* need to be notified of the change so they can update the information they're displaying.

Consider the situation illustrated in Figure 12.7.

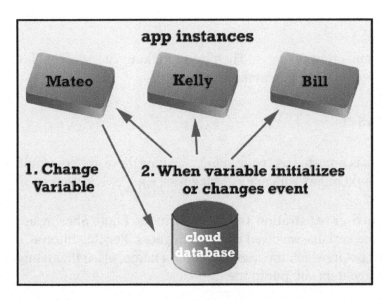

Figure 12.7. When a user sets a variable, all app instances are notified.

Mateo, Kelly, and Bill have all downloaded an instance of the same shared guessing app. If Mateo makes a guess, Kelly and Bill's app instances should immediately be notified so they can display the new guess.

Fortunately, when a cloud variable is changed, Thunkable sends a notification to everyone. The notification is just another event—the when <variable> initializes or changes event, which is found in the "Variables" folder.

As Figure 12.7 illustrates, when Mateo submits a guess, the change to the cloud variable feedbacklist triggers the when cloud feedbacklist initializes or changes event in all app instances, including Kelly's, Bill's, and even Mateo's. It is your job as a programmer to code that event handler to update each app instance's user interface.

Drag in a when cloud variable feedbacklist initializes or changes event handler from the "Variables" folder. Inside it, code it so that the ListViewer displays the updated feedbacklist, as shown in Figure 12.8:

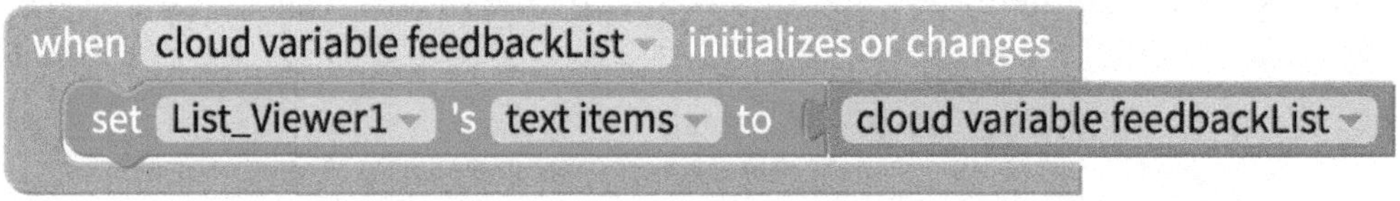

Figure 12.8 This event will trigger in all app instances

With these blocks, the ListViewers in all app instances will be immediately updated when a user makes a guess—everyone will see everyone's guesses!

Test the App

Once again, test the app on two devices. Then begin making guesses from both devices. Does each app update when the other app makes a guess?

Name the Guesser

Currently, each guess is reported as "your guess…". Since there are now multiple players involved, the app should report who made each guess, e.g., "Sylvia's guess…"

You could add full-on user registration and login, as in the Photo Sharing app of Chapter 11, and then use the username variable involved to tag each guess. For this tutorial, do something simpler: add a TextInput in which the user can enter a name, place that name in a variable, and use it as the tag on each item you put in the feedbacklist.

Consider for a moment: how should you designate the variable name—should it be an "app", "stored", or "cloud" variable?

"stored" is the best answer. You want the name to be persistent so the user doesn't have to reset it each time the app is closed and reopened. But you don't want a single name, you want a name for each user. Thus, "stored" is the right designation for the name variable.

Define the "stored" variable name and add a TextInput for the user to change it. With any stored or cloud variable you need to initialize it in the when Screen1.opens event handler. Figure 12.9 shows the blocks:

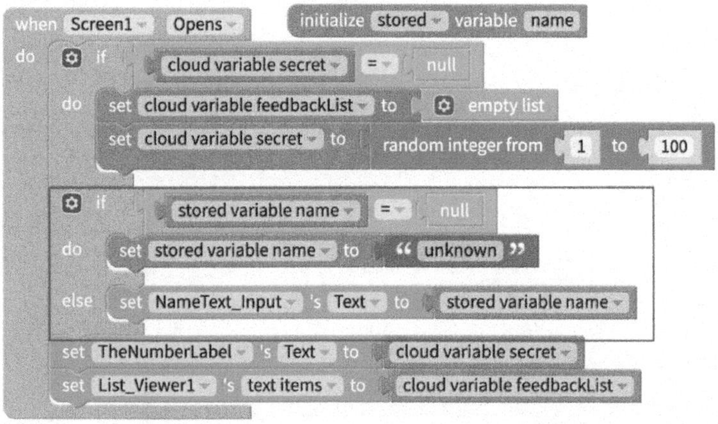

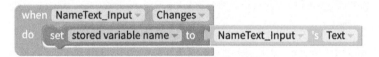

Figure 12.9. Display the name the user previously entered

When the user types in the NameTextInput, you need to update the name variable. Open the blocks for NameTextInput, and you'll see a changed event. Drag that in and add blocks so that when the user changes NameTextInput, the name variable gets changed, as in Figure 12.10:

Figure 12.10. Modify the variable "name" as the user types

Now that the user can enter a name, you're ready to use that name to tag the items you add to feedbackList on a user guess. Figure 12.11 shows the modified blocks:

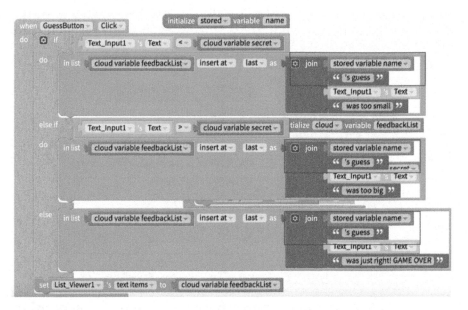

Figure 12.11. Tag each guess with the user's name

Test the app with multiple devices. Does the feedback list now show who made each guess?

USE FIREBASE FOR YOUR CLOUD VARIABLES

By default, the data for your cloud variables is stored in a Thunkable-controlled database along with the data for the cloud variables of all Thunkable developers! If some other Thunker had a cloud variable named secret, that app could overwrite your data!

One strategy is to give your cloud variables descriptive and unique names, e.g., "DaveWolbersSecret", but clearly that is not a secure way to build an app. Storing your cloud variables in a Thunkable-controlled database also presents another issue—you can't view or access the data. This makes debugging your code challenging, and also precludes you, as the app administrator, from managing the database (e.g., removing items)

Instead of using the hidden default database that Thunkable provides, you can instead connect your app to a database that you create and to which you have unimpeded access. The scheme is based on Firebase, the tool introduced in Chapter 11 for storing user information. In this chapter, you'll use Firebase to store your cloud variable data.

Follow these steps to create a database at firebase.com[1]:

- Go to firebase.com and register for a free account.

- From the Console, click on "Add project". Enter a project name like, "GuessingGame", and disable the use of Google Analytics. Click on "Create Project".

- Create a "web app" by clicking on the web icon </>, as shown in Figure 12.12:

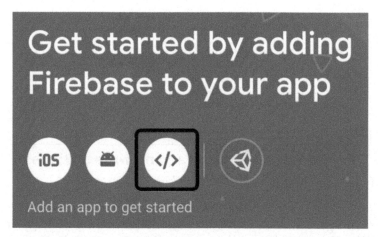

Figure 12.12. Click on the web app icon </>.

Enter "guessing game" for the app nickname and leave the box for setting up hosting unchecked. Click on "Register app".

- Click on "Realtime Database" in the left-menu and "create database". Choose "production mode" and in the next dialogue choose a location closest to you for the server farm in which your database will be stored.

---

[1] Firebase's user interface may change. See https://draganddropcode.com/bookCh12/ for updates.

- On the "Database" screen there is a tab for "Rules". Select it and then carefully change the rules so that "read" and "write" are set to "true" as shown in Figure 12.13:

Database   🖳 Realtime Database ▾

Data   Rules   Backups   Usage

```
1 ▾   {
2 ▾     /* Visit https://firebase.google.com/docs/databa
3 ▾     "rules": {
4          ".read": true,
5          ".write": true
6        }
7     }
```

Figure 12.13. Set the read and write settings to "true"

- After modifying the rules, choose "Publish".

- You need two properties from Firebase. Click on "Project Settings" and scroll down to find the APIKey. Copy it without the quotes. You also need the Database URL. Choose "Realtime Database" again, and the "Data" tab. You'll find the Database URL at the top.

- In Thunkable's Designer, choose the project settings icon on the left and scroll down until you see the Firebase settings. Set the two properties from Firebase as shown in Figure 12.14:

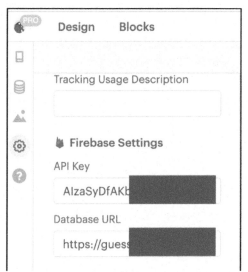

Figure 12.14. Place the Firebase settings into Thunkable properties

Test the App

Test your app. If you've configured the settings correctly, the app should work exactly as before. However, behind the scenes the data is stored at the database you configured at Firebase.com. Make a couple of guesses and confirm that they appear in the ListViewer of your app.

Then check that you can view the data at Firebase, as you'll want to do this for debugging and app administration. Back at Firebase, go to the Database screen and click on the "Data" tab. You should see that data with the tags "feedbackList" and "secret" has been created, as shown in Figure 12.15:

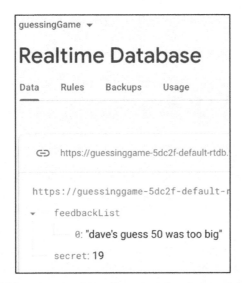

Figure 12.15 You can view the app's data at Firebase.com.

If you are seeing the data you entered, congratulations! You've successfully created and connected your app to your own Firebase database.

S U M M A R Y

Apps with dynamic data are abstract and challenging to code. The data is not explicitly part of the code, as with an app like the "Slideshow" of Chapter 4. Instead, you must envision the data that will be generated through user input or other means, and envision scenarios of user actions and how the app's memory and database will appear after those actions.

The Guessing Game app is relatively simple. But realize that you now know how to create apps with a database that is shared amongst users. Your magical powers have increased dramatically!

Thunkable's persistent variables make database coding simple. The system takes care of all the bookkeeping in terms of storing variable data to and from a database—other languages require you to do this explicitly.

RAFIKI BREAKS IT DOWN

Imagine building an app that is an extension of your user's memory, a convenience that many of them would probably appreciate. Your app could remind your mother of the last five songs she played, or your grandfather of how many times he's played, "So What", by Miles Davis. This is possible because every time they close your app their data slate is preserved instead of wiped clean—it persists until the next time they open the app. Your job is to be diligent in understanding the strengths that Thunkable places at your fingertips—in this case persistent variables—and then apply brain power to creatively take advantage of them.

VOCABULARY VIBE

PERSISTENCE

Persistence is the state of your data being accessible over time. Transient data disappears as soon as an app is closed. Persistent data is the opposite. It doesn't do a disappearing act. It stays around.

It's present to be called upon, time and time again, in the memory of the user's mobile device or in the cloud. Many experiences extend beyond a single moment and thus the data that drives such experiences needs needs to be always at the ready and available upon command.

CONCEPTUALIZE

1. Define the term "persistent data". Is all persistent data cloud data? Is all dynamic data persistent data?

2. Describe the difference between "app", "stored" and "cloud" variables. For which types of apps should each be used?

3. Explain the purpose of the when variable changes or initializes event handler. When is it triggered? Be sure and use the term "app instance" in your answer.

CUSTOMIZE

1. In either the private or cloud version of the "Guessing Game" app, timestamp the guesses so that they include date and time information. Check out the Device folder for the blocks you'll need.

2. Modify the "Slideshow" app of Chapter 4 to allow the user to take additional pictures to be included in the Slideshow, and store them persistently. You may initialize the picture list with some existing pictures, or have it start as an empty list.

4. In the "Asteroids" app of Chapter 8, keep score in some manner, and define a persist variable to keep track of the scores of all previously played games (i.e., a high score list).

CREATE

1.Build an app of your own design which allows the user to store data persistently in a private or cloud database (stored variable).

2. Build a chat app.

Share your creative apps with your authors and other *Drag and Drop* coders:

- Use #DragAndDropCode and #MadeWithThunkable on your social media platforms.

- @ us at @DragAndDropCode on Twitter and Instagram.

Chapter Resources: <u>draganddropcode.com/bookCh12/</u>

.

CHAPTER 13. DEFINING FUNCTIONS

App:"MathBlasterFunctions"

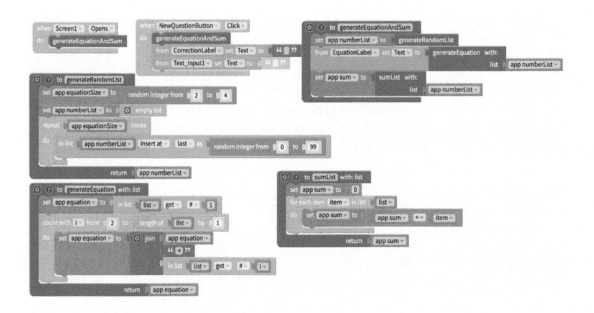

The apps you've built consist of event handlers, some of them quite long and detailed. In this chapter you'll learn how to define functions-- building-blocks for organizing your code hierarchically. Such organization is crucial to software engineering, especially for large apps developed by teams (which fits most software projects!).

INTRODUCTION

Abstraction is a key concept in problem solving and coding. Simply put, an abstraction gives a name to a set of details. In coding, it is most often applied in the realm of functionality—giving a name to a sequence of detailed operations.

When parents tell their child, "Go brush your teeth," they really mean, "Take your toothbrush and toothpaste from the cabinet, squeeze out some toothpaste onto the brush, swivel the brush on each tooth for 10 seconds (ha!), and so on. "Brush your teeth" is a functional abstraction: a name for a sequence of more detailed instructions.

Humans become overwhelmed when faced with a problem consisting of hundreds of steps. Solutions are best organized hierarchically, broken into five or so major steps, with those steps broken down into multiple sub-steps, and so on, until a hierarchical blueprint for a solution is understood. Abstractions help us divide-and-conquer large problems.

Abstractions are also key for team-based projects as they allow teams to communicate at various levels of detail. At times the group can communicate at a high-level and discuss the major steps, ignoring the details of the sub-steps. At other times, sub-groups can delve into the details of one of those sub-steps, or the sub-steps of those sub-steps.

Software is problem-solving, and thus abstraction is key to productive software engineering. *Functions* are the basic coding construct for abstraction. A function provides a name for a sequence of operations. You can then *call* the function, causing all of its operations to be performed. In Thunkable, a function is a new block you create that represents a set of blocks you define. No matter what language you use, the function is a basic building block for software.

You've become familiar with event handlers, which are like functions in that they define a sequence of operations to perform. The difference is that event handlers are triggered by an external event (e.g., Button.Click), while functions are called explicitly from within the app, either from an event handler or another function.

DEFINING FUNCTIONS IN THUNKABLE

Recall the "MathBlasterEQ" app in Chapter 9 which generates arithmetic equations for the user to solve. When the app launches, it generates a random list of numbers, generates an equation from that list for display, then calculates the sum of the numbers.

Figure 13.1. shows the when Screen1.Opens event handler, with the three subtasks outlined.

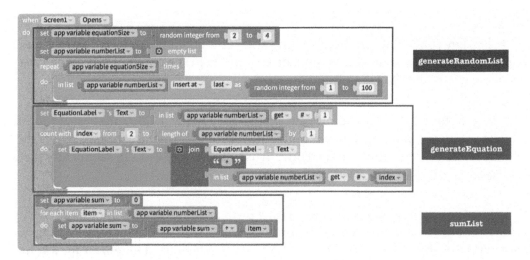

Figure 13.1. The three sub-tasks in the Screen.Opens event handler

All of the code is directly within the event handler. An experienced programmer, however, would have identified the separate subtasks and coded them as separate functions, then called them from the event handler. The three sub-tasks are named in the dark blue boxes to the right of Figure 13.1. To learn about functions, make a copy of the "MathBlasterEq" app from Chapter 9 and name it "MathBlasterFunc". Then, in the Blocks Editor, drag in a **to** "do something" block from the Functions folder, as shown in Figure 13.2:

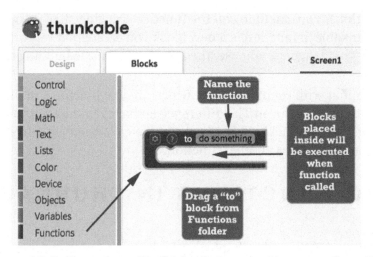

Figure 13.2. Drag in a "to" block to create a new function.

Name the function by changing the text "do something" to "generateRandomList". Then move the blocks in the top blue rectangle in Figure 13.1 from the when Screen.Opens event handler into the function. The function should appear as shown in Figure 13.3:

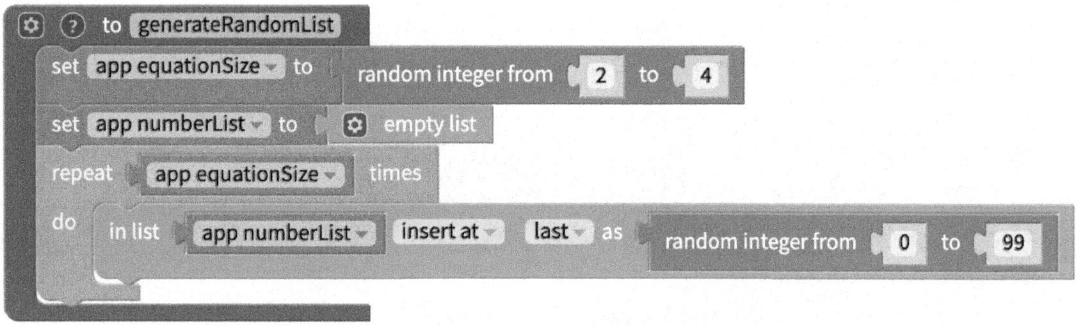

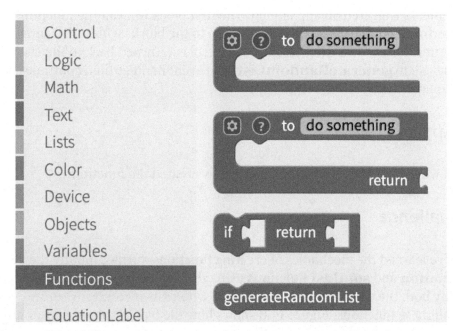

Figure 13.3. The function "generateRandomList"

When you create a function, a new call block is generated in the "Functions" folder. If you open the Function folder, you'll see a call block labeled, "**generateRandomList**" as shown in Figure 13.4.

Figure 13.4. When you create a function, a new block is generated.

Congratulations, you've created a new block!

Though the **generateRandomList** block doesn't include the keyword "call", it indeed calls, or invokes, the function. Drag in the **generateRandomList** block and place it within the when Screen.Opens event handler, replacing the blocks that you moved into the function. Figure 13.5 shows the updated blocks for the when Screen.Opens event handler:

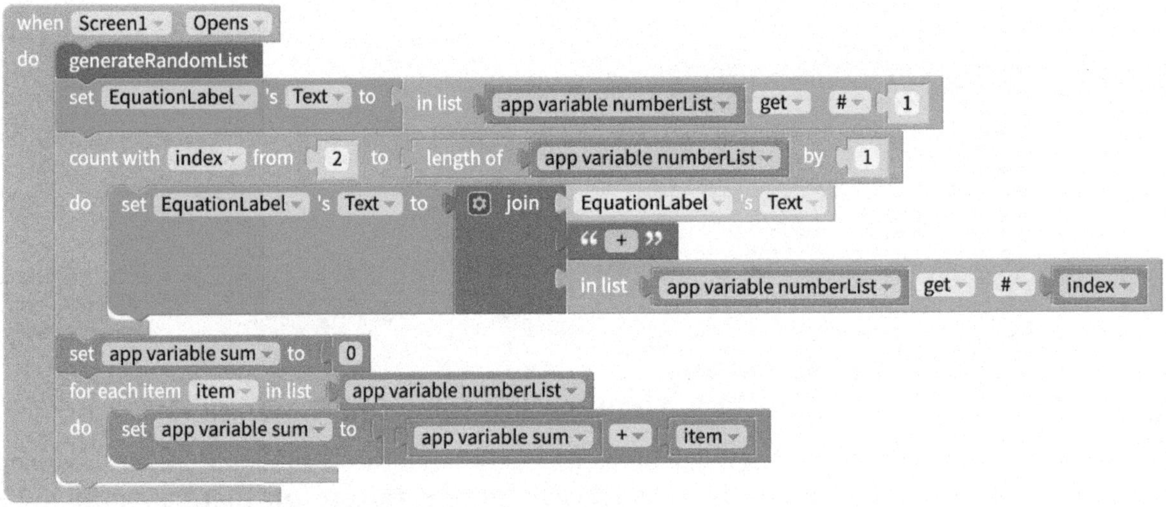

Figure 13.5. The event handler now calls the function

The event handler is triggered on app launch. The first block will call the function **generateRandomList** and cause the app to jump to the blocks within that function (see Figure 13.3). After those blocks are performed, control is returned back to the event handler, right below the call to **generateRandomList**. The event handler then continues on, starting with the set EquationLabel's Text block.

Test the App

If the app still works as before, you have successfully created the function!

Coding Challenge

Now that you've learned the mechanics of creating functions, further modify the app by defining **generateEquation** and **sumList** functions using the outlined code specified in Figure 13.1. as a guide. Modify both the when Screen.Opens and when NewQuestionButton.Click event handlers to call these functions. Figure 13.6 shows how the blocks should appear after your changes.

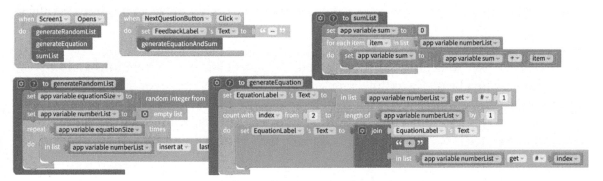

Figure 13.6. The app with three functions

Refactoring is when you change the internal code of an app without changing how it behaves externally, for the user. You just refactored the app by defining three functions, moving code blocks into those function, and calling the functions from the two event handlers.

THE ADVANTAGE OF WELL-STRUCTURED CODE

What was gained from refactoring the code? The app now has a hierarchical structure. One can read the blocks inside the event handlers and get a high-level understanding of the tasks involved, and view the code within the functions only when necessary to understand the details of those tasks. You have created three new blocks—three abstractions—which can be used in the app and in communicating about the app.

If this design had been put in place prior to coding, each member on the project team could have been assigned one or more functions to code. Each individual could code their function(s) and test them separately before integrating them back into the larger code base.

The new version also eliminates some redundant code. In the original app, the two event handlers had duplicate copies of all of the blocks. In the new version, most of the duplicate code is replaced with function calls. Now there is only one copy of the detailed blocks to generate a random list, to generate an equation, and to sum a list. Originally those blocks were in both event handlers.

Novice coders tend to use copy-paste to reuse code blocks in multiple places, as was done in the Chapter 9 version of "MathBlaster". When apps get large—and useful ones always do—such duplication can turn the code base into "spaghetti code" that is especially hard to modify.

Eliminating redundant code is a key to software maintenance, that is, coding software that is easy to change. Software is fluid—all code bases are subject to significant change, either because bugs appear, the client changes the specification, or the app is remixed to create something new.

Duplicate code makes change difficult, as you have to find all the duplicates (spaghetti noodles) and make any change in all of them.

As you gain experience, you'll think abstractly from the outset and define functions and sub-functions before coding begins, avoiding copy-paste and the introduction of duplicate code. But even experienced programmers will often refactor code once they've delved into a problem and discovered the need for additional abstraction. The key is to gradually improve the code base so that when a change needs to be made, it can be made easily and without introducing bugs.

FUNCTIONS CALLING FUNCTIONS

The solution in Figure 13.6 still has some redundancy: both event handlers call the three functions and in exactly the same order. This redundancy can be eliminated by introducing another function, **generateEquationAndSum**, which calls the three other functions. Figure 13.7 shows the blocks:

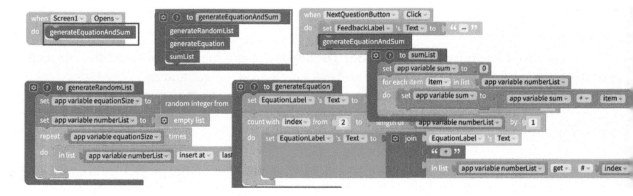

Figure 13.7. The app with no redundant code

This solution eliminates the redundancy. It also creates a three-level function call hierarchy: the two event handlers both call the function **generateEquationAndSum**, which then calls the three other functions. This solution also illustrates how a function can be called by another function, not just an event handler.

SOFTWARE BLUEPRINTS: STRUCTURE CHARTS

One job of a *software architect* is to break down a large software problem into smaller and smaller parts and create blueprints like the structure chart shown in Figure 13.8.

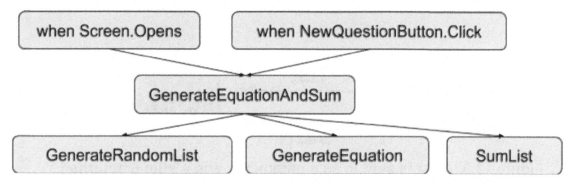

Figure 13.8. A partial structure chart for the app

Each node in the chart represents an event handler or a function, and the arrows represent function calls. After the software architect creates such a blue-print, the functions can be assigned to different coders on the development team.

The blueprint can also include the input and output parameters of each function on the arrows, and specifications for the task each function should complete.

FUNCTIONS AS INPUT-OUTPUT BOXES

So far in this chapter, "MathBlaster" has been organized into distinct functions, but those functions don't have input parameters and outputs. The functions rely on "app" variables that are *globally* known to all event handlers and functions. One tenet of quality software development is defining each function as a black-box, with explicit input and return outputs (results) to the caller.

You have used Thunkable's built-in functions, sending in input parameters and receiving outputs in return. The input parameters are the data that the caller sends to the function so it can do its job. A function return value is the opposite of an input parameter—it is the output of the function, the result that a function sends back to the caller. In this section, you will learn to define inputs and outputs for functions that you define.

Consider again the **sumList** function and consider what should be defined as its inputs and outputs. If you asked **sumList** to do its job, and **sumList** could talk, it would ask, "which list should I sum?" Thus, the function should be defined with an input parameter named "list".

The result (output) of **sumList** is also clear: it is the sum computed from adding the numbers in the list. Thus, the function should return a number. The information flow for **sumList** is illustrated in Figure 13.9:

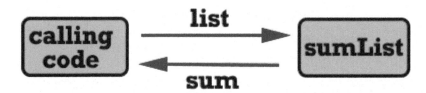

Figure 13.9. A list is sent in as a parameter, and a sum is returned.

When **sumList** is called, a list is sent in. When the function completes, it returns a sum. Coding the function in this manner will allow it to work on any list and return its value to any variable.

SPECIFYING INPUT PARAMETERS

In previous chapters, you called Thunkable's built-in functions and plugged in input parameters into their slots. Now you will learn how to specify input parameters for the functions you define.

To specify an input parameter for a function, you click on a function's blue mutator icon, as shown in Figure 13.10.

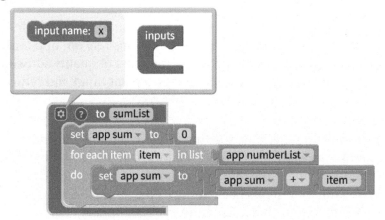

Figure 13.10. Click the blue icon to define the input parameters.

You then drag the "input name" block from the left side into the "inputs" slot on the right, and change the name from "x" to something that describes the parameter. For **sumList**, a parameter named "list" is appropriate. After you define an input parameter for a function, it appears after the keyword "with" in the top part of the block, as shown in Figure 13.11:

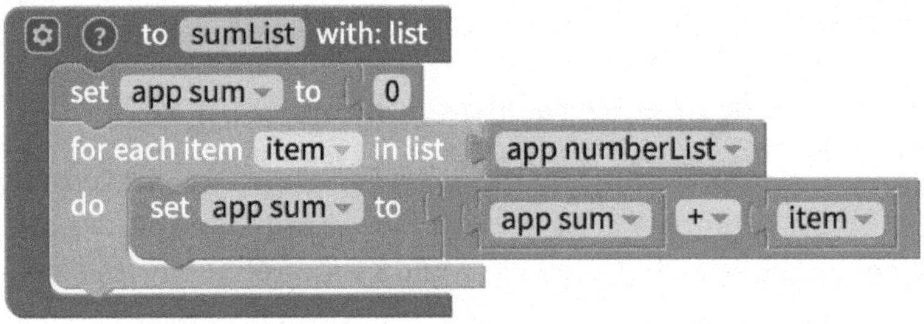

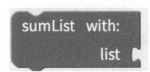

Figure 13.11 Parameters appear after the "with" keyword

Even though the input parameter list has been defined, the **sumList** function must still be modified to actually use it. The blocks within the function still refer to the particular variable, app numberList, and don't refer to the parameter "list". When a parameter is defined for a function, a new block is generated for it and placed in the "Variables" folder. For **sumList**, a block list appears there. That block should replace app numberList in the function's code, as shown in Figure 13.12:

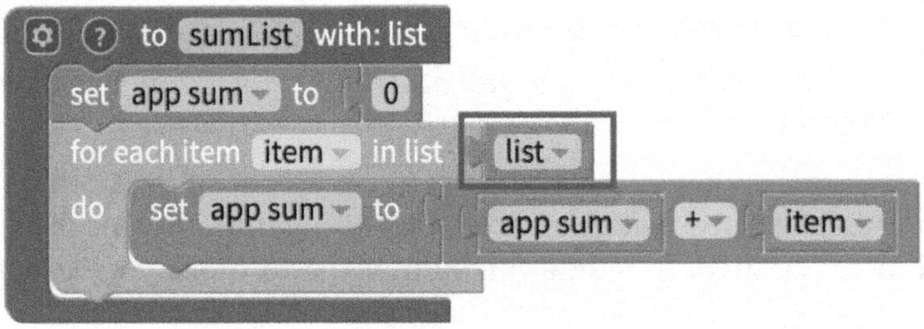

Figure 13.12. sumList sums the items in the input parameter "list"

With this change, the function will work on the variable that is sent in as the parameter as opposed to the particular variable app numberList.

After a parameter is defined for a function, a slot appears in the call block for the function. For **sumList**, the function call block is automatically updated as shown in Figure 13.13:

Figure 13.13. An incomplete call to sumList

The caller must fill the slot to specify the particular list to be totaled. Figure 13.14 shows two such calls:

Figure 13.14. Two calls to sumList

The call on the left is appropriate for the "MathBlasterEq" app, since the variable numberList is used in that app to store the generated numbers. But if the app or another app needed a different list variable to be totaled, that variable could be slotted in, as illustrated by the blocks on the right of Figure 13.14.

In this way, input parameters make a function more general-purpose. The earlier version of **sumList** worked on the particular list, numberList. With the parameter defined, it can be used to add up any list.

SPECIFYING A RETURN VALUE

Besides accepting input parameters, a function can also return a value. Unlike Thunkable's built-in functions, which can return multiple *output parameters*, programmer-defined functions can only return one value.

A function that returns a value is defined using a different **to** block than the one used in the samples above. It is found in the "Functions" folder just under the **to** block you've been using, as shown in Figure 13.15:

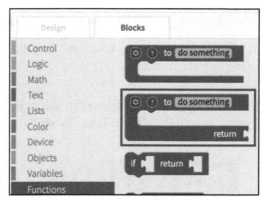

Figure 13.15. The second "to" block returns a value

The **to** block that includes a return slot is the second-from-the-top in Figure 13.15. You place a variable or formula in this slot to specify the result of the function.

For the **sumList** example, drag in the **to** with return block and move all of the original **sumList** blocks into it. Then plug a reference to app sum in the return slot, remove the original **sumList** function and give its name to the new one. The function should appear as shown in Figure 13.16.

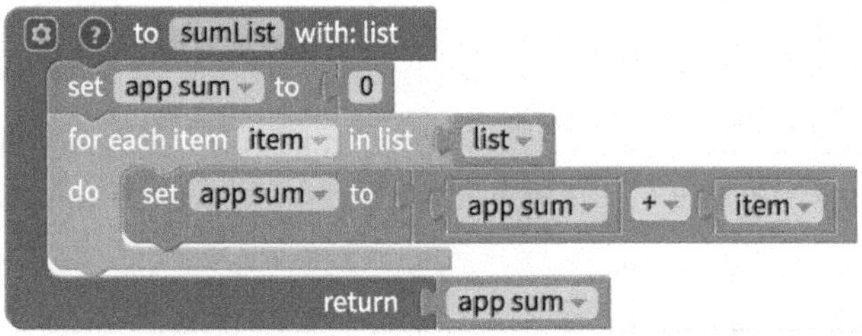

Figure 13.16. sumList with an input parameter and return value

After defining **sumList** with a return value, the purple **sumList** call block will have a knob sticking out of its left-side, as shown in Figure 13.17:

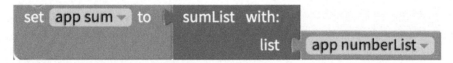

Figure 13.17. The left-side knob signifies a return value

The knob signifies that the function returns a value. Envision the function **sumList** doing its job, computing some value as the sum, and that value being returned from the function directly to that knob.

The code that calls the function is responsible for *catching* the return value. The caller must plug the knob into an open slot, often a block that sets some variable. For the "MathBlasterEq" app, the return value is plugged into the set app sum to block. The variable sum *catches* the value returned, as shown in Figure 13.18:

Figure 13.18. A call that sends in a parameter and catches the result

Just as an input parameter allows a function to be called with different data, the return value allows the function result to be placed in any variable. For example, Figure 13.19 illustrates a call to **sumList** which sends in the variable scores and places the returned value in the variable total:

Figure 13.19. Calling sumList with a different input and "catcher"

The other functions in the "MathBlasterEq" app can also be defined with input parameters and return values. The app structure chart in Figure 13.20 shows a blueprint for such a refactored app:

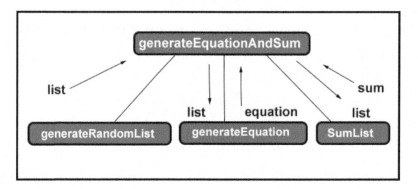

Figure 13.20. Structure chart showing inputs and return values

In this design, the **generateEquationAndSum** function calls **generateRandomList** with no input parameter and the generated list is returned to the caller. list is then sent as an input parameter to **generateEquation**, with equation returned as the result. list is also sent to **sumList** which returns the sum.

Figure 13.21 shows code that implements the blueprint:

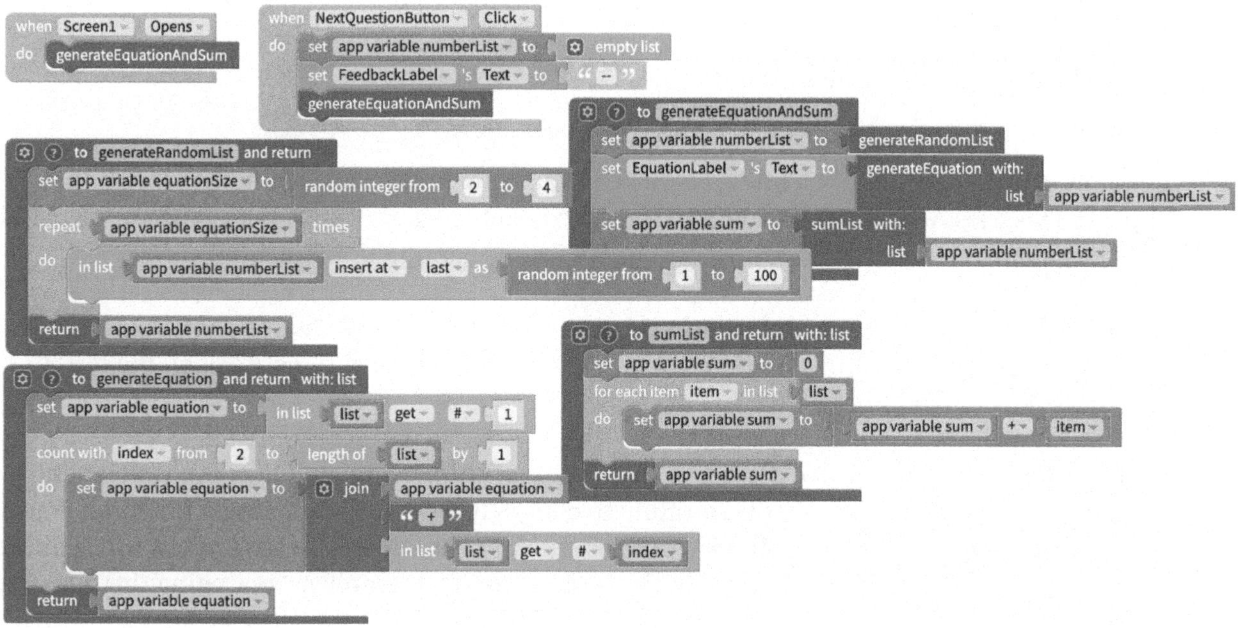

Figure 13.21. MathBlaster with input parameters and return values

From the user's viewpoint, the app will behave the same as the solutions earlier in the chapter. But each of the functions now has explicit input parameters and a return value. The code is better organized, easier to read, and the functions are more reusable.

SUMMARY

Abstraction is a key concept in problem solving. The function is the key building-block for abstraction in code. Instead of your app consisting of event handlers with lots of detailed blocks in them, you can organize an app hierarchically, placing detailed code into functions and calling those functions when needed.

Defining an app in this hierarchical way makes the app easier to read and modify. You can eliminate redundant code so that required changes can be made in just one place. You can also define functions with parameters and return values, making them more general purpose and more reusable.

A well-structured app with reusable functions becomes even more important when you move on to larger software projects. Real world apps tend to have thousands or even millions of lines of code, and a team of developers. A hierarchical design and clear blue-print is a necessity.

If an app is useful, it will live forever and be remixed into other apps. Software always needs to be tweaked and fixed, so its design and architecture are crucial.

RAFIKI BREAKS IT DOWN

For a bit of levity, let's remix a line from Schoolhouse Rock. If you're not familiar with that popular TV series, which aired from the early 1970s to the early 2000s, take a minute to check out this clip provided for your enjoyment: http://bit.ly/conjunctionJunction[2].

"Captain Function, explain your junction. I take control on the run, when something needs to get done. Captain Function, explain your adjunction. When operations stack by the ton, I march then forward as one."

Back in Chapter 3, you learned about the operations within an app and how multiple operations often depend upon each other, collaborating to complete a task. By creating a function, you can efficiently package a set of operations together. Once you create it, you have a new block and can perform a complex job with a single call. Or as our little jingle implies: "marching them forward as one".

VOCABULARY VIBE

FUNCTION

A function is a named sequence of operations. All functions are not the same. Some functions are "built-in", that is, pre-defined by Thunkable, and work with the components of a mobile device.

There are also programmer-defined functions, which you, the app developer, can create. You can give a name to a sequence of detailed operations and thereby create a new block. Functions allow you to extend the grammar, and genie-power, of Thunkable!

INPUT PARAMETER

When a function is called upon to execute an action, it needs data to act upon. That data is called an input parameter. A parameter is a slot that the caller of the function gets to fill in. The function opens up, becomes more flexible, and thus more general-purpose useful.

---

[2] https://ia803205.us.archive.org/6/items/ConjunctionJunction/Conjunction_Junction.mp4

CONCEPTUALIZE

1. How is a function similar to an event handler? How is a function different than an event handler? How is each invoked?

2. What is an abstraction and how are abstractions important to the software development process?

3. When you define an input parameter for a function, it makes the function more general-purpose. Explain.

4. What does it mean to "refactor" code in order to eliminate redundancy?

CUSTOMIZE

Go over the apps you've built and identify functions that would be appropriate, then refactor the code by defining the functions and calling them.

CREATE

It is now time to build that app you've been wanting to build! Choose such an app, but before coding determine abstractions (functions) that can be used as building blocks for the app, and design a structure-chart blue-print specifying the calls between event handlers and functions.

Share your creative apps with your authors and other *Drag and Drop* coders:

*   Use #DragAndDropCode and #MadeWithThunkable on your social media platforms.

*   @ us at @DragAndDropCode on Twitter and Instagram.

Chapter Resources: draganddropcode.com/bookCh13/

CHAPTER 14: OBJECTS

Apps: "WorkoutApp", "Black-Owned Businesses" , "GoogleBooksAPI"

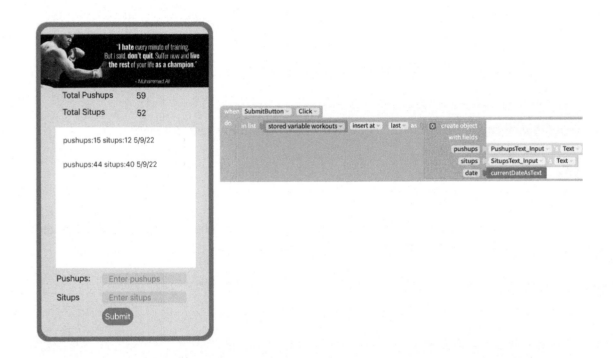

You may have heard the term object-oriented programming. In this chapter, you'll learn to code using objects, which allow you to organize your data into packages, you'll learn techniques for creating apps with complex data, and you'll learn how to use an API to access external software and process the JSON that is returned.

INTRODUCTION

The world is becoming ever more digital, with complex data that is hierarchical and interrelated. Think of the data stored on your social networking accounts—your personal information, your posts, who you follow, and who follows you. Or think of the web link and ranking data stored by Google to provide you with the great search results you use every day.

In Chapter 13, you learned about functions and how they serve as building blocks for complex app logic. In this chapter, you'll be introduced to *objects*, and how they serve as building blocks to organize the complex *data* in an app.

You'll build three apps, each of which uses objects. The first is a workout app for recording pushups and situps. The second is an app to encourage the support of black-owned businesses; it brings in data from a spreadsheet into a list of objects. The third is an app that retrieves data from the Google Books API into a list of "book" objects. When you complete these apps, you'll understand objects and be primed to build apps with complex data.

OBJECTS

In coding, an *object* is a multi-dimensional entity with one or more properties and a set of functions that work on that object. A "person" object might have properties "firstName" and "lastName" with values "David" and "Wolber", as shown by the key-value pairs in Figure 14.1:

Key	Value
FirstName	David
LastName	Wolber

Figure 14.1. A "person" object.

The key names the data, the value is the actual data. A "person" object would also contain functions that work with the data, e.g, a *getFullName* function.

Thunkable allows you to create your own objects in order to package data items together. For instance, the blocks shown in Figure 14.2 create a "person" object.

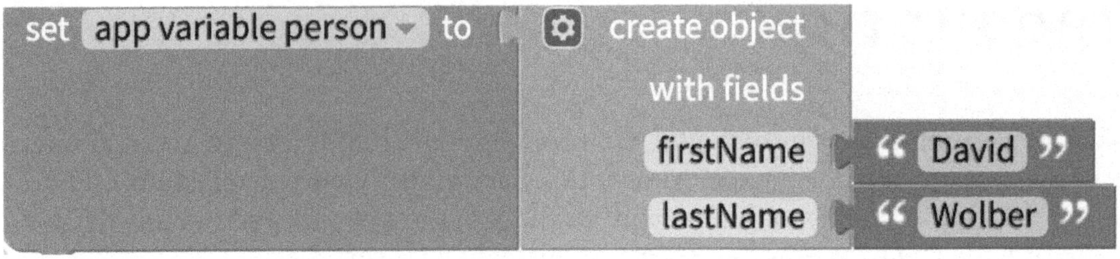

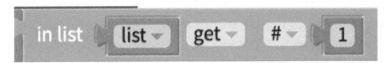

Figure 14.2. A block for creating a "person" object with two properties.

The create object block uses the term "fields" to refer to key-values. The first field is named "firstName" and its value is "David". The second field is "lastName" and its value is "Wolber". The two fields together make a single object named "person".

OBJECTS COMPARED TO LISTS

The apps from previous chapters organized data with a multi-part entity called a list. Lists, like objects, package data items together. You reference each item of a list with a numerical index—e.g., the block in Figure 14.3 refers to the first item in the list, "list".

Figure. 14.3. Access the items of a list with an index.

With an object you refer to each data item with a property name (key) instead of an index. For example, the get property block in Figure 14.4 gets the value of the "firstName" property of the object stored in the variable person and puts it in the variable first.

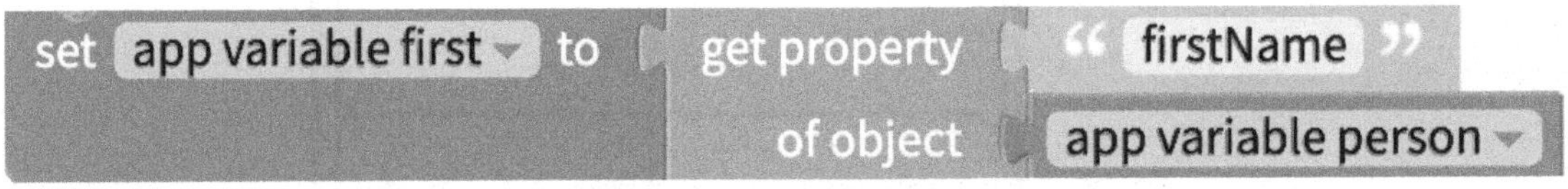

Figure 14.4. Access the parts of an object by property name

Typically, you define a *list* when you want to package items of the same type, e.g., a set of scores in a game app. You define an *object* when each item in the collection represents a different kind of data that can be named (e.g., firstName, lastName).

WORKOUT APP

Consider the "Workout" app shown in Figure 14.5.

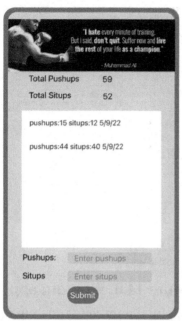

Figure 14.5. The "Workout" App

The app allows the user to enter the number of pushups and situps completed for each workout session. Previously recorded sessions are displayed in a ListViewer along with a date, and the totals are listed at the top.

Design the User Interface

In the Designer, create the interface to look something like that in Figure 14.5:

- Drag in a Label with the text "Total Pushups:" and a second Label, named TotalPushupsLabel, where you'll display calculated data (it is showing 59 in Figure 12.5). Drag in two Labels to display the text "Total Situps" and the value for total situps as well.

- Drag in a ListViewer underneath those labels.

- Drag in a Label and a TextInput underneath the ListViewer. Name the TextInput PushupsTextInput. Add another Label and TextInput for situps as well.

- Drag in a Button at the bottom with text, "Submit" and name it SubmitButton.

Code the Workout App Behavior

Figure 14.6. shows the blocks for a first version of the "Workout" app.

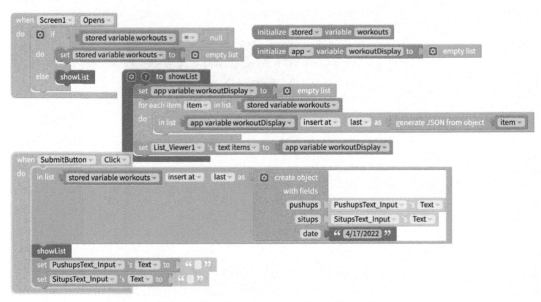

Figure 14.6. Workout app, first iteration

This version doesn't calculate the total number of pushups and situps yet, and it displays the recorded workouts in a rudimentary manner.

The variable workouts is initialized as "stored" because the list should be persistent and private for each user.

The when Screen1.Opens event handler checks to see if there is data in the workouts variable and initializes it to the empty list if not. If there is already data in workouts, it calls the function **showList** to display the list (discussed below).

The when SubmitButton.Click event handler is called when the user has entered the number of pushups and situps for a session and clicked "Submit". An object is created with three parts. The pushups property is set to the number entered in PushupText_Input, the situps property is set to the number entered in the SitupsText_Input property, and date is set to some fixed text (you'll fix this later). In the Designer you can set the keyboard type of the TextInput components to "numeric" so the user can only enter a number.

The created object is inserted into the workouts list. The app then calls the function **showList** to display the updated list, and blanks out both of the TextInputs.

Display an Object

The **showList** function is necessary because you can't directly display a list of objects in a ListViewer—it only knows how to display a list of text. For display purposes, you must create a list of text corresponding to the list of objects, and have the ListViewer display that list.

The **showList** function in Figure 14.6 builds a text list named workoutDisplay, then sets the ListViewer's text item property to it. The basic scheme is to initialize an empty list, then loop through the list of objects, adding a text representation of each object to the new list.

Converting an object into a text representation is called *serializing* an object.

Thunkable provides the generate JSON from object block, shown in Figure 14.7, for serializing an object into a text representation:

Figure 14.7. Generate a JSON text representation of an object

JSON stands for *JavaScript Object Notation*, which is a standard and extensively used notation for representing data. JSON encloses the data of an object with curly brackets, separates keys from values with colons, and separates the various key-value pairs with commas.

For example, the JSON generated from a workout object would be of the form:

{"pushups": 12, "situps": 10, "date":"6/15/20"}

The generate JSON from object function is helpful as a quick way to display data as you debug your app, but typically you'll code custom blocks to display an object in the format you'd like. An example will be provided in the next section.

Test the App

Test version 1 of the "Workout" app. You should be able to add workouts and view them in the ListViewer. However, the date field will be the same for each entry and the items will be displayed in a less than ideal manner.

Serializing an Object

Figure 14.8 shows a function that serializes a workout object in a better formatted way than the generate JSON from object:

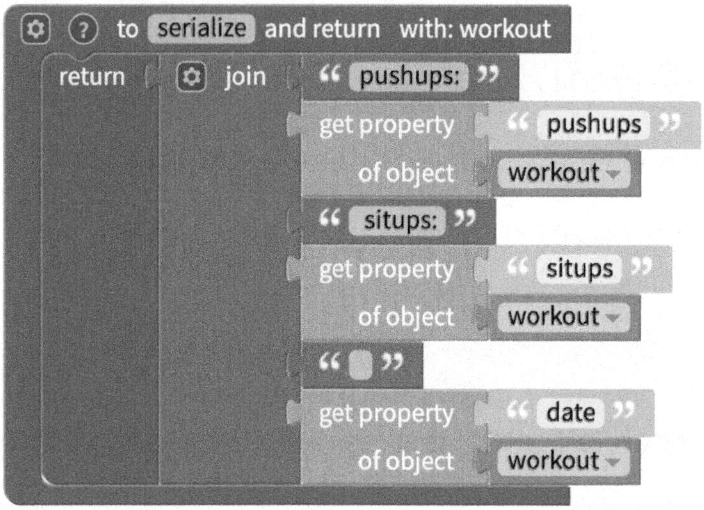

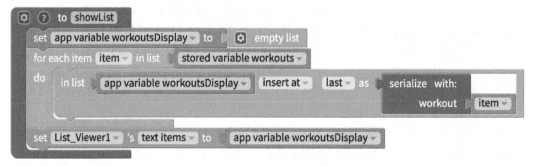

Figure 14.8 Serialize returns a text representation of an object

The function's input parameter is a workout object and it returns a text representation of that object. If the workout parameter is an object with 10 pushups, 12 situps, and a date of "6/15/20", the function will return the text "pushups: 10 situps:12 6/15/20".

Modify your code to add the new **serialize** function and call it from the **showList** function, instead of generate JSON from object, as shown in Figure 14.9:

Figure 14.9. Create workoutsDisplay to show in the ListViewer

As each item in the list is processed, it is sent as a parameter to **serialize**, which returns the text representation (e.g., "pushups: 10 situps:12-- 6/15/20"). That text representation is added to workoutsDisplay, the list that is displayed in the ListViewer.

Accessing the Current Date and Time

The Device folder provides blocks for accessing the current day and time. If you drag in a **current month** block and click the upside-down triangle, you can view the various functions that are available, as shown in Figure 14.10:

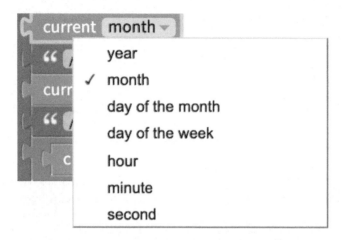

Figure 14.10. The "current" blocks

You can use these blocks to code a function that returns a text representation of the current date/time. The **curDateAsText** function, shown in Figure 14.11, returns the current date including month, day, and year:

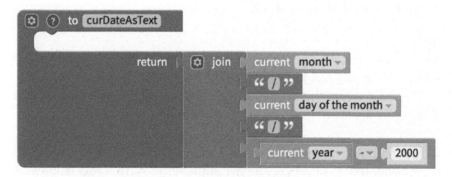

Figure 14.11. A function to return mm/dd/yy

After creating this function, you should call it from the when SubmitButton.Click event handler, as shown in Figure 14.12:

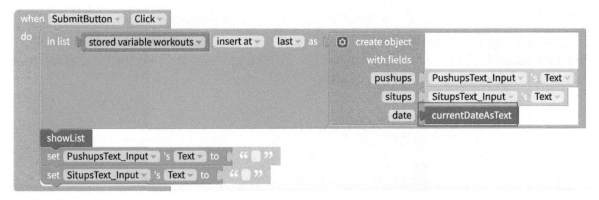

Figure 14.12. Call the curDateAsText function when you create an object

Test the App

Test the app. Does the current date appear now on new entries? Is the display of each item suitable? Play around with the blocks to get it to display how you want.

The workouts variable is "stored" so the data is persistent. Each time you test, the old workout data should still be there. As you debug, you may want to clear out the data. One way to do this is to change the when Screen1.Opens code temporarily so that it sets workouts to the empty list. Run the app once to reset the variable, then change the code back to how it was.

WHY USE OBJECTS?

As the previous section shows, there is a fair amount of bookkeeping required to display a list of objects. One might ask: why not just store the data as formatted text originally, e.g., "pushups 10, situps 8, 5/10/22"? When the user enters the data, why not use a join to create a long text string with delimiters separating the property values?

The reason is that an object is easier to process than a text value with delimiters. With an object, you can call "get property" to access each part of the data. With a text value and delimiters, you have to code complex blocks to separate each part of the text.

If you don't need to run calculations on the data, the "text" solution is reasonable. Often, however, you'll need to process the items in a list, e.g., select all workouts before a certain date, or add up the total number of pushups in all workouts. Using objects simplifies the solution.

COMPUTING THE TOTAL PUSHUPS AND SITUPS

Challenge: Add a feature to the Workout App such that the total number of pushups and situps for all previously input workouts is displayed.

In Chapter 9, you learned how to add up a list of numbers. For this challenge, you need similar functionality, but you'll need to get the numbers—the pushups and situps—from each object.

Begin by coding a function **totalPushups** that takes a list of workout objects as an input parameter and returns the total number of pushups. Figure 14.13 shows the code.

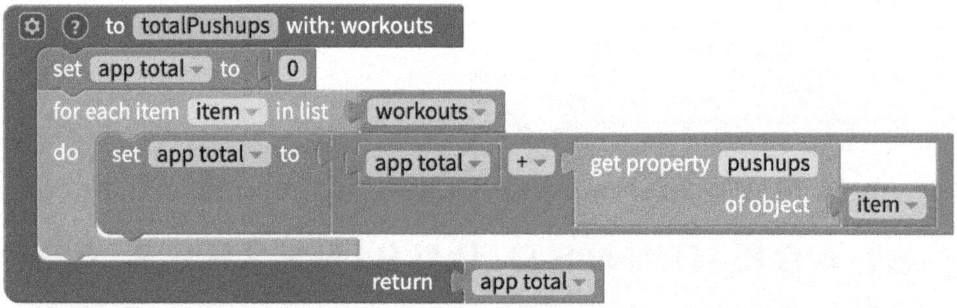

Figure 14.13. A function to total up the number of pushups

This code is very similar to the "add up a list" code in the "MathBlaster" app of Chapter 9 (which was re-coded as a function in Chapter 13). The only difference is the items in the list are objects, not numbers, so the get property block is used to get the pushups property from each item as you iterate through the list.

The **totalSitups** function is similar, only you'll get the "situps" property instead of "pushups". Code that function, and then modify your code so you call them from when Screen.Opens, to display the totals on app launch, and from when SubmitButton.Click, so that each time a new entry is added the totals are updated. The code for these event handlers is shown in Figure 14.14:

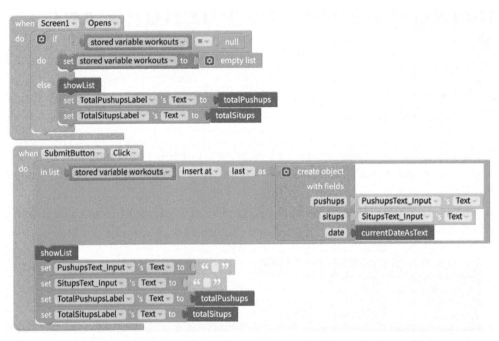

Figure 14.14. Workout app event handlers that now call functions

THE BLACK-OWNED BUSINESSES APP

Today there is an abundance of data at our fingertips, and individuals and organizations around the globe are figuring out how to harness it. With the Photo Sharing app of Chapter 11, and the Workout app in this chapter, the apps generated *new* data from the user's input. In this section, you'll learn how to incorporate data that already exists into your apps. You'll use objects, and you'll learn about another 3rd party tool, Airtable, which provides a more sophisticated database option than Google Sheets.

Consider the Black Lives Matter movement and how it has amplified the inequalities in our society. The challenge is, "how do we make real and lasting change for equality?" One straight-forward way is to encourage the support of black-owned businesses. An app which makes it easy to find black-owned businesses can help, and that is what you'll build in this section.

Creating such an app requires some data collection as well as the capability to get the data into the app. In this section, you'll create an app that displays spreadsheet data on Bay Area Black-owned businesses, as shown in Figure 14.15:

Figure 14.15. Black-owned business app: home and info screen

You'll build the app in a simple, straight-forward manner, but the template will provide a basis for further creation: you can remix the app and extend it with images, websites, and sound clips; you can add location information to the data; and you can add additional features like the ability for businesses to provide coupons or customers to record their purchases and support. Our goal is for the readers of this book to use this app as a basis for creating black-owned business apps for every town in America!

Collect the Data

The first step is to do some research and find data for the town or city on which you'd like to focus. As a sample, we did this for San Francisco, and came across this site: https://sfist.com/2020/06/04/you-can-find-black-owned-businesses-to-support-with-these-apps-and-online-lists/. The site led us to a list of spreadsheets with information on black businesses in the San Francisco Bay Area. For illustrative purposes, we chose one of them[3] and imported the spreadsheet into a database at Airtable.com, as shown in Figure 14.16.

---

[3] https://docs.google.com/spreadsheets/d/1X5U0MKi6jy-g0CfZMKVo_xG2HT0jmpDQrGPdijyE170/edit#gid=0

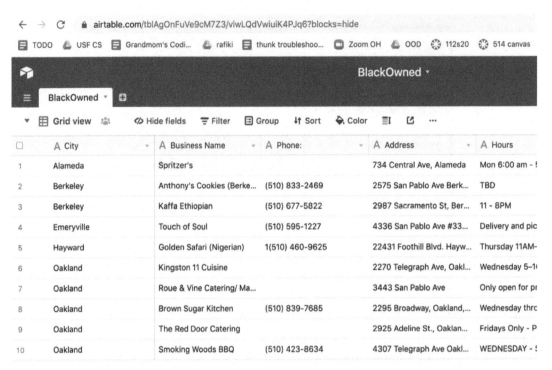

Figure 14.16. A black-owned business spreadsheet in Airtable

Build the App

At Thunkable, create a new app and name it "BlackOwnedBusinesses". In the Designer, add two Labels, one with the text, "Black-Owned Businesses", and one with the text, "Bay Area", and also add an Image component. Set the Image's Picture to one of your own choice or the one at https://draganddropcode.com/bookCh14/. Configure the Labels and Image so the top of the screen appears similar to the app shown on the left of Figure 14.15. Then drag in a Data Viewer List which will display the data.

Create a Database at Airtable

Airtable is a cloud database tool, like Firebase, but it provides a spreadsheet-like view of the data similar to that of Google Sheets and Excel. It is more sophisticated than Google sheets and offers more features.

Airtable can be used for apps like "Workout" that start with a blank data slate. It also facilitates the import of existing spreadsheets into the database, so you can build apps that incorporate existing data along with user-generated data.

Register for a free account at Airtable.com. Then click on the "+" button to "Add a base" and choose to "import a spreadsheet". Copy the rows of data in the table at https://Airtable.com/shrLYNLGdUeDREpXq and paste them into your table (this link is also at draganddropcode.com/bookCh14). Name the base "BlackOwnedBusinesses" and rename the single default table that comes with it from "Table 1" to "BlackOwned".

As shown in Figure 14.16, the sample table comes with a number of columns, including "City", "Business Name", "Phone", "Address", and "Hours". The table has several other columns to the right of those shown, including the website for the business, which you'll incorporate into the app.

Connect your Thunkable App to your Airtable database

Thunkable's data source capabilities can be used with Google Sheets, Airtable. WebFlow or Thunkable's own spreadsheet type. The advantage for a developer is that the same exact data source blocks are used to access the data no matter which database type you use.

In the Designer, add a new Data Source, choose "Create New" and choose Airtable as the type. A dialog will appear asking for some settings from your Airtable table as shown in Figure 14.17:

Figure 14.17. The settings for an Airtable component in Thunkable

At Airtable, click on the account icon and you will be prompted to create a personal API key. Create it and use the result to set the APIKey property in the dialog shown in Figure 14.17. Once you do that, you can choose the Base you created above.

The table name and view name are displayed near the top-left of your database. In the base shown in Figure 14.18, the table name is "BlackOwned" and the view name is "Grid view."

Figure 14.18. TableName="BlackOwned", ViewName="Grid view"

DISPLAY THE DATA ON THE HOMEPAGE

On Screen1, add a Data Viewer List and connect it to the Data Source you just created, as shown in Figure 14.19.

Figure 14.19. Connect the DataViewer to the Source

You'll show only the "Business Name" and "City" on the home screen list. Later, you'll add an information screen that shows more data for a chosen business.

Test the App

Test the app. If the names of the businesses from the Airtable spreadsheet appear then your app and the Airtable database are configured correctly. If you don't see the data, double-check the properties of your data source to see if they match those on in your AirTable table.

AN INDIVIDUAL BUSINESS INFO SCREEN

Screen1 just lists the names of each business. Add a second screen, InfoScreen, to show detailed information about each business. InfoScreen should look something like the screen to the right in Figure 14.15: two Labels to display information, a Button labeled "go to website", a WebViewer component, and a back button. The WebViewer shows a web page within an in-app browser.

After you design InfoScreen, add some code to Screen1 so that it opens up InfoScreen when the user clicks on an item in the ListViewer. When the user chooses an item, set a variable chosenRow to the row selected by the user. Later, in the code for InfoScreen, you'll use that variable to select and display the correct business. Figure 14.20 shows the addition to Screen1:

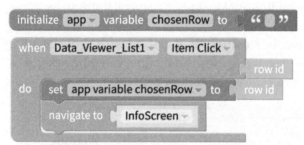

Figure 14.20. set chosenRow then open InfoScreen

InfoScreen's code could retrieve the data from the spreadsheet a single property at a time, as was done in the "MeetMyClassmates" app of Chapter 5. But its more efficient to load an entire spreadsheet row into an object, and then just access the properties from that object for display. The object will have a property corresponding to each column in the Airtable table. Figure 14.21 shows the code: only the "Business Name", "Address", and "Website:" properties of the table are accessed, though the other properties could have been as well.

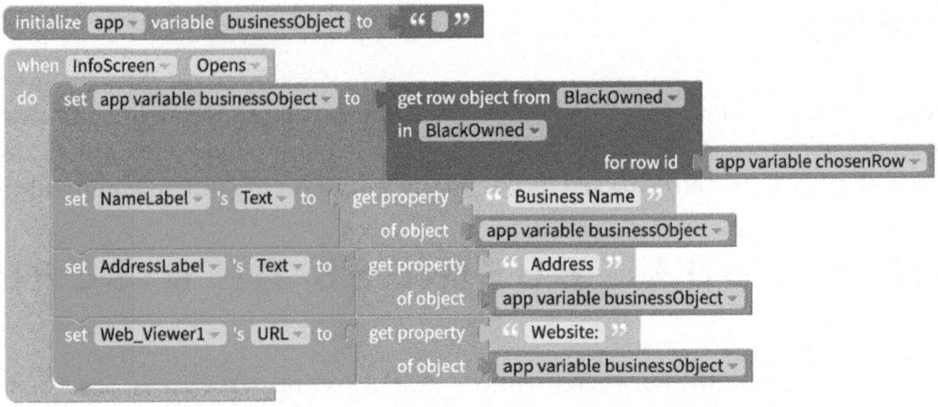

Figure 14.21. The code for when InfoScreen.Opens

get row object from is called to retrieve a row of data—a single business—from the spreadsheet. That row is transformed into an object and placed in the variable businessObject. The blocks then access desired properties from the object: "Business Name" and "Address" are displayed in Labels and the "Website:" is used to set the page of the WebViewer.

Note that the "get a row" scheme of accessing spreadsheet data is different than that used in the Photo Sharing app (see Figure 11.21). In that app, spreadsheet *columns* are placed into lists, and then those lists are traversed to grab each piece of information.

The "Website:" property for the business is also used with WebsiteButton. When WebsiteButton is clicked, the app opens the web page for the business in a browser. Use the open link function, found in the Control folder, as shown in Figure 14.22.

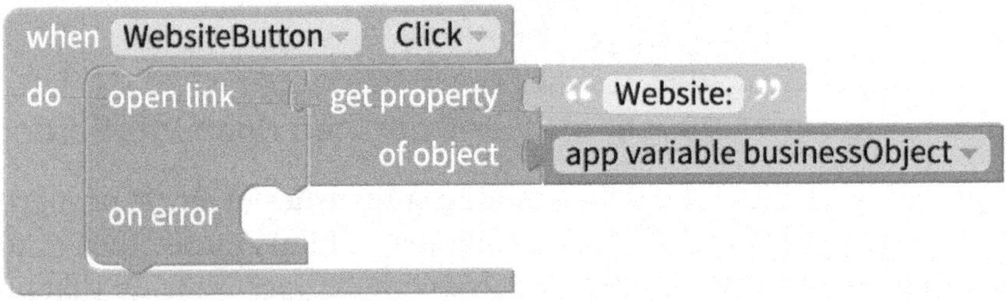

Figure 14.22. Open the website in a browser when button is clicked

The "Black-Owned Business" example is illustrative of an app that makes use of existing data, uses an AirTable database, and uses an object to process the data.

In the app, data was discovered on the web and copied from the web into it. One downside of this scheme is that if the original data on the web changes, you must manually update your copy as well. In the next section, you'll learn about Web APIs and a more maintainable way to share data.

WEB API

Web APIs provide an alternate method of accessing web data. A web page is used by a human, a web API is used by an app. Most software companies, including Facebook, Twitter, Amazon, and Google, have APIs along with their websites: they serve both people and computers! Because of this, you can create apps that use web APIs to gather live data from the web.

API stands for *application programmer interface*. An "application programmer" is you—the creator of an app. "interface" refers to a computer-to-computer interface, not a user-interface. The API specifies how an app talks to a data source on some server.

APIs work in the following manner: the app sends a URL request to the data source server in the format defined by the API. The server processes the request by gathering data and performing calculations. It then returns data to the app in a standard format like JSON. Unlike HTML, JSON isn't well-suited for human readability—it's meant to be processed by software.

In this section, you'll build a book search app that talks to the Google Books API. The user will enter keywords and your app will send a request to the Google Books API, which will return a list of books that match the keywords, in JSON format. Your app will convert the JSON into human-readable form and display it for the user, as shown in Figure 4.23:

Figure 14.23. An app displaying info from Google's Book API

Most APIs require you to set up an account and obtain a key to authorize your URL request, which is somewhat complicated. Fortunately, the Google's Book API is one that doesn't require authorization. Type https://www.googleapis.com/books/v1/volumes?q=baseball into a browser. The response will come back in JSON format. Figure 14.24 shows the top part of the JSON returned from a Google Books API request performed in the Spring of 2022:

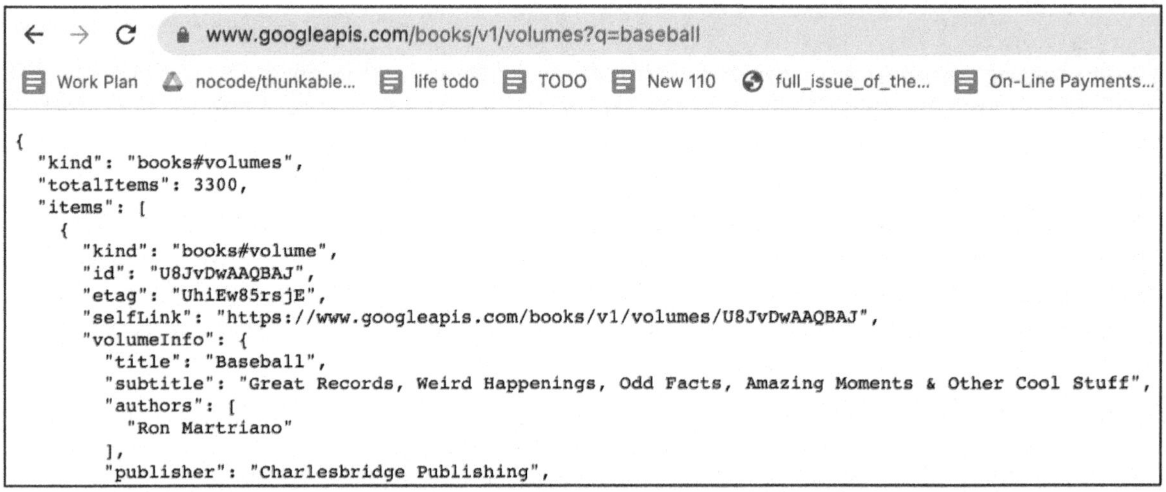

Figure 14.24. The JSON returned from a call to the Google Books API

This JSON data returned is not meant for a browser or a human—the API should really be invoked by an app which will process the JSON, possibly combine it with other data and process it, and eventually display it in human-readable form. Each API returns data in a particular format so you have to examine it to understand the structure of the data. The data returned from Google Books includes "kind", "totalItems" and "items". "items" is a list and each of its items has its own properties ("kind", "id", "etag", "volumeInfo" etc.). "volumeInfo" is itself an object with properties for the "title", "subtitle", "authors", etc.

You'll call the API, process the resulting JSON into human-readable form, and place it into a spreadsheet. That spreadsheet will be a list of book records, and the app will display it to the user using a Data Viewer List.

Your app will basically do what you did when you typed
https://www.googleapis.com/books/v1/volumes?q=baseball into a browser. In the Blocks
editor, you'll open up the "Advanced" folder and create a WebAPI component. You'll then use
the **Get** block, shown in Figure 14.25, to perform the request.

Figure 14.25. "Get" is the app equivalent of typing a URL in a browser

The response output parameter will contain the data that the Web API returns, in this case a text
string like that in Figure 14.24. The app's job is to process that text so as to display it to the user.

Create a new app named "GoogleBooks". Add a Data Source, choose "Create your own table" to
create an internal spreadsheet, and name it "GoogleBookResults". Give the table three column
headings, "title", "author", and "thumbnail". This internal sheet will store the processed results
for each user search query.

On the home screen, add a Data Viewer List, connect it to the spreadsheet you just created, and
map it to show the three data items in the spreadsheet. Then add a TextInput for entering
keywords, and a SubmitButton.

Then code blocks as shown in Figure 14.26:

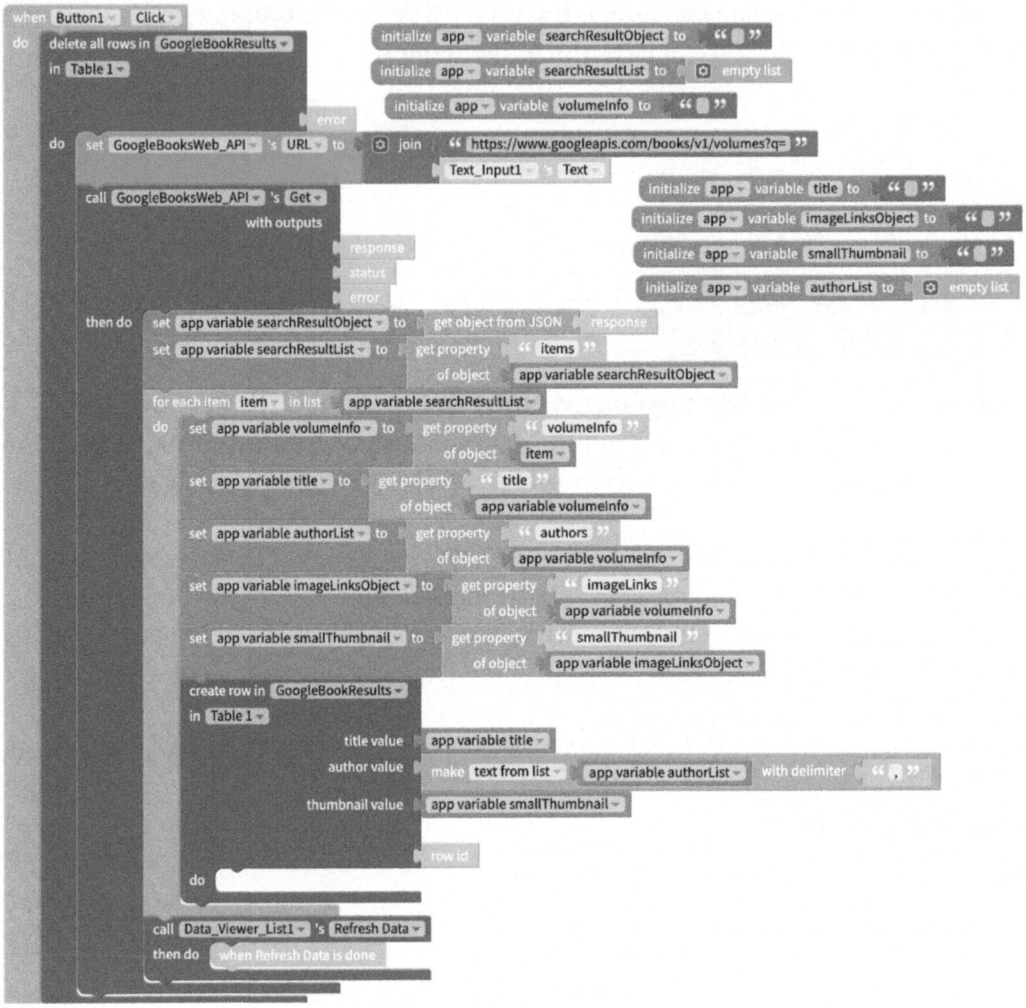

Figure 14.26. Call Google's Book API and process result

The code first sets the Web_API1's URL property, which specifies the URL for the request. In this case, the URL is for Google's Books API. A URL parameter follows the "?" in the request. The parameter's name is "q" (for "query") and its value is the text the user has entered. If the user entered "baseball" in TextInput1, then the URL referred to earlier, https://www.googleapis.com/books/v1/volumes?q=baseball, would be sent to Google.

Once the URL is set, **Web_API1.Get** is called to make the request. The Google Books API does a search for all books on "baseball" on their server, and returns JSON data in the response output parameter. The call to get Object from JSON converts the JSON into an object.

Once you get the APIs response in object form, the detailed work begins. You must analyze the JSON that is returned from the particular API to see which properties the object will have. In this case, the code accesses the "items" property of the object to get the list of book items into the variable searchResultList. It then loops through those items and accesses the "volumeInfo" property of each. The "title", "authors", and "imageLinks" properties are accessed from "volumeInfo", and then the "smallThumbNail" is accessed from the "imageLinks". All of the data is then inserted as part of a new row in the GoogleBookResults spreadsheet. Refer back to Figure 14.23 to see the app in action, with the user entering "baseball" as the keyword.

The Web API component is powerful, but coding with it is complex. As mentioned, most APIs require accounts and authorization (Google Books is an exception). You also must analyze the result JSON of each API you access in order to code the blocks correctly and collect the data you need. It can be almost as difficult as learning another coding language. Most APIs provide documentation, e.g., the Books API documentation is at:
https://developers.google.com/books/docs/overview.

Though complicated, with practice you can become fluent in JSON and feel comfortable with APIs. The reward is access to a world of data!

SUMMARY

Objects package together related data items into a single multi-dimensional entity. Objects are made up of properties, and each property is a key-value pair. You can create objects, and you can use the get property function to access each property.

This chapter presented three samples of apps which use objects. The "Workout" app stores a list of objects, one for each workout recorded by the user. Each object has three parts: the number of pushups, the number of situps, and the date of the workout. A stored variable was used to store the list of objects, so they were persistent and private to the user.

The "Black-Owned Businesses" app uses **get row object from** to bring each spreadsheet row into an object within the app. The object's properties correspond to the columns in the spreadsheet.

The "Google Books API" app uses the Web API component to access book information. The API returns JSON in text format, and you use the get Object from JSON function to convert the JSON into an object. The Web API component is general-purpose and can be used to access any data source on the web. The language of APIs, URLs and JSON is complicated, but mastering it opens up the world of data to you.

With these samples, you now have the fundamentals for creating apps in which complex data is entered by the user or imported from a data source. Your magical powers have increased dramatically!

RAFIKI BREAKS IT DOWN

Objects in Thunkable are multi-dimensional packages that provide structure for complex collections of data. They are similar to spreadsheets, where each column in a row is uniquely named and stores a separate element of data for that row.

In the Black Business app, each business featured is an entry or a row and the column names include Business Name, Zip Code and Business Type. Because each part of the row (object) is tagged, you can easily access all the businesses that are food related, or that are from a particular zip code.

You can also extend the Black Business app to draw upon various different databases, in order to give your users a rich composite of information about a business. These could include data from the Better Business Bureau (BBB), the local Chamber of Commerce, the Health Department, or reviews pulled from social media. Organizing the data as objects helps you cut through the mountains of data and surface detailed and exact subsets of that data.

VOCABULARY VIBE

OBJECT

An object is a data package, with each thing in the package called out by name.

CONCEPTUALIZE

1. How is an object similar to a list? How is an object different than a list?

2. If you couldn't use objects in the "Workout" app, what kind of data structure would you use instead? Describe how your app would be different.

CUSTOMIZE

1. Make a copy of the "Workout" app and modify the code so that it records the exercises you perform in your personal workouts, e.g., bench press, burpees, jumping jacks, etc.

2. Modify the "Workout" app so that it records the hour and minute as part of the date, e.g., "6/29/20 11:43am"

CREATE

1. Create a "CloudWorkout" app, using cloud variables or Airtable, which you and your friends can use to share your progress and compete.

2. Add a high score facility to the Asteroids game or another game you've built. Use a cloud variable for the scores list, and code it so each score in the list is an object with properties for user account, score, and date/time.

3. Extend the "Black-Owned Businesses" app: display more information, incorporate a map or website in app, or create one for a different city/area; Contact some businesses and incorporate coupons or discounts into the app; add a feature whereby users can post notes about a business, or record their support with a photo of a receipt or picture at the establishment.

4. Build your own app that incorporates data from a spreadsheet. Build a"Latin-X-Owned Businesses" or "Female-Owned Businesses" app, an app that displays and analyzes COVID-19 data. Wherever your interest lies, do some research and build an app that adds value to data.

Share your creative apps with your authors and other *Drag and Drop* coders:

•   Use #DragAndDropCode and #MadeWithThunkable on your social media platforms.

•   @ us at @DragAndDropCode on Twitter and Instagram.

Chapter Resources: draganddropcode.com/bookCh14/

APPENDIX A. ANSWERS TO CONCEPTUAL QUESTIONS

Chapter 1. Event-Response Coding

1. The terms aligned with their definitions:

Term	Definition
Event	Something that happens to the app/device
Function call	When the app performs a task such as speaking words or playing a sound clip
Response	The sequence of operations performed when an event occurs
Event Handler	An event and the response it triggers.

2. An **app's behavior** consists of a set of event handlers. An event handler has an event and a response consisting of a sequence of operations.

3. The purple box encloses an **event** and the red box encloses an **event handler**. The green box encloses an operation and specifically a function call.

4. Button1.Click and the passing of time (when Timer.Fires) are considered **events** in a Thunkable app. **say** is an operation and specifically a function call.

Chapter 2. I Have a Dream 2022

1. The green box outlines an **event handler**. The blue outlines an event. The yellow outlines a single operation (and specifically a function call). The red outlines the response to an event (made up of three operations).

2. The "I Have a Dream 2022" app has **four** event handlers that specify what should happen when each of the three buttons is clicked.

Chapter 3. Conditional Blocks and an App's Hidden Hemory

1. A spreadsheet's memory cells are named by their row and columns, e.g., "A3" refers to the cell at row A and column 3. Thunkable's memory cells are component properties (or variables which you'll learn about in the next chapter). Properties are referred to with descriptive names that include the component and property names, e.g. Button1's Text.

2. A set operation changes the value in a memory cell. A get operation retrieves a value from a memory cell.

3. a. The blocks **increment** the value in CountLabel.Text. Since CountLabel.Text starts as 5, these blocks will change it to 6.

    b. The set block on the left can't be executed until its parameter (the blocks inside it) is evaluated. The blue "+" block can't be evaluated until its parameters are evaluated. So the first block performed is the lighter green get block: the current value of CountLabel1.Text (5) is retrieved from memory. Once the value arrives, the + operation can be evaluated to 5+1=6. Finally, the set operation can be executed and 6 is placed into CountLabel.Text.

    c. The row of blocks **increment** CountLabel.

4. From the user's viewpoint, Button1's Text displays "Go" no matter how many times the button is clicked. The property does change, internally, to "Stop", because the first if-block evaluates to true. But as soon as it changes to "Stop", the second if-block executes and also evaluates to true, and thus Button1.Text is set back to "Go". All of this happens on each click.

    Note that even though the property changes for an instant internally, the user interface doesn't update until the event handler completes. The text on the button seen by the user doesn't change at all, not even for a microsecond.

5. Operation 2 will be executed if A is false and B is true. It won't be executed if A is true because the "else if" won't even be considered. Operation 3 will be executed if both A and B are false.

Chapter 4. Lists and Iteration

1. If the code compares index to a particular number, like 4, it will work only if there are exactly 4 items in the list (as in the Slideshow example of the chapter). If the number of items in the list is changed, the code will no longer work unless you modify it. Thus, for flexibility and so you can use your code for more than just the current problem you are working on, it is better to compare index to the *length of the list*. In general, your code shouldn't refer to fixed numbers other than initialization numbers, e.g., 0 or 1.

2. The slideshow algorithm in Chapter 3 is essentially, "if the picture is displaying the first picture, show the second. If it is showing the second picture, show the third" and so on. The code refers explicitly to the data, in this case the names of the picture files. In the "list" solution of chapter 4, the algorithm is essentially, "Increment the index and see if it is within range of the list. If not, get the next picture in the list". This algorithm *abstractly* refers to list items and doesn't explicitly refer to particular file names. The data is only referred to in the list variable definition.

    Separating the algorithmic code from the data definition is important. For apps with fixed data, it makes it easy for the programmer to reuse code by changing only the data definition (e.g., modifying the picture file list). More importantly, it allows the algorithmic code to work even for dynamic, user-generated data, e.g., a slideshow in which the pictures can be taken with the camera or uploaded by the user. For an app with dynamic data, the algorithm must work abstractly.

3. The given blocks illustrate an error that beginners often make as they become comfortable with lists and indexes. The key issue is that the variable index never changes—if it starts at 1 it will stay 1.

    The last row of blocks does have an expression "index + 1", but this expression is not slotted into a set index block, and the only way to change a variable is with such a set block. Thus, the index variable never changes.

    On the first click, things will work fine as the last row will get the item in the index+1 slot (the 2nd item), and show the second picture. But since index doesn't change, on the next click the app will continue to show the picture in the 2nd slot.

Chapter 5. Apps with Data

1. You could reuse "MeetMyClassmates" simply by modifying the data in the spreadsheet. In "TriviaApp", the data is encoded into variable initialization blocks, so you have to change the "code" to change the app.

In general, separating code from data is important for flexibility. As you'll see later in this book, it gets even more important as your data becomes dynamic and specific to each user.

2. The spreadsheet has a "hidden" column named ID, which is a long text string uniquely identifying each row.

3. You can't add 1 to a rowId because the rowId is a text string, not a number.

Chapter 6. Calling Functions

1. The **timer recording** function call has a single input parameter named "number of seconds". The actual parameter plugged in is the number 5. The output parameters are "audio file" and "error".

2. An input parameter is something the coder must provide when calling a function. It is information that the function needs to do its job.

3. An output parameter is information the function returns when it completes its job. The caller can make use of that output data within the "do" slot of the function call block.

4. Output parameters such as translated text can only be referenced in the "do" slot of a function call. In this case, translated text is referenced below the entire function call, so it will not hold the output from the function and SpanishLabel's Text property won't be set properly.

Chapter 7. Processing Text

1. When working with a list or text string, which is really a list of characters, you'll often define a variable which keeps track of the current position in the list as it is being processed. Customarily, such variables are named "index" or "i".

2. In coding, "character" refers to a key on the keyboard, including letters as well as digits, punctuation, and control characters (e.g., tab).

3. An "app abc" block accesses the value in a variable (memory cell). A red text "abc" refers to the literal text string—the letters "a", "b", and "c".

4. Prior to selecting a character from a string, you should check that your index (current position) is less than or equal to the length of the string.

5. "e"

Chapter 8. Build Animated Games

1. A sprite's speed property specifies how fast a sprite is moving and is defined in pixels per second.

2. If a sprite's angle property is set to 270, it will move straight up toward the top of the screen.

3. A sprite's x and y properties specify where its *center* is located. If a sprite is located at x=0, y=0 its left side and top side will be off-screen (though Thunkable will adjust in some instances so that the image appears on-screen).

4. Most components in Thunkable are statically created, meaning you specify them in the Designer and they exist when the app launches. Dynamically created objects, on the other hand, are created as the app runs. Sprites are the only component for which there is a create block to create new ones on the fly. So, for instance, your Asteroid game might create any number of asteroids as the game goes on.

Chapter 9: Repeat Loops

1. The count with block initializes a counter variable to a number, then on each iteration increments it and checks if it has reached its limit. The repeat while doesn't do any of these things automatically.

2. The for each item block initializes a variable to the first item in the list, then on each iteration places the next value in the list into the variable, until the end of the list is reached. The repeat while doesn't do any of these things automatically.

3.The trace for the blocks in Figure 9.19, given that the random numbers generated are 2,8, and 11.

equationSize	numberList	EquationLabel.Text	sum	item
3	[]	2	~~2~~	~~8~~
	[2]	2+8	~~10~~	11

[2,8]	2+8+11	21
[2,8,11]		

Chapter 10: Maps and Location

1. A "?" in a URL signifies that the first parameter is next. So "xyz.com/func/?index=4" has a parameter named index (with a value of 4). "&" is used to separate parameters. So xyz.com/func/?index=4&zoo=99 has two parameters, "index" and "zoo".

2. URLs are like function calls in that you are invoking some function on a server somewhere, sending parameters using the "?" and "&" syntax, and receiving something back (a web page or JSON data, usually). In "xyz.com/func/?index=4", "func" is the function call.

Chapter 11: Build a Photo-Sharing App

1. Because the photos are meant to be shared amonst users, they need to be uploaded into a web database (the cloud). The files selected from the Photo Chooser are local references to files on the particular user's device and have no meaning to other users. When you upload to Cloudinary, you get a URL that anyone can use to view the photo.

2. The **create row** block adds a row of data to the bottom of a spreadsheet.

3. The spreadsheet "RecentPostsFirst" is used to re-order the data from the "Posts" spreadsheet, which places the most recent posts on the bottom. The code places the posts in "RecentPostsFirst" in reverse order so the user sees the most recent at the top.

4. The **list of values in** block retrieves a column of data from a spreadsheet into a variable. Once you have the data in a variable, you can process it, e.g., add up a bunch of scores, or in the "Photo Sharing" app, loop through the variable backwards to re-order how the list is displayed.

Chapter 12: Persistent and Cloud Data

1. "persistent data" is dynamic data that lives on even if an app is closed and reopened. Data must be stored in a database for it to be persistent (stored and cloud variables do this for you automatically)

   Not all persistent data is cloud data—an app can also store data in a private database that lives on the computer/device and not on the web.

Not all dynamic data is persistent—an app might keep track of data that it does not need to save in a database because it shouldn't appear the next time the app is launched.

2. An "app" variable stores data for the life of a single run of the app, but not persistently. A "stored" variable stores data persistently on the user's device so it is not shared with others. A "cloud" variable stores data persistently in a database on the web. All instances of the app can access a cloud variable.

3. The when variable changes or initializes event handler is triggered when a cloud variable is modified in some app instance. It essentially notifies all app instances that a change in a shared variable has occurred. Typically, the code in the event handler just updates the user interface based on the change (e.g., shows the newly entered post).

Chapter 13: Defining Functions

1. A function and event handler are similar in that both enclose sequences of operations (blocks) to be executed. They are different in that a function is invoked by *calling* it from elsewhere in the app, either from an event handler or another function, while an event handler is *triggered* by an external event like a button click or the passing of time.

2. An abstraction gives a name to a set of details. The function construct is the way you do this in coding. It is important in software engineering because it allows one to break a solution down into sub-solutions, each defined as a function, and build a hierarchical blue-print for how to proceed. The software team can talk at various levels of abstraction, ignoring details at times, then delving into them at others.

3. When a function doesn't have input parameters, it works on specific variables and specific data. If a function has an input parameter(s), the calling code is allowed to specify some of the data on which the function will work and thus the function can be used for different purposes.

4. To "refactor" code is to change an app internally without changing how it works for the end-user. The purpose is to modify the code for readability or reusability and it is often performed in order to eliminate redundancy in the code. If you can place redundant code into a function, it is then in one place and any changes to it only need to be applied once.

Chapter 14: Objects

1. An object is similar to a list in that they both can store multiple items. An object typically stores different kinds of items and each item has a name (the property names). A list typically stores homogeneous items and each item is named only with an index (position in the list).

2. If objects couldn't be used in the "Workout" app, each workout record could be stored as a list. list[1] would store the #pushups, list[2] the #situps, and list[3] the date. The variable workouts would then store a list of lists, with each sub-list being a single workout.

Each workout record could also be stored as text, with the different properties separated by a delimiter, e.g., "p:12, s:11, 7/15/20". The code would then need to split the string into parts in order to, say, count the total number of pushups across all workouts.

APPENDIX B: MORE THUNKABLE COMPONENTS

This book doesn't cover all the components in Thunkable, which is continually updating its component library to add new capabilities. With the fundamentals you've learned, you are ready to explore and make use of all of the components and functions Thunkable provides. This appendix provides you with a head-start.

NAVIGATORS

Navigators are those menu bars at the top or bottom of an app that allow the user to navigate easily between screens.

You create a Navigator by clicking the "+" near the word "Screens" in the top-left panel of the Designer. Figure B.1 shows the different types of Navigators.

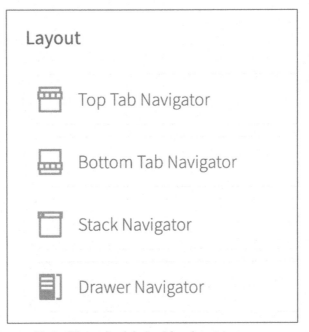

Figure B.1. Thunkable's Navigator components

Navigators come with some template screens for Home, About, etc. You can remove any of these you don't want in your app.

The Screens you already have in your app will not be within the Navigator by default. Using the top-left panel, you can drag them in. Figure B.2 shows the Screen organization of the "Login and Profile" app.

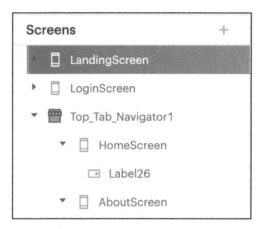

Figure B.2. Drag the screens within the Navigator

Note how HomeScreen and AboutScreen are indented within Top_Tab_Navigator1 (a UsersScreen and ProfileScreen are as well, but not shown). Because of this configuration, the top navigation menu will have items that when clicked open thos screens, as shown in Figure B.3:

Figure B.3. Top Tab Navigation

Clicking on the top menu items takes the user to that screen. You can change the item names that appear in the menu by selecting each Screen in the Designer and changing some properties (e.g., Top Tab Navigator has a Title and Tab Bar Label properties).

VIDEO

The Video component plays video. As of July 2020, it must be set to a .mp3 extension: either one you've loaded or a web URL with a .mp3 extension. You cannot set it to a YouTube URL.

The Video component allows you to provide great content in your apps. For instance, you could create a "Slideshow" or quiz app which played a video instead of showing static content.

AUDIO RECORDING AND RECOGNIZING

Thunkable provides blocks for both recording audio and recognizing it. Figure B4 shows the pertinent blocks:

Figure B.4. Sound recording blocks

The audio blocks on the left are in the "Sound" folder of the Blocks Editor. The end result of a recording is an mp3 file that you can replay or store to Cloudinary.

The **recognized speech** block is in the "Speech" folder and returns a text transcription of the user's speech. Like Siri or Alexa, your app can then process that text.

The audio recording blocks could be used to build a soundboard app in the form of the "I Have a Dream 2022" app, but one in which the user can set the clips that are played. With such an app you might record your friends saying funny things so you can replay them later, or record grandchildren clips for an app for your grandmother or grandfather.

APPENDIX C: TEAM-UP WITH THE THUNKABLE COMMUNITY

Thunkable has an amazing on-line community of app builders with whom you can collaborate, get help from, share code, and talk coding.

GET AND GIVE HELP

Thunkable has useful documentation on all of its components and functions. You can mouse over a component or block to view a description. The documentation page is at docs.thunkable.com.

You can also collaborate with the on-line community of Thunkable coders at community.thunkable.com. Always perform a search first to see if there are already posts on a topic you're interested in or bug you're experiencing. If you don't see anything on your issue, post a new issue and be as specific as possible. I typically post snapshots of my code blocks as well as a "share" link to my app's code. You will receive answers from both the Thunkable staff and other coders.

You can contribute back to the community by reading through the issues of other users and making suggestions where you see fit. Teaching is a great way to learn, and you may be surprised how much you can help others, especially if you've mastered the material in this book!

SHARE YOUR SOURCE CODE

Click on the "share" icon in the top-right menu to share a copy of your app, including its source code, with another Thunkable coder. A link is generated that you can email others. Clicking the link launches Thunkable with a copy of the app open. It is not your version—they can't edit that—but a copy that they can remix.

Your Thunkable apps are by default "open source", meaning the source code (really, blocks) is available for other to view and remix. The apps you build are automatically public and will appear in the Thunkable gallery by default. To designate apps as private, you need to become a paying "Pro" member.

You can also show off your completed apps in the "Made with Thunkable" category within the Community tab.

The awesome aspect of Thunkable's open source nature is that you can find existing code on just about any topic, both to learn from and to remix. Few software development projects start from scratch—most coding involves becoming familiar with an existing code base and remixing it into something different.

GET SOCIAL

Even as your working on your apps, share them on social media! Provide a screenshot, description of what you're doing, and the "Share" link to your source code (if you want to share that). Tag your apps with #MadeWithThunkable and #DragAndDropCode, which is the hashtag for this book's community of authors and readers. You can also @ us at @DragAndDropCode.

PUBLISH YOUR APPS

When you test your app with "Thunkable Live" on a phone or tablet, you are simulating the execution of the app. Your app is running within the "Thunkable Live" app and is not in a form for distributing to others.

iPhone and iPad
You cannot get an executable directly on your computer—you must go through the Apple Developer program. First, register as an Apple Developer, which costs about $99 a year. Once you register, click on "Publish" and Thunkable will step you through publishing your app to the App Store.

The Apple Developer program provides the "Test Flight" tool which allows you to test an app with a restricted set of users. Once it is tested, you submit it to Apple for compliance. Once it passes their tests, your app will appear on the app store.

Android
You can create an executable Android app for install. Click Download in the top Thunkable menu and choose "Download Android". Thunkable downloads an executable Android app (".apk" file) directly to your computer. The ".apk" file can be emailed to anyone and they can install it on their Android device if they set their phone to accept apps from "unknown sources".

You can also publish on the Android Play store by registering as a developer for a one-time $25 fee.

Web App
Thunkable provides one other option for app distribution, the mobile web app, but you must pay for a "Pro" membership to use it. A mobile web app runs within a browser on any type of phone

or tablet and is not "native" to either iOS or Android. Mobile web apps can be distributed widely with a link and without going through an app store.

For more and up-to-date information on downloading and publishing apps, see https://docs.thunkable.com/download.

GO PRO

Thunkable is free to use and you can build each of the apps in this book with the free version. You may also want to consider Thunkable's "pro" version, and purchasers of this book can take advantage of an exclusive offer. Here are your choices:

1. Use Thunkable's Free Version: Building apps with Thunkable is free! Register for a free account at thunkable.com and work on up to 10 apps at a time.

2.GO PRO! Special "App Camp" License, exclusively for purchasers of *Drag and Drop Code with Thunkable*. You get "pro" features for a major discount! Unlimited apps, downloads, and publishing!

Scan this QR code to take advantage of this exciting offer.

BOOK ERRATA

Please report errors in the book at https://draganddropcode.com/book-errata/. Your feedback can help make future editions better!

APPENDIX D. TRANSITIONING TO TEXTUAL CODING

If you've completed most or all of the apps in this book, you now have magical powers that few people possess. You also have a basic knowledge of the language of code, which is completely foreign to most people. Terms like "event handler", "if condition", "repeat loop", "function call" and "input parameter" are fundamental to all coding languages. Being able to talk this talk is extremely beneficial in communicating with coders and engineers, which is more and more common in the workforce.

The coding concepts you've learned in this book will also translate if and when you transition to coding in a more traditional, textual language like Python or Java.

Figure D.1 shows some Thunkable blocks with the corresponding Python code:

Thunkable	Python
set app index to (app index + 1)	index=index+1
repeat while (app index ≤ length of app numbers) do set app item to in list app numbers get # app index set app total to (app total + app item) set app index to (app index + 1)	while index<len(numbers): item=numbers[index] total=total+item index=index+1
set app total to sum with: list app numbers	total = sum(numbers)

Figure D.1. Thunkable Blocks and Python Code

The code is essentially the same, just in a different medium. With Python, you type the code in as opposed to dragging and dropping blocks. It is easier to make mistakes with Python, and the error messages you receive can be difficult to understand, which is especially frustrating for beginners.

Traditional textual languages also differ from Thunkable in that event handlers are not primitive constructs in the language, and the languages don't provide mechanisms for easily connecting a user interface to back-end code. With traditional languages, it can take months or years of fundamentals before you reach the point of building apps with user interfaces. Fortunately, the knowledge you've learned with Thunkable will make this learning easier and quicker.

There are many on-line resources for learning Python and other languages. For a quick start, try https://www.codecademy.com/learn/learn-python-3

APPENDIX E: VOCABULARY VIBE

Coding introduces a language all its own. Mastering the vocabulary of code is vital to communicating in our digital world. This section collects all of the "Vocabulary Vibe" entries from the various chapters.

EVENT and EVENT HANDLER

An event is something that your app can respond to, such as a user swiping a screen, clicking a button or the inflow of data from GPS satellites or sensors. The *agents* that facilitate such responses are event handlers and the process of them doing so is event-response.

OPERATION

An operation is an action that an app performs. *A genie's hands clappin' makes an operation happen.* The two operation types are **function call** and **set.** It often takes a collection of operations to execute a full cohesive action.

BOOLEAN

The foundation of all computation is binary, a matter of 1s and 0s, on or off. The computing concept of boolean, true-false, mirrors this.

To the average ear, the word boolean rings kind of different. Actually, it's a nod to George Boole; a self-taught 19th century mathematician and logician who's work in algebraic theory laid the foundation for digital circuit design and all that followed from that—namely the Internet.

IF

The world is full of possibilities. Not everything aligns on a single track. To accommodate for this type of complexity in coding, there are conditional statements, all starting with if.

if is like a traffic light giving direction based on circumstances at hand. When conditions are a certain way, then proceed; if not. then move in a different direction.
A simple concept, but imagine the knot that traffic would be tied into without this single factor: the traffic light. Consider this as well: by adeptly combining if-else conditions, you can engineer any artificial intelligence you want.

VARIABLE

A variable is a named memory cell or cells, whether it is a single point or collection of many points. Designing how your app will remember things and recall them is a critical element to effective app design and delivery of a great user experience. Any good app has to call forth and manipulate data at the speed of light and variables are an essential power in their ability to do so.

Varying types of data flowing through an app, and even between apps, constantly or upon request, is much like an orchestra. The melody of it all depends on precision, not approximations or guessing. Harmony and rhythm require the same exactness. If coders are the orchestra conductors of the data music in an app, then variables are the tools they use to ensure that the data notes end up where they belong and in the correct measure.

FUNCTION CALL

"Hey, Sound Card, you're needed to play the audio of Kamala Harris's vice-presidential acceptance speech." This is an example of a function call, a request by your app to a component of your mobile device to get involved with helping to fulfill a user's wish.

With Thunkable, such genie-power is as easy as pulling the appropriate block onto the screen.

STRING AND CHARACTER

As an English-speaker, your command of language involves primarily the twenty-six letters of the alphabet and the ten numeric digits. There are also the various punctuation marks you see on your keyboard.

In a computer's memory, there aren't really any symbols. Instead, each letter, digit, and punctuation mark is represented as a number. The set of 128 characters is known as the American Standard Code for Information Interchange, or ASCII for short. It forms the basis for Unicode, which is the internationalized form of ASCII.

Recall that computers really only understand 1s and 0s. Each 1 or 0 is stored in a bit, and each character is stored in an 8- or 16-bit package called a byte. You then combine a sequence of ASCII characters to store a text string like "Genie in an app". The table below illustrates this:

Binary	01000111011001010110111001101001011001010010000001101001011011100001000000110000101101110001000000110000101110000011100000010111 0
ASCII Bytes	(G) 01000111 (e) 01100101 (n) 01101110 (i) 01101001 (e) 01100101 (sp) 00100000 (i) 01101001 (n) 01101110 (sp) 00100000 (a) 01100001 (n) 01101110 (sp) 00100000 (a) 01100001 (p) 01110000 (p) 01110000 (period) 00101110
English Text	Genie in an app.

ITERATION

An app often needs to perform an operation or sequence of operations over and over, sometimes thousands or even millions of times. Iteration—also known as looping—is the process of repeating operation(s).

You certainly don't want an unwieldy number of blocks in your app, so all coding languages provide a way to specify iteration. Thunkable provides a number of repeat blocks which say, "do the blocks within me multiple times", in different ways.

PERSISTENCE

Persistence is the state of your data being accessible over time. Transient data disappears as soon as an app is closed. Persistent data is the opposite. It doesn't do a disappearing act. It stays around.

It's present to be called upon, time and time again, in the memory of the user's mobile device or in the cloud. Many experiences extend beyond a single moment and thus the data that drives such experiences needs to have as long a shelf-life as is required by the experience.

FUNCTION

A function is a named sequence of operations. All functions are not the same. Some functions are "built-in", that is, pre-defined by Thunkable, and work with the components of a mobile device.

There are also programmer-defined functions, which you, the app developer, can create. You can give a name to a sequence of detailed operations and thereby create a new block. Functions allow you to extend the grammar, and genie-power, of Thunkable!

INPUT PARAMETER

When a function is called upon to execute an action, it needs data to act upon. That data is called an input parameter. A parameter is a slot that the caller of the function gets to fill in. The function opens up, becomes more flexible, and thus more general-purpose useful.

OBJECT

An object is a data package, with each thing in the package called out by name

Index

ABOUT THE AUTHORS

David Wolber is a leader in teaching beginners how to code. His focus is empowering artists, designers, kids, women, men, people of color, humanity majors, business students—makers of all types—to add coding to their creative arsenals. He was the lead author of the App Inventor 2 book, along with MIT App Inventor lead Hal Abelson and Google developers Ellen Spertus and Liz Looney. That book, and Dave's video-based site appinventor.org, have introduced thousands of new app builders to the world of code.

David is a professor of Computer Science at the University of San Francisco. He taught one of the first App-Inventor-based courses in 2009 and has provided USF students from across the university with their first coding experience. His appinventor.org course-in-a-box teaching materials have served as a template for hundreds of courses at the K-12 and university levels, as well as for the Mobile Computer Science Principles (MobileCSP.org) Advanced Placement (AP) curriculum. David has taught using Thunkable for the past four years and now runs the site draganddropcode.com.

Rafiki Cai has vested over twenty-five years towards ensuring that emerging technology can be a tide to lift all boats. His work has taken him from a tech writer for national media outlets, to a trusted tech advisor on Capitol Hill, to a bridge builder in academia and Silicon Valley. Iconic, world-renowned figures have sought out and valued his strategic counsel on things digital and his passion for creatively executing the strategies he suggests. He has been a co-founder of a Washington, D.C. based digital divide non-profit, a tech educator at the University of San Francisco and, most recently, a co-author of bioinformatic research on Cancer Disparities Among African American Communities.

Before coming to technology, Cai served in the fields of ministry and social work; working in communities in Colorado and New Jersey. He brings to technology the same passion for making a difference in lives and showing persons the potential power that lies right within them. He currently serves as the chief technology officer (CTO) of Friends of The Congo, a non-governmental organization working to empower and uplift everyday people in the Democratic Republic of The Congo.

65709039R00162